Fadó

Fadó

A Memoir of Life, Liberty, and the Pursuit of Happiness

Kevin O'Donnell

Xlibris

Philadelphia

To order additional copies of this book, contact:
Xlibris Corporation
1-888-795-4274
www.Xlibris.com
Orders@Xlibris.com
55798

To Rory

Map of Arranmore Island, County Donegal, Ireland.
Drawn by author © 1985

CONTENTS

ༀ

CHRONOLOGY 1592-2009

IRELAND

NORTH AMERICA

IRELAND		NORTH AMERICA
Hugh Roe (Red Hugh) O'Donnell escapes from Dublin Castle where he was held prisoner for 4 years.	1592	Central Algonquian Indians lead semi-mobile lifestyle around lower Great Lakes.
Hugh Roe O'Donnell defeated at the Battle of Kinsale, end of O'Donnell reign in Ireland. Flees to Spain. Dies there at age 30.	1602	
	1607	Jamestown, Virginia founded. First permanent English settlement in North America.
Rory O'Donnell, 33, Prince of Tyrconnell dies in Rome.	1608	
British banish 30,000 military prisoners to South America & West Indies plantations.	1612	
	1620	English Separatists (Pilgrims) land the *MAYFLOWER* at Plymouth, MA. First permanent European settlement in New England.
Mary Stewart O'Donnell writes to Cardinal Antonio Barberini seeking assistance from his uncle, Pope Urban VIII.	1635	
Mary Stewart O'Donnell dies a widow in Prague.	1649	
Oliver Cromwell begins his Reign of Terror slays 30,000 in Drogheda, Ireland.	1649	
Slaughter at Cave of The Innocents occurs on Arranmore Island. 70 islanders massacred by Cromwell's army.	1650	

Seán Mac Mánus Óg O'Donnell escapes the British, arrives on Arranmore and settles on nearby islands.	1650	
Irish slavery peaks. 100,000 Irish Catholic children and 58,000 women and men are rounded up by Cromwell and "Barbadosed" to the British West Indies.	1650-62	
	1673	Father Jacques Marquette & Louis Joliet first Europeans to explore northeast Illinois and canoe the Des Plaines River. They claim the land for France.
Irish defeated at the Battle of The Boyne.	1690	
Irish defeated at the Battle of Limerick. Ireland comes under full subjugation of English rule. Penal Laws enacted and ruthlessly enforced.	1695	
Protestant Ascendancy begins in Ireland. "The Long Peace," no major political violence for nearly 100 years.	1700	French fur trappers trade with Native Americans at Fort Hill, north of modern-day Mundelein, IL.
Famine kills 400,000.	1740-41	
	1763	Seven Years War ends between British and French. France cedes all lands east of the Mississippi River to Great Britain.
	1775	American War of Independence begins.
	1776	Declaration of Independence signed.
	1781	Cornwallis surrenders at Yorktown.
Commercial fishing on Arranmore fails completely.	1793	
	1795	Treaty of Greenville. Native Americans "sell" all lands east of the Great Lakes to US Government.

United Irishmen Rebellion. 30,000 Irish Catholics killed.	1797-98	
Charles Connaghan born in Cloughglas, Co. Donegal. (g-g-grandfather).	1801	
	1802	Fort Dearborn constructed on the banks of the Chicago River.
	1803	Louisiana Purchase from France doubles the size of the U.S.
	1809	Abraham Lincoln born near Hodgenville, Ky.
Meave Eoin Rodgers born on Arranmore Island. (g-g-grandmother).	1811	
Arranmore lighthouse constructed.	1817	
St. Crone's, the first permanent church Built on Arranmore with the help of Charles Connaghan.	1825	
Irish Penal Laws repealed under the Catholic Reformation Act.	1827	
Arranmore's population 1,141.	1832	Indians cede all land east of the Mississippi River to the US Government.
	1833	Chicago incorporates. Population, 300.
Sale of Irish as slaves to the "sugar islands" ends after more than 150 years.	1834	
	1835	Peter Shaddle settles on the banks of Mud Lake. William Fenwick builds a cabin nearby along Diamond Lake, IL.
Night of The Big Wind, January 6th.	1839	English settlers escaping the industrial depression settle near Shaddle's cabin in Illinois and name the place Mechanics Grove.

Charles Connaghan (41) and Meave Eoin Rodgers (31) marry.	1842	
The Great Famine begins. Brian Oge O'Donnell born on Arranmore. (g-grandfather).	1845	
Potato crop on Arranmore a complete failure. Comes to be known as "Black 47."	1847	
Brigid (Biddy Charlie) Connaghan born on Arranmore. (g-grandmother). John Charley (Beag) buys Arranmore for £1500 and begins deporting tenants.	1848	Diamond Lake School established.
John Charley banishes 161 islanders at once.	1851	Mechanics Grove, Illinois renamed Holcomb. Wolf bounty $8 per pelt.
	1856	John (Strac) O'Donnell arrives on Beaver Island, MI. Convinces many from Arranmore to emigrate.
Hugh (Stokes) Rodgers born on Arranmore Island. (g-grandfather).	1860	Abraham Lincoln elected President. More than 50 families from Arranmore now living on Beaver Island.
	1861-65	Civil War.
Charles & Meave Connaghan leave Arranmore. Settle on Beaver Island, MI.	1871	Great Chicago Fire & Great Peshtigo Fire.
	1872	George Mundelein born in NY.
Condy Bryan Og O'Donnell born on Arranmore Island. (grandfather).	1879	
Mary (Stokes) Rodgers, oldest of 22 children, born on Arranmore Island. (grandmother).	1883	
Arranmore fishing industry revives.	1890	
	1891	Charles Connaghan, 90, dies in Marinette, WI. (g-g-grandfather).

	1901	
Arranmore's population 1,308.		
Cornelius (Condy Bryan Og) O'Donnell And Mary (Stokes) Rodgers marry on Arranmore Island. (paternal grandparents).	1902	
	1909	The village of Holcomb, IL changes its name to Rockefeller and incorporates. In July, 1909 changes its name again to Area.
	1911	Meave Eoin Connaghan, 94, dies in Marinette, WI. (g-g-grandmother).
John (Mary Hughie) O'Donnell born on Arranmore Island. (father).	1920	Construction of St. Mary of the Lake Seminary begins.
	1924	Area changes its name to the Village of Mundelein in honor of George Cardinal Mundelein.
Mary (Stokes) Rodgers dies of consumption on Arranmore Island. Edward & Celia Boyle (maternal grandparents) emigrate from Roshin Acres, Co. Donegal to Bayonne, NJ.	1926	George Cardinal Mundelein hosts the 28th Eucharistic Congress at St. Mary of the Lake Seminary, Mundelein, IL. 500,000 attend.
	~	Teresa Boyle born 4 months after parents immigrate. (mother).
The Great Arranmore Disaster. 19 drowned.	1935	
Father forges birth certificate and joins the British Navy. Sails the Mediteranean.	1937	
	1939	George Cardinal Mundelein, Archbishop of Chicago, dies at his villa in Mundelein.
	1941	Father re-enlists in the Royal Canadian Navy.
	1946	Father honorably discharged from naval service. Enters US for the first time. Moves to Chicago.

	1949	Father moves to Bayonne, NJ and meets Teresa Boyle. (mother).
Electricity comes to Arranmore Island. Population 1,131.	1950	John O'Donnell & Teresa Boyle marry in Bayonne, NJ.
	1955	Author born, May 8th, Bayonne, NJ.
	1956	Celia Boyle (maternal grandmother) dies, Bayonne, NJ. John & Teresa (parents) move family to Waukegan, IL.
Cornelius O'Donnell 80, dies on Arranmore Island. (grandfather).	1959	John & Teresa O'Donnell move family to Mundelein, IL.
Father returns to Arranmore Island. His first visit in 38 years.	1977	
Authors first visit to Arranmore Island.	1979	
	1983	Teresa O'Donnell, 56, dies in Libertyville, IL. (mother).
Author returns with father to Arranmore.	1985	
Arranmore population 596, lowest in more than 300 years.	1987	John Mary Hughie O'Donnell, 67, dies in Mundelein, IL. (father).
Arranmore Island & Beaver Island twinning ceremony. Island monument erected.	2003	
	2009	Mundelein celebrates its centennial of incorporation. Fadó memoir published.

PROLOGUE

ᖷᐣᕉ

HIS TURNED OUT TO BE a far different project than when it began. In fact, it began not as a book but as a collection of essays from my childhood that I called "Rory's Stories," after my son, Rory, who asked for them as his graduation gift from high school. I was flattered that he asked and eager to accommodate his request. However, I found the more I wrote, the more I had to explain to him the *Irishness* behind what I was writing, compliments of the commanding influence of my father, who died shortly before Rory was born. To give a better understanding of the deeper meaning of these stories, I felt compelled to interject my family's rich traditions; the influence of music; of history; and the impact the Catholic Church had in shaping the stories of my life. They, in fact, *are* the stories of my life. Before I knew it, I was at 35,000 words and counting. At the encouragement of my family and friends, I was persuaded to extend those stories into a book. Not convinced that *my* life was all that interesting, I began to link the chronological events of my family in Ireland prior to the Great Famine in 1845 with events of my boyhood hometown, Mundelein, Illinois, which was settled by Europeans about the same time. The confluence of these parallel cultures occurred in 1959 when my family (to my shock and surprise), moved to the remote suburb forty miles north of Chicago. Chronicling these two places to that point in time provided some surprising historical connections and ironic twists. But that was only half the story. The other half, of course, was how these events, taken retrospectively and told in a series of interjecting flashbacks in first person narrative, helped usher me into adulthood.

My research has taken me on an incredibly surprising physical and emotional journey that has lasted more than two years and spanned more than 18,000 miles of travel from: Rome, Italy, in search of various papal connections to my boyhood hometown, my exiled Irish ancestors, and the tomb of an Irish Prince; to Arranmore Island, Ireland, the remote Gaeltacht community off the coast of County Donegal that fisherman-farmers like my father called home and where I returned many times over the years to experience first-hand his island and its centuries-old traditions; to Dublin, Ireland, where I scoured through archives and antique book shops to chronicle and document the darkest chapters in my family's history; to the National Archives and National Portrait Gallery in Washington, D.C., in search of a deeper understanding of the development of America during the antebellum; to the working-class town of Bayonne, New Jersey, where all this began for me on Mother's Day, 1955; and finally, to my boyhood hometown, Mundelein, Illinois.

I have sifted through countless books and on-line records, and combed through stacks of family photographs. I have pored over my own personal diaries, pages of notes, and hours of interviews that I have been collecting for more than thirty years from relatives in Ireland, Scotland, Chicago, New Jersey, and Beaver Island, Michigan, all in an effort to fill in the spaces that my memory cannot. Subsequently, I have developed a database of more than seven hundred names in my genealogical records. All of these resources have made important contributions to these chapters.

Fadó, pronounced *f'doe*, is an Irish expression meaning "long ago" or "in years past." The term was commonly recited as an introduction to old Irish stories related by a *Seanchaidh* (*shana-'kee*), a teller of tales, an antiquarian, or historian. Coincidentally, Fadó in Portuguese means "destiny" or "fate." It is also a form of folk music characterized by mournful melodies and lyrics; a yearning, often about the sea or the life of the poor.

There are numerous words in Irish scattered throughout this book. They are italicized when they are first introduced and generally followed by their pronunciation and definition in English.

PART ONE

⌐∿⌐

"How will we know it's us without our past?"

—John Steinbeck, *Grapes of Wrath*

CHAPTER 1

∽

BEFORE THE WAKE

AUGUST, 1987: DEPRESSINGLY GREY, MISERABLY wet, and unspeakably sad. My six siblings and I, with our families in tow, scurry up the steps of Kristan Funeral Home in Mundelein, Illinois. It is lashing rain. My sister, Sheila, and I made all of the arrangements two days before. Pete Kristan, the funeral director's son hurries to greet us in the darkened lobby. Our families know each other informally, having grown up in the same small, mid-western town, attending the same church and the same schools. We have siblings around the same ages. Sheila and Pete were grade school classmates at Santa Maria del Popolo. Pete takes the time to express his condolences to each member of the family as we shake off the rain and crowd into the narrow foyer. We had been through this routine with Pete's father, Albert Kristan four years earlier, when Mother passed away. But the heir apparent to the family's modest mortuary business takes a personal interest in the arrangements this time, going well out of his way to accommodate us.

Pete turns his lanky frame and pushes open the double doors at the rear of the chapel. We file in silently. Several floral arrangements flank the bronze candelabras on either side of the coffin at the opposite end of the salon. I count them. Twenty-seven. About one hundred folding chairs are meticulously aligned down the center of the room. It's not going to be enough, I say to myself. Along the walls are heavily draped windows, several sofas, tables, and upholstered chairs. The wake won't be open to visitors for another hour. This is the family's time to grieve. No one talks. We sit and weep over the loss of our family patriarch and the realization that now we are orphans reaches critical mass.

Several minutes pass before I muster enough courage to approach his casket. I fight the unbearable sadness which I know might suddenly and violently overtake me at the sight of my father's lifeless body. I kneel down in front of him.

I brush my fingers lightly along the sleeve of his sport coat—a rough-hewn tweed of blue and grey. I recall how I encouraged him to purchase the jacket in McGee's on the Diamond in Donegal, Ireland, when he, Sheila, and I were on our way to Arranmore Island two summers before. It would be his last visit home to his native land. His crisp white shirt stands in bold contrast to the complementary blue and grey wool necktie that I bought for him in a little shop in the town of Gweedore (*ge 'door*) during that same visit. The Windsor knot is perfect. Pete made sure of it. Although decades apart in age, Pete and Dad were friends and shared a mutual admiration and respect for each other over quiet conversations and countless pints at the quaint lake-side tavern south of town, known as The Irish Mill.

"So," I whisper in resignation, "it has come down to this, has it?"

I am, for better or worse, very much like my father—both in personality and physical appearance. I'd like to think that I inherited only his finest qualities; in truth, I believe I possess in equal parts the best of his virtues and the worst of his faults. He is—or was—by those who knew him best, a good and a decent man. He had a difficult early life and fought hard to earn every scrap of respect that he gained through sheer determination and with practically no formal education. His mother died when he was six. He first left home at age twelve to work in the misty fields of Scotland and fled his despot father and the hard-scrabble existence of his tiny island home in Ireland for good when he was seventeen, forging his birth certificate and enlisting in the British Navy on the eve of the Second World War. Eventually, he made his way to America, where he met and married my mother, became a US citizen, raised a family, worked hard, and drank hard. He struggled for a lifetime in the dingy, rusting factories of American capitalists in order to provide for his family as best he could. And he instilled in me an abiding love for my family heritage, history, and music. He was my good friend. He had precious little time to enjoy the fruits of his labor and he leaves this world too soon—but he leaves it a better place than when he entered and when all is said and done, you can't ask any more of a man than that.

And now, here we are.

I admire with profound sadness how handsome he looks. My every tear carries with it its own special memory. I know well the lines on his face and the stories they tell.

CHAPTER 2

✢

ISLAND HOME

THE COASTAL ROAD THAT HUGS the red granite cliffs known as the "Bloody Foreland" is narrow and unfamiliar. I cautiously negotiate our rented Ford Fiesta over the patchy blacktop. We are in *na Gaeltacht* (*ne gale 'tock*) one of the few remaining pockets in Ireland where the Gaelic language is still commonly spoken. I grow impatient with my father's faded memory as he struggles to translate the road signs from the Irish to English, attempting to get us back to the modest fishing village of Burtonport. We have a place reserved for our car on the tiny ferry, *MISNEACH* (*meesh 'neh*, Courage), which will return us, come evening, to my father's birthplace and boyhood home, *Árainn Mhór Oileáin* (Arranmore Island). It is the last scheduled ferry of the day; miss it and we will have to spend the night in a B&B somewhere along the road in *na Rosann* (*ne ross 'n*, The Rosses), the desolate, naked headlands central to the Donegal coast.

This area of Ireland is often overlooked or dismissed by tourists who prefer the less challenging terrain, kitschy banquet castles, and crystal factories depicted in the splashy vacation brochures so prevalent in the counties to the south. An extract from *The Topographical Dictionary of Ireland Survey of 1837* by Samuel Lewis, describes *The Rosses* as "a dreary wilderness of rugged mountain wastes and heaths, unfavourable for either grazing or tillage." But western Donegal's haunting desolation, jagged coast, and independent people are exactly what I find so endearing and what has brought me back here for the third time in six years.

"We dilly-dallied too long in town," my father insists. He gazes out the rain-spattered window at the Derryveagh Mountains. "We'll never make the ferry now."

He is referring to the fact that we had stopped for a pint and a walk about the Gaeltacht village of Gweedore. We browsed the shops and I bought a fine wool necktie of blue and grey plaid. I presented it to him when we returned to the car. He smiled when he realized how well it complemented the new sport coat he purchased earlier in the day in Donegal town.

"No sense breaking your neck to get there, son" he says, folding the tie and placing it on his lap. "There will be no ferry at the dock."

I dismiss his pessimism, which I notice is increasing with the onset of age, and I am determined to prove him wrong. I set a new strategy: as long as the Atlantic Ocean remains off to our right we will eventually get to where we need to be. But will it be in time?

I speed recklessly past the clusters of confusing signposts beside the trout lakes and blanket bogs unique to the region. I wonder how in the world generations of families have been able to sustain themselves on such barren land. I intuitively drift over to the right-hand side of the road and jerk the wheel to the left narrowly in time to avoid an oncoming car. I wave to the driver as we pass. He looks perplexed. Not many tourists on these secondary roads.

"Jaysus Christ! Slow down, will ye," my father whines, "you're gonna get us all bloody killed!"

My sister, Sheila, and my first cousin, Brian Fisher, are wedged in the back of our tiny, sub-compact. They try to remain quiet as my father becomes increasingly agitated.

"You'll want to keep to the left now so ye will, Kevin," Brian says calmly, reminding me of the Irish style of driving.

I push the Dan Dooley rental to its limits, beating it like a government mule. If the car hire company knew I was traveling on these roads, in this remote part of the country, they would never have leased it to me.

"Goddammit!" my father yells. "Slow down. We're never going to make it in time so just slow down. I'm tellin' ye, we're late. The ferry will be gone!"

"We'll make it, we'll make it," I say with casual arrogance. "Hang on!"

The car leaps into the air as we dart across a small stone bridge in the town of Keadew (*Kay jew*) south of Kincasslagh. Suddenly, everything seems to go silent and in slow motion—like a scene from "The Dukes of Hazzard." The car noses downward. Anything that is not battened down becomes airborne: maps, candy wrappers, my father's new tie, cigarettes, and in the rear view mirror I see Brian and Sheila—out of their seats, frozen in time, with their faces pressed against the headliner on the roof of the car. We slam to the ground, jolting everyone back into their seats and back into real-time. I am laughing hysterically and can barely maintain control of the car. Brian and Sheila try unsuccessfully to smother their laughter. My father is not amused. He's screaming at me, expectorating all over the windshield, his voice high-pitched and trembling. I remain cool and calm but soon realize that I missed a turn and that we are now inland, headed toward Meenbannad on the Roshin Acres Road. I slow to a crawl to maneuver through a herd of sheep that had wandered onto the pavement. I roll down my window and try to coax them out of the way with words of encouragement. Another black-and-white signpost, *Ailt an Chorráin 2* (Burtonport 2). The car shudders in protest as I downshift and round the curve at St. Columba's Church. It is where my mother's parents, Edward and Celia Boyle, were married in 1918. We rattle down the long hill into Burtonport. A few hundred yards ahead I see the ferry. I slow down, mindful of the pedestrians and activity around the pier. The car jerks to a stop at the end of the dock.

We missed the ferry. It had backed away from the dock seconds before and was getting ready to come about and make for the harbor entrance.

My father is still admonishing me, "Ye see? Ye see? I told you we wouldn't make it. No, ye wouldn't listen to me, would ye? No! Ye had to drive like a bloody madman, nearly get us all killed! And for what?"

I pay no attention to his rant. I peer through the windshield and make eye contact with the ferry boat captain above in the wheelhouse. His name is Charlie Daly but the islanders call him Charlie the Lighthouse. He and I had a long conversation over a pint a few days before on the island, in Phil Bánn's Pub. I open the car door and stand with one foot on the pier. The engine idles roughly. Charlie recognizes me and nods once. He instructs the deckhands to make ready to dock. Much to everyone's astonishment, the boat returns to the pier and the draw-gate lowers. One of the crew guides me onto the overcrowded deck. I turn off the engine, wink at Sheila and quip, "See Dad, I knew we'd make it."

He glares at me.

A panoramic view of Arranmore Island gradually reveals itself as we sail past the small islets that surround and protect Burtonport harbor. The cottages and houses that comprise the various hamlets on the island dot its hillsides like scattered flocks of grazing sheep. Most houses lie near the shore. The rest fade up the gently draping long green veil of *Cur na Naoíbh* (*coor ne neebf*, The Mount of Saints). Arranmore is, at twelve square miles, the second largest island in Ireland and often confused with the three smaller Arran Islands off the coast of Galway to the south. To make the distinction, the word *mhór* (*more*), meaning great or large, is commonly added. But to locals, the island is simply known as Arran.

I recognize one of the deckhands, my cousin, Tony Gallagher, whom everyone calls Tony Patsy. It's a funny thing, these island names. They are given to identify individuals of specific families and typically include a location, a profession, or some physical attribute. Anthony Bonner, the postman, is known as Tony the Post. Little Barney O'Donnell is called Barney hen; Charlie Daly, the lighthouse keeper, Charlie the Lighthouse; and so on. But more often than not, with only a handful of family names on Arranmore, you have to go back several generations in surnames just to keep the lineage straight. "The son of / daughter of" rule is often applied—Tony Patsy, for example.

Besides my father's people, there are several other distinct families of O'Donnells on Arranmore. My father's mother's name was Mary, and her father's name, Hugh. Hence, my father's island name: John Mary Hughie (John, the son of Mary, the daughter of Hugh). On my initial visits to Arran, the islander's called me Kevin John Mary Hughie from America or Kevin John Condy from Chicago. But when that required too much effort, they eventually gave me my own name, Kevin the Singer (for reasons that will later become obvious).

O'Donnell is arguably the most eminent name in Irish history. We are fortunate in that we have always had excellent chroniclers to record the deeds and genealogy of our clan and are probably the best documented of all the Irish pedigrees. There have been many celebrated O'Donnells as soldiers, churchmen, authors, and politicians. O'Donnells are generally associated with County Donegal but there are fairly large septs in other parts of the country, particularly in Galway, Limerick, and Tipperary. The O'Donnell's of Arranmore have been among the custodians of the island long before records were kept.

The Donegal O'Donnells date back to the 13th century. They are descended from Donal, a direct relation of King Niall of The Nine Hostages (379-405 A.D. and pronounced *ny ill*). The Boyles, my mother's family, are also descended from this king, leaving my family "tree" shaped more like a giant wreath. Niall of The Nine Hostages was so named because in his early reign he consolidated his power by taking prisoner members of opposing royal families. He didn't discriminate either. He frequently raided each of the five provinces that then constituted Ireland, as well as the four surrounding countries of Scotland, Saxony, Brittany, and France. The opportunistic warlord amassed numerous wives as spoils during his conquests and sired dozens of children. He is considered to be the patriarch of the Ui Neill, meaning "the descendants of Niall," a group of dynasties that claimed the high kingship and ruled the northwest and other parts of Ireland for six centuries. If he was indeed the patriarch claimed in folklore, and recent genetic fingerprinting provides strong evidence that he was, Niall of the Nine Hostages would rank 2nd behind Genghis Khan as the most prolific male in history. An estimated 12,000,000 people can be genetically traced back to the randy Irish ruler.

Tradition holds that during his forays in Briton, Niall captured and sold into slavery a sixteen-year-old boy who later escaped, it is said, on orders he received from God in a dream, only to return to Ireland years later as a priest. He brought Christianity to the pagan masses, drove all the snakes from the emerald isle (to where is still a mystery) and used the native wood sorrel (or *seamróg*, shamrock) to demonstrate the concept of the Holy Trinity. The populace bought into it in a big way. More than fifteen centuries later we *still* celebrate his feast day, March 17th, and the Christian world recognizes that priest to be the apostle of Ireland, St. Patrick. But Patrick is just *one* of several patron Saints of Ireland. Most people don't know there are others. Patrick, it seems, had better PR. Even his contemporaries could not compete with his popularity. Legend tells that the obscure St. Urho of Finland, for example, tried to upstage Patrick's notoriety by making the preposterous claim that he drove the grasshoppers from the vineyards of Finland. Snakes are one thing, but grasshoppers and vineyards in Finland? Ludicrous! And who, outside of the Iron Range of Minnesota, has ever heard of St. Urho?
I rest my case.

My relatives of the renaissance were an interesting bunch. There is much written of the 16th century Kings and their families, and the Prince of Tyrconnell, *Aodh Roe* (*aid row*, Red Hugh) O'Donnell, is celebrated as the most famous. His well-chronicled adventures are the stuff from which legends, and as it turns out, Disney films, are made.
It seems from birth Hugh fulfilled many prophecies including one from his 6th century relative St. Colmcille—"there will come a man glorious, pure,

and exalted who will cause mournful weeping in every territory; he will be
the god-like prince, and he will be king for nine years."[1]

Red Hugh, the first-born son of his father's second marriage, ascended
to the throne in fulfillment of another prophecy, one that stated that an
O'Donnell with a *ball dearg*, (red spot) would rise to save and unite Ireland.
Hugh had a distinguishing Port-wine birthmark. The conspicuous stain,
impossible to disguise, covered a considerable portion of his face and head,
exalting him among his countrymen while targeting him among his enemies.
Many of his descendants are also said to have inherited this mark. (I have
such a stain, as did my father. My "red badge of courage" is comparatively
small and its geographical proximity is much farther south than Red Hugh's,
witnessed only by doctors and a few women I have known.).

Red Hugh's mother, Ineen Dubh (*doov*, black), conspired to have
the sword arm of the first-born son of the first marriage disabled, thus
eliminating him from election to high office. She later hoodwinked her senile
husband into believing that her darling Red Hugh should become the next
Ó Domhnaill (O'Donnell, or high king).

As a child, Hugh was fostered by several of the noble houses in Ulster
and "continued to grow and increase in comeliness and urbanity, tact and
eloquence, wisdom and knowledge, goodly size and noble deeds, so that
his name and fame spread throughout the five provinces of Erin among
the English and the Irish, even before he passed the age of boyhood and
completed his fifteenth year."[2]

Kidnapped in Donegal at the age of sixteen when he and a few friends
were lured aboard a vessel disguised as a Spanish wine merchant ship and
invited to sample its cargo; Hugh and his party were seized, disarmed,
and secured below deck. His English assailants made for deep water and
returned to Dublin where Hugh, at the insistence of Queen Elizabeth I, was
incarcerated in the tower at Dublin Castle. He and a comrade successfully
made their daring escape four years later in January 1592, by means of a silk
cord which had been smuggled into the prison. They fled the city barefoot
and nearly naked, and made fast for the Wicklow Mountains. When the
winter rains turned to snow, they sought shelter in a shallow cliff dwelling
in the near impregnable valley of Glenmalure. Covered with ice and near
death, Hugh was narrowly rescued by supporters of an ally Chieftain. His
comrade was not so lucky and died of exposure. Red Hugh suffered severe
frostbite of both feet from the ordeal and had both big toes amputated, which
left him lame for the rest of his life. Within a few months of his escape, he

was well enough to co-lead the Nine Years War against his captors, storming castles built by the English and slaughtering those unable to speak his native Gaelic language. He was ultimately defeated in the climactic Battle of Kinsale in 1602, after which he retreated to Spain seeking help from King Phillip III. Red Hugh O'Donnell died at the young age of thirty, at Castillo Simancas in central Spain while organizing a new invasion of Ireland. His death was a terrible blow to his countrymen and marked the beginning of the end of the O'Donnell reign.

With news of O'Donnell's death came rumor that he was poisoned by an English agent of Queen Elizabeth I. She approved a plot to have Red Hugh killed after he decimated nearly 20,000 of her finest troops during the Nine Years War. This theory was accepted by both English and Irish until recently—the English because they liked to believe that a traitor was safe nowhere; the Irish because it was further evidence of English treachery and elevated Red Hugh to immortal hero status.

Hugh's countless escapades made for an adventure story that Walt Disney himself couldn't resist bringing to the big screen. Buena Vista Pictures released *The Fighting Prince of Donegal* in October 1966, based on the book *Red Hugh, Prince of Donegal*, by Robert T. Reilly.[3] The cinematic melodrama extols the virtues of the young, swashbuckling Irish prince as only Disney Studios can relate. Red Hugh's death, however, was far less romantic in reality, and omitted from the movie. Recently-found documents concur that Red Hugh suffered an illness which lasted for seventeen days. A few days before his death he vomited a huge worm, which historians conclude was a tapeworm,[4] a disease quite prevalent in those days, but a death unbecoming an Irish hero; hence, the ready acceptance of the poisoning theory.

Hugh's brother, Prince Rory O'Donnell, was forced to renounce his lordship after his brother's death, and in an effort to sue for peace and retain as much of his territory and income as possible, he was compelled to kneel before the Queen and accept the English title, First Earl of Tyrconnell. Rory was a staunch defender of the Catholic Church and when he was exiled after the Nine Years War (a watershed moment in Irish history known as the Flight of the Earls), he made his way to Rome to visit his ally and fellow enemy of the British, Pope Paul V. Rory and his party of about one hundred were given a palace by the pope. (Currently the Columbus Hotel on Via della Conciliazione, on your left just before you enter St. Peter's Square.) Rory witnessed the building of St. Peter's Basilica, and had the royal privilege of ascending the Scala Regia at the Vatican. Some decades later, Italy's most famous and prolific sculptor, Gian Lorenzo Bernini, restored the Scala Regia and placed a sculpture of his own making there, an equestrian statue of Emperor Constantine. Bernini re-designed the Royal Staircase such that light shines down through a window from above, with Constantine's motto in Latin overhead, *In Hoc Signo Vinces* (under this sign you shall conquer). The motto and cross was adopted by the O'Donnells and said to date back to the time when St. Patrick imparted a cross with his staff held in his left hand, on the shield of Niall of the Nine Hostages' eldest son, Conall, promising and predicting that "such of his race as would carry that sign on their standard should never be overcome in battle." The motto and passion cross, held in the left hand (the O'Donnell Family Coat of Arms), appear beneath the window over the Scala Regia, prominently placed on a sculpted unfurled ribbon. All monarchs and royalty thenceforth visiting the pope would be reminded on leaving to follow the Cross, as O'Donnell had, and upon turning right and entering the atrium of St. Peter's Basilica would, ostensibly, be so inspired.

Rory O'Donnell died in Rome on the 28th of July, 1608, probably of malaria. He was thirty-three years of age. The revered Earl was given an elaborate Vatican funeral and buried at the foot of the high altar at San Pietro Montorio on Rome's Janiculum Hill. The Spanish Franciscan Church, commissioned by King Ferdinand and Queen Isabella of Spain (who also financed an expatriate by the name of Christopher Columbus for his expeditions to the New World), is built on the historical site of St. Peter the Apostle's inverted crucifixion.

Rory's youngest daughter, Mary, also left a lasting impression on posterity. Born in England in 1608 shortly after her father's death, she was given a large sum of money, raised in the old faith, and given the name Mary Stuart O'Donnell by King James I of England, the first Stuart King (formerly James VI of Scotland). The king and Mary shared a common Stuart ancestry. They were ninth cousins. She was raised in England by her grandmother, The Dowager Countess Kildare, the notorious Ineen Dubh as she was formerly known, suggesting that her mother, too, had died. Mary was introduced to the English Court when she was only twelve. She had many suitors and every inducement was held out to her to renounce her religion and marry one of the Protestant nobility. She refused and incurred the displeasure of those in high places.[5] Gradually she fell into disfavor. With her future precarious, Mary donned male attire, and with her maid and a manservant, escaped to Ireland. It is said that "whenever her disguise aroused any suspicion, she allayed it by making passionate love to a girl, or offering to fight a duel!"[6] The Old Gaelic Order was gone when her family went into exile and Mary had no cause to stay in Ireland and soon made her way to Flanders. From there she crossed to Genoa where she married Don John Edward O'Gallagher, like Mary, another descendant of the prodigious Niall of the Nine Hostages. What exactly became of Mary is a bit of a mystery; it is said that when she was expecting her second child she wrote in great distress to Cardinal Antonio Barberini at his family's sprawling villa in Rome, seeking assistance from the cardinal's uncle, Pope Urban VIII. (Nepotism was at work on a grand scale in the church hierarchy during the Baroque.) The pope was impressed with Mary's fame and commended her for her defense of her religion. But between trying to get the up-start astronomer Galileo Galile to recant his theory that the sun was at the center of the Solar System, waging war to expand his territory, and bankrupting the Vatican while purchasing art and amassing great wealth for his own family, the supine Pope Urban was otherwise distracted. The last that was heard of the remarkable Mary Stuart O'Donnell was that both of her children died in infancy and she faded into obscurity as a widow living in Prague, around 1649.

It appears from my review of the plethora of records, that my family is descended from either Aodh Roe and Rory O'Donnell's father, *Aodh Dubh* (Black Hugh), or (and more likely) through their lesser known uncle, Mánus *Óge* (*Oag*, junior, young), who was Black Hugh's brother and son of the 21st Chieftain.

The first possibility documents how Red Hugh, as the first-born son of his father's second marriage, "inherited" the title of king upon his father's death. The first born son of his father's first marriage was *Donncladh* (*den 'cle*, Dennis), whose fighting arm was permanently maimed at the behest of his wicked stepmother, Ineen Dubh. Dennis was subsequently appointed by his father as steward of *The Rosses* where he was known ever after as *Donncladh Scaite* (*Den cle skate cha*). His descendants are said to be numerous in *The Rosses* and surrounding areas to this day.

The second and more likely possibility stems from Red Hugh and Rory's uncle, Mánus, whose son, Seán, had land in the Inishowen Peninsula in northern Donegal. Seán took no part in his cousin's Nine Years War, but after the Flight of The Earls the English moved into Donegal and it became quite apparent there would be no recognition of Seán's good behavior. He was forced to make one last stand to defend his homeland, but he was outnumbered and the struggle was short lived. Knowing that the situation was hopeless, Seán retreated briefly to Tory Island where the family had a fort. His departure from Tory was so hasty that he left his wife and family behind. As his boat pulled away from the island under the cover of darkness, he came within oar's length of the English boats approaching the island but they were too preoccupied with landing their craft to notice the fleeing Seán. His next refuge was Arranmore.[7] How long he remained on the island is unclear but he fled from there to *The Rosses* mainland, assumed the alias Seán Mac Mánus Óg, and successfully eluded the English. No more appears on record except that he eventually settled on Inis Saile, a small island between Burtonport and Arranmore. Some accounts contend that he later returned to the larger, more hospitable island of Arranmore. Historians have every reason to believe that he and his heirs took up residence there and that his descendants are scattered throughout Arran and the lesser islands.

There is further evidence to support the theory that members of Red Hugh O'Donnell's family settled on Arranmore. Having failed in their attempt to conquer England in 1588, the Spanish Armada was homeward bound when the ships foundered off the west coast of Ireland. The O'Donnell clan came to their rescue. In gratitude, King Phillip III of Spain sent gifts to Red Hugh. Among the bounty was a set of four pearls. According to the 2006 book *Arranmore Island*, published by the island co-op, Comharchumann, the pearls were said to "vary in colour from silver-grey to cream-rose. Each pearl is encased in a mother-of-pearl shell as one piece, with the largest pearl being the size of an English Shilling, 13/16 in., and their gross weight is 132.93 grains." The pearls are estimated to be worth over one million dollars today.

Prior to fleeing Ireland for Spain in 1602, Red Hugh left the pearls in the care of Tony O'Donnell, who was said to be his heir. Tony settled on Arranmore and the islanders referred to him as "the uncrowned King of Donegal." The pearls remained on the island and were handed down through the generations, until the early 20th century when they were entrusted to Mary O'Donnell. Mary, who never married and had no heirs, moved to London as World War I was coming to a close, taking the pearls with her. She bequeathed them to a friend (and some say her husband) Earnest Chapman in 1928. Mary passed away in 1942. For safekeeping, Chapman stored the pearls in a London bank vault. He died in 1965 with no mention of the O'Donnell Pearls in his will. Their present day location remains an unsolved mystery.

There is one additional theory beyond circumstantial evidence and legend that has been overlooked, but leads me to believe O'Donnell nobility settled on the island. The Boyles and the Gallaghers were prominent chieftains in this region of Ireland and were most notable as the Gallowglass, mercenaries assigned to protect the king and the O'Donnell family. The names Boyle and Gallagher along with O'Donnell have remained the three most prominent surnames on Arranmore since the mid 17th century.

There have been many other famous O'Donnells through the ages. *The Annals of the Four Masters*, the detailed chronicle of medieval Irish history, lists the exploits of no fewer than three hundred O'Donnell chiefs and military leaders. In more recent times, Cardinal Patrick O'Donnell (1856-1927) was, at the age of thirty-two, the youngest Bishop in the world. He came from the townland of Glenties, not far from Arranmore, and eventually became the Primate, or head of the Catholic Church, for all Ireland. By coincidence, his calling brought him thirty-five hundred miles across the Atlantic Ocean in June, 1926, to my boyhood town of Mundelein.

The family name appears in other unusual and surprising places. Amid the pan and the prairie dogs of west Texas stands a dusty little crossroads called O'Donnell, named after a pair of local railroad promoters, T. J. and A. F. O'Donnell.[8] The brothers named the whistle stop after themselves in 1910, as was common among railroad men in that part of the country. There is a Pennsylvania Railway station by the same name, as well as similar references in Maryland and Wyoming, and an O'Donnell dormitory on the campus of Marquette University in Milwaukee, Wisconsin.

One hundred miles to the south of Milwaukee, William "Klondike" O'Donnell, a well known Chicago gangster, hit man, and big shot labor racketeer, infiltrated the city's Coal Teamsters & Hikers Union during the 1920's and 30's. He ran "a horde of homicidal hoodlums" in Cicero for his boss, Al Capone.[9] His 1926 police photo bears an uncanny family resemblance.

O'Donnell is inscribed on the base of the lighthouse at the entrance to Havana Harbor, Cuba, and I traversed a street called Calle de O'Donnell on my first visit to the old city of San Juan, Puerto Rico. I spent the better part of a beautiful tropical day in the Carnegie Library in Old San Juan investigating this peculiarity. I found both are in reference to Leopoldo O'Donnell y Jorris, Duke of Tetuan, a Spanish General and statesman who was appointed Governor of Cuba from 1843-1848. He is descended from the Donegal O'Donnells as a result of the Flight of the Earls.

Back on the little island of Arranmore, the O'Donnells of the 18th, 19th, and 20th centuries were concentrated in the middle and west end of the island, particularly in the townlands of Ballintra, Aphort, and Torries. These locales are a considerable distance from the island's harbors and afford panoramic views. They remain well fortified with rugged coastlines, steep hills, and scores of Gallagher and Boyle families in direct proximity who have occupied the same cottages for generations. Documentation not withstanding, this leads my imagination to believe that this island was indeed the likely home of routed O'Donnell nobility.

∾

This theory continues to drive my curiosity as I study the geography from aboard the sturdy ferry. She plies across "Arran Roads," the open stretch of water between the mainland and the fabled island, and I wonder: what compels the inhabitants to live in such a geographically remote and unusual place?

Inasmuch as *The Rosses* has a distinctive identity separate to the rest of Donegal, Arranmore has a distinctive identity separate from the rest of *The Rosses:* its own customs, culture, Gaelic and English dialects, and folklore. It has changed very little from the time medieval kings walked its hills.

During the 18th century, herring were plentiful in the waters around the Donegal islands and said to be of the highest quality throughout all the British Isles. But as the shoals were fished out, the herring ran further and further out to sea, beyond the reach of the little island boats. In 1793, commercial fishing failed completely. It was later revived for a few decades beginning around 1890, employing as many as six hundred residents in the coastal townlands and islands that comprise Templecrone Parish. Many of my grandparents' generation made their living from the sea. My maternal grandmother, Celia Boyle, is said to hold the Burtonport record for gutting herring, sixty in one minute. By 1920, the effects of international competition and civil unrest severely limited local commercial fishing.

Even in the best of economic conditions, their island life has always been a struggle and most men and children went off to *The Lagan* (the unknown lands east of *The Rosses*) seeking work at local hiring fairs in Letterkenny, Ballybofey, or Strabane. Others, like my father, joined the spring "tattie-hoking" squads in Scotland, cultivating and harvesting potatoes, cabbage, and corn. Nearly all returned to their desolate shamrock shores in the fall. Most who eventually broke away immigrated to America where some of their progeny have taken the time to trace their island heritage back two centuries or more, but Irish history under British rule has not made it easy to do so.

In 1695, shortly after the decisive Siege of Limerick, in which Ireland came under full subjugation of the English Crown, the terms of the treaty of surrender were subsequently rejected in the Protestant-dominated Irish Parliament. It was important that as a British colony all vestiges of Gaelic culture were removed, beginning with the language; many of the family names were Anglicized. A spate of laws upon the Irish Catholic population were enacted, and re-enacted, with the deliberate intent of reducing the people to "insignificant slaves" by forcing them into extreme destitution and degradation. They were officially known as "the Laws in Ireland for the Suppression of Popery," but were commonly called the Penal Laws. "The purposes of these laws were clear: to deprive Catholics from all civil life, reduce them to a condition of ignorance, disassociate them from the soil, and expirate the race."[10] This deliberate and systematic destruction of a population is defined by The Merriam-Webster New Collegiate Dictionary as *genocide*.

A partial list of the new Penal code forbid all Irish Catholics to practice their religion, enter a profession or trade, vote, hold public office, engage in trade or commerce, or secure a loan. They could not own a horse of greater value than five pounds. They could not purchase, lease, or inherit land, or reap any profit from their land in excess of one-third their rent. They could not be educated nor seek to educate themselves or their children and upon death could not leave infant children to Catholic guardianship. Engaging in "sin-forming" acts was encouraged as an honorable service. Priests were banned in Ireland. Priest hunting was treated as a sport. All priests who came to the country were hanged.

These laws were ruthlessly enforced throughout Ireland even in the most remote regions such as *The Rosses*. No register of births or marriages could be kept and civil registration for the general population did not begin until 1864, all of which makes finding and recovering documentation an often frustrating task and the reason so many records are incomplete. The first record of my family I can substantiate appears in the late 18th century when Conall O'Donnell, son of Phillip, was born on Arranmore in 1815. Prior to that there is a gap of approximately eight generations (160 years), going back to the time of Seán Mac Mánus Óg.

A glimpse of everyday island life during my great-great-grandfather's boyhood in 1823 is depicted in a letter sent to the absentee landlord of the island by his agent at that time, Nathan Forster:

> "It appears Arranmore contains 207 families that pay rent, one half of whom have no livestock to countervail it. There are also several cottiers [squatters] who pay no rent, not taken into account, whom by adding to the number of mouths, only help to increase the general distress.
>
> One half, at least, of the inhabitants are miserably poor, in a complete state of destitution of every malsary [sic] to any domestic comfort. This I presume arises from the following causes: an overlooked population, want of regular habitual industry, and their attachment to, and too frequent use of illicit spirits. For the island gives barley of a very superior description, which increases the temptation to making illicit whiskey."[11]

Throughout that year the agent sent several letters to the landlord referring to the condition of the people in vivid terms: "Their poverty generally speaking, is beyond conception . . . "[12]

The local inhabitants lived in abject poverty and squalor but were otherwise healthy—drunk, but healthy.

Until the Catholic Emancipation Act of 1829, when the Penal Laws were repealed, Catholics were forbidden to assemble for worship. On Arranmore, The Eucharist was clandestinely celebrated outdoors at a place called "Mass

Rock," a solitary granite boulder which served as an altar, today marked with a cross and plaque. It is located in the townland of *Plughoge* (*plo hug*), not far from my father's boyhood home.

The agent again writes to the landowner as the Penal Laws are gradually repealed: "They seek a rood of ground to erect a church on—perhaps half an acre would be of no great consideration to your Lordship."[13]

The island's first church, St. Crone's, was built in 1825. The first permanent priest, Father Neil Houston, was installed ten years later. "A good sailor and oarsman" whose stories of courage in braving the high seas to attend to the sick on the island are still told.[14]

The remoteness of Arran was a blessing and a curse and a testament to the resiliency of her people who have occupied her hills since the early Iron Age.[15] They survived successive waves of invasions from neighboring tribes, Vikings, Normans, and most recently, the British. They experienced the extermination attempts from Cromwell's armies in 1649 (known locally as the Slaughter of the Innocents), followed by the harshly enacted and brutally enforced 18th century Penal Laws, and re-plantation. Despite all this, the island population remains 100 percent Roman Catholic.

By the mid-nineteenth century, crop failures of cataclysmic proportions posed a very different threat, and it was starvation, disease, and deportation that eventually brought twenty-six hundred continuous years of habitation on Arranmore to the brink of extinction. Through it all, the people persevered, unlike those on the neighboring islands, Innishfree, Ichter, Owey, and Rutland among them. This harrowing time in the country's history has forever since been referred to by the islanders as *An Drochshaol* (*an dro sho hull*, The Great Hunger).

My father's British Navy photo, Liverpool 1941, looking every bit as hard as the gangster in the 1926 Chicago police photo below.

(1) William "Klondike" O'Donnell looking pleasant before a camera at the Detective Bureau. (2) Building in which was located a beauty shop which stopped machine gun bullets believed intended for "Fur" Sammons, one of "Klondike's" henchmen. (3) "Three-finger" Jack White, another "Klondike" O'Donnell ace.

A Chicago gangster in the family? Bearing an uncanny family resemblance, the caption reads: (1) William "Klondike" O'Donnell looking pleasant before a camera at the detective bureau. (2) Building [in Cicero] in which was located a beauty shop which stopped machine gun bullets believed intended for "Fur" Sammons, one of Klondike's henchmen. (3) "Three-finger" Jack White, another "Klondike" O'Donnell ace.—excerpted from Hal Andrews book *X Marks The Spot—Chicago Gangland Wars in Pictures*. Chicago. Maltese Publications, 1933.

Sign along Route 87 entering O'Donnell, Texas (pop 1,011). Named after brother promoters of the Pecos and Northern Texas Railway. The town was the boyhood home of actor Dan Blocker, better known as Hoss Cartwright on the NBC Television series, Bonanza.—*Photo courtesy of Byron Browne.*

A mariner's view of the Castillo del Morro lighthouse in Havana, Cuba. The name O'Donnell is carved into its base. Built in 1845 by then Governor of Cuba, Leopoldo O'Donnell y Jorris, like me, a descendant of the Donegal O'Donnells.—*Photo courtesy of Martijn Tersteeg.*

An 1849 Depiction of Brigid O'Donnel [*sic*]
and her two children during the famine.

"Her story is briefly this:—'... we were put out last November;
we owed some rent. I was at this time lying in fever... they
commenced knocking down the house, and had half of it knocked
down when two neighbours, women, Nell Spellesley and Kate
How, carried me out ... I was carried into a cabin, and lay there
for eight days, when I had the creature (the child) born dead. I
lay for three weeks after that. The whole of my family got the
fever, and one boy thirteen years old died with want and with
hunger while we were lying sick.'"—*Illustrated London Times, 22
December 1849*

CHAPTER 3

⌀⌀⌀

STARVATION, EVICTION, DEPORTATION

*A*N GORTA MÓR, OR THE Great Famine, began quite mysteriously in August 1845, the year my great-grandfather, Bryan Óge O'Donnell (Conall's son), was born on Arranmore Island. The local peasantry noticed that the leaves on their potato plants suddenly turned black, curled, then rotted, seemingly the result of a fog that had wafted across their fields. The cause was actually an airborne fungus (*phytophthora infestans*) originally transported in seed potatoes in the holds of ships traveling from Mexico and the United States to England and Belgium. Winds from southern England carried the fungus to the countryside around Dublin. The blight spread throughout the fields as fungal spores settled on the leaves of healthy potato plants, multiplied and were carried by the millions on cool breezes to surrounding plants. The problem was compounded when the parasitic spores were washed into the soil from the country's famously frequent rains, attacking healthy young tubers. Under ideal moist conditions, a single diseased potato plant infected thousands more in just a few days. The nation's entire crop was susceptible to the mold. The scientific community had not evolved techniques for developing genetically diverse and mold-resistant hybrid seed potatoes.

The attacked plants fermented while providing the nourishment the fungus needed to live, emitting a nauseating stench as they blackened and withered in front of the disbelieving eyes of the people. There had been crop failures in the past due to weather and other diseases, but this strange new failure was unlike anything ever seen. Potatoes dug out of the ground at first looked edible, but shriveled and rotted within days.

The people of Ireland formulated their own unscientific theories of the cause of the blight. Perhaps, it was thought, static electricity in the air resulting from the newly-arrived locomotive trains caused it. Others reasoned that "mortiferous vapors" from volcanoes emanating from the center of the earth were to blame. Catholics viewed the crisis in religious terms as Divine providence for the "sins of the people," while others saw it as emblemic judgment against abusive landlords and middlemen.

In England, religious and social reformers viewed the blight as a heaven-sent blessing, hoping that the scourge would finally provide the means necessary to transform Ireland by ending the cycle of poverty they believed resulted from the people's mistaken dependence on the potato.

Though County Donegal did not suffer the keen distress of the famine as in such counties as Mayo or Cork, reports document a period of much hardship, want, distress, and disease. The Parish of Templecrone was seriously affected and the greatest of hardship was felt on the islands, especially on Arranmore.[16]

In the years leading up to the famine the people of Arranmore held their land in a system called Rundale, whereby small plots of tillable ground were subdivided when necessary to provide an allotment for a son or daughter in marriage. In time, these sons and daughters subdivided their allotments to provide dowries for their own children. As the demand for the limited agricultural land increased, more land of inferior or marginal value was pushed into service. This lowered the living standards of people compelled to live on the land. Even in years of good harvests, it invariably placed them on a level of bare sustenance and starvation. Prior to the famine, Arranmore Island had a population around fifteen hundred clinging to infinitely small pieces of arable land along the leeward coastline. They shared the rest of the island with their neighbors as commonage, where they grazed their sheep and cattle. These family farms were so small, so irregular, and so infertile, that they could never produce enough food to sustain a growing family. Such areas of the country came to be recognized as "congested districts" attributed not to the density of the population, but to the inability to sustain them agriculturally and keep them from pending starvation.

"The means of earning money are scanty and limited in the extreme; and scarcely have the poor inhabitants a choice in the mode of expending it. After the demands on them for rent, tythes and taxes have been discharged, very little remains for the supply of food and apparel."[17]

On the eve of the Great Famine, Charles Conaghan, who had arrived on Arranmore several years earlier from nearby Cloughglas on the mainland, was a bachelor nearing the age of forty. He decided it was time he married. He was a skilled carpenter who helped to build the island's first church in 1825, as well as the barracks and several island cottages. His skills rewarded him handsomely following *Oíche na Gaoithe Móire* (*e ha na gee ha more*, the night of the big wind), the 1839 storm in which hurricane force winds swept across Ireland and destroyed many island houses. He had a sizable dowry to bargain with, as the vast majority of marriages on Arranmore in those days were "match-made." The church strongly discouraged company keeping, or courting, and the priests on the island had a reputation for chasing courting couples with blackthorn sticks in an effort to quell such sinful behavior. Charles went to the house of John Rodgers one night, as matchmaking was always done at night, and asked John for his only daughter, Meave *Eoin* (*Owen*). He likely had the usual consignment of *poitín* (*pote cheen*, moonshine) to help facilitate the negotiations. He mentioned at the pre-arranged meeting that he had a house and land, a few cattle and sheep, and he convinced old John Rodgers that he would be a good provider. Meave, approaching the spinster's age of thirty, had limited prospects. The two were married at the same time as several other island couples, the week before Shrove Tuesday (Fat Tuesday). Marriages were not permitted during Lent or between Advent and Christmas.

Charles and Meave had four of their six children between 1842 and 1850, covering the famine years. They all endured the darkest chapter to befall the country since Oliver Cromwell's campaign of slaughter and slavery two centuries earlier. The Conaghans survived the horrible ordeal and carried with them a lifetime of indelible and bitter memories of pestilence, disease, starvation, and death. The story of their survival provides a fortuitous thread of lineage and is the genesis of this memoir. Charles and Meave Eoin Conaghan were my great-great-grandparents.

The degree of poverty specific to the Arranmore islanders in those pre-famine days is vividly depicted by Thomas Campbell Foster, a London

attorney who was engaged by the London Times to report on conditions in
Ireland in 1845-46. His letters published in the Times convey a grim picture
of the squalor and destitution he encountered in the Irish countryside during
his journey. Reporting from the town of Gweedore on September 3rd, 1845,
he describes his recent visit to Arranmore:

> "I landed at a village called Labgaroo [Leabgarrow] containing
> 24 cottages and almost the whole of it shockingly destitute, and
> a half-naked shoeless population immediately swarmed out and
> surrounded me, begging me to go into their cottages—such of
> them at least could speak English—and look at their misery.
> Some thrust scraps of paper into my hands with petitions written
> on them, praying for assistance to keep them from starving, for
> medical assistance, to have their rents reduced, and so on. Such
> an assemblage of wretched beggar-like human beings I never saw.
> These scraps of paper, or petitions were ready written, and some
> of them old and worn. They appeared to me to be intended to
> be ready to present any stranger who might chance by during the
> summer visit to the island.
>
> Picture to yourself the beggars who sometimes on Sundays lie
> about the pavement in the streets of London, dressed up to
> excite commiseration and who write with a piece of chalk on
> the flags, 'I'm starving', and then lay themselves down beside
> the scrawl crouched up in a violent shivering fit as the people
> pass them from church, and you have the exact facsimile of
> the kind of people around me—the tenants of the Marquis
> Conyngham. At times I was informed, and I can well believe
> it from what I saw, that their destitution is horrible. They are,
> however, but a degree worse than the tenants of the mainland
> opposite."[18]

It is difficult to imagine that these were the conditions *before* the
famine. The Marquis Conyngham, mentioned by Mr. Foster, was the
British absentee landlord who owned Arranmore and large tracts of the
mainland adjacent, then called the Barony of Boylagh. He was responsible
for this inhumanity. He never once visited his 75,000 acre estate. During
the summer of 1845 he concentrated all of his time and effort on a new pet

project: using his considerable influence with Queen Victoria to have the privileges of the Royal Yacht Club (which later became the Royal Saint George Yacht Club) conferred in Dun Laoghaire (*dun leery*), Co. Dublin (then Kingstown). Conyngham left the management of his property in the hands of his English agent, Benbow, who, after replacing Nathan Forster, visited the island only once a year to collect rents.

The rhythm of island life dictated that once the spring crops were planted, the able-bodied men and boys went off to local hiring fairs of *The Lagan* or to Scotland to seek work. The women remained at home to tend to the little patches of potatoes to help ward off starvation in the ensuing winter and early spring. As a result, the Arranmore people were ill-prepared to face the calamity to beset them in the upcoming years of 1846-1849. As early as August, 1845, the general blight of the potato crop had become apparent in the Innishowen peninsula of northern Donegal. But the blight behaved capriciously in the baronies of Boylagh and nearby Kilmacrenan, which comprise the poorest soil in the county, and many areas went practically unscathed. However, before summer rolled into autumn the following year, reports of new areas of blight in the region became more frequent and widespread. A correspondent to the Derry newspaper said that he had seen enough of the potato disease in *The Rosses* to convince him that famine was awaiting epidemic proportions if the people did not get immediate relief.

> "I do not exaggerate," he stated, "when I say that I have not seen one sound pit of potatoes out of ten and, in almost all, one fourth at least is damaged—and the disease frightfully progressing!"[19]

But such reports to government officials were down-played and sanitized by the landowners, fearing any intervention would upset the balance of trade in the grain market, and the loss of their property. When assistance finally did arrive, it was too little, too late.

As the summer of 1846 progressed the searing blight began turning healthy fields into a putrid blackened mass. The disease had spread so rapidly that within a week's time in August it had consumed the whole of the island. It became a common sight to see gaunt-looking figures combing the fields in search of a single potato which might have escaped the ravages of the disease. As summer gave way to autumn and the cold pale skies of October enveloped the island, the wind moaned dolefully, and the now starving and panicking population began slaughtering sheep on the mountainsides.

Soon throughout the county people began to live off wild blackberries, nettles, turnips, old cabbage leaves, edible seaweed, shellfish, limpets, and roots. Their teeth were stained green from consuming roadside weeds and grass. Not only were dogs, donkeys, horses, cattle, and fowl eaten, but so were foxes, hedgehogs, frogs, rabbits, and badgers. Many began selling their personal belongings—boats, nets, cattle, even the clothes that they wore—all in an effort to save themselves from impending starvation. Barns were raided at night in the hope of finding a hidden cache of the crop.

It was reported to authorities in Burtonport that a woman by the name of Mary Gallagher on Arranmore was caught one night by a neighbor while raiding his potato stores. To brand her as a pilferer, he cut off her ears with a reaping hook.[20]

A pall blanketed the island. Hedgerows were silent of any birds as both wild eggs and the birds themselves had been eaten. The stillness was only interrupted by the wail of banshees who cruised "pinky hill" at night, lurked among "*the dreen*" (the brambles that hug the roadside in Fallagowan), hid in the hobs and hollows, and rattled the bothy doors of the fearful islanders. Charles Conaghan did his best to protect his family and provide for his wife Meave, young daughter, Nellie, and infant son, Owen.

Famed American author and social reformer Mrs. Asenath Nicholson spent 1847-49 traveling throughout Ireland recording her observations of the Famine. She paints a horrifying description of the desolation and destitution of the Donegal people:

> "The dogs ceased their barking, there were scarcely any cocks to be heard crowing in the morning, and the glad-some mirth of children everywhere ceased. O! Ye, whose nerves are disturbed at the glee of the loud-laughing boy, come to this land of darkness and death, and for leagues you may travel, and in house or cabin, by the wayside, on the hill-top, or upon the meadow, you shall not see a smile, you shall not see the sprightly foot running in ecstasy after the rolling hoop, leaping the ditch or tossing the ball. The young laughing full faces, and brilliant eyes, and buoyant limbs, had become walking-skeletons of death! When I saw one

approaching, with his emaciated fingers locked together before him, his body in a bending position, as all generally crawled along, if I had neither bread nor money to give, I turned from the path; for, instead of the 'God save ye kindly,' or 'ye look wary, lady,' which had ever been the salutation to me on the mountains, I knew it would be the imploring look or the vacant sepulchral stare, which, when once fastened upon you, leaves its impress for ever."[21]

The few islanders who were fortunate to have a remainder of the 1845 crop on hand held on to it in the hope the scarcity would drive up the price when the merchants from Skerries on the east coast of Ireland and from Scotland arrived as they did every year for cargos of potatoes. The *SMACK MARINER* which anchored at neighboring Rutland Island to take on potato cargo was attacked by a large party of island men in boats. Her rigging was torn and her deck fittings smashed. A similar fate was met by the *LADY FRANCIS* and the *SEA FLOWER* from Dublin when they arrived to collect potatoes. So desperate was the situation that in the autumn of that year the government was forced to rush a shipload of Indian corn meal, chosen by the British government to replace the potato as the staple article of food, to the islands off the Donegal coast.[22] The steamer *WARRIOR* sailed up from the main depot in Sligo and weighed anchor off Rutland Island for distribution of the coarse meal among the starving Arranmore people.[23]

The corn meal was not without its own problems. Normally, the islanders ate huge meals of boiled potatoes three times a day. A working man might eat up to fourteen pounds daily. They found Indian corn to be an unsatisfying substitute. Peasants nicknamed the bright yellow substance "Peel's brimstone," after British Prime Minister, Sir Robert Peel, who imported it from America. It was difficult to cook, hard to digest, tore at the intestinal lining, and caused diarrhea. Most of all, it lacked the belly-filling bulk of the potato. It also resulted in scurvy, a condition previously unknown in Ireland due to the normal consumption of potatoes naturally rich in Vitamin C. Among the Arranmore people, Peel's brimstone was known as *min dipsy*.[24] (I heard my father use this term whenever he faced a plate full of unappetizing food. Only now do I understand what he meant.) What meager amount of min dipsy arrived on Arranmore was usually "in a rancid and sodden state, heavily infested with maggots, weevils and other impurities. To make it fit for human consumption it was necessary to simmer it over a slow-burning fire until all the foreign bodies and impurities formed a scum on the surface. This was then skimmed off and the meal was brought to a boil."[25]

In deciding their course of action during the Famine, British government officials and administrators rigidly adhered to the popular theory of the day, known as *laissez-faire*, which advocated a hands-off policy in the belief that all problems would eventually be solved on their own through "natural means." Great efforts were made to sidestep social problems and avoid any interference with private enterprise or the rights of property owners. After years of successful political foot-dragging, the government was pressured to intervene and finally got its meal scheme underway. But the entire country was in crisis by this time, with over half the nation's potato crop failed. Hardest hit was western Ireland.

Areas such as Arranmore and *The Rosses* were seriously lacking in services and utilities necessary for establishing the government relief scheme. There were no merchants of sufficient size and means in remote Western Donegal who could be depended upon to import and distribute adequate quantities of the coarse Indian corn. There was also great risk that convoys of corn meal coming from Derry and Letterkenny would come under attack and piracy in the mountainous areas of Muckish Gap, Glendowan, Glenswilly, and Barnsmore Gap on their way to *The Rosses*. Coupled with this was the complete unpreparedness and neglect by many of the landlords, especially the Marquis Conyngham.[26]

As 1846 drew to its bleak close, the following year would bring no hope of relief to the people. It would forever come to be known throughout all of Ireland as Black 47. The destruction of the potato crop that year was total. Not a single healthy potato stock could be seen throughout the island and Charles and Meave Conaghan were expecting their third child. Now there would be five hungry mouths to feed.

The government begrudgingly sent supply ships around the coast and when they anchored off nearby Rutland Island, the delighted people of Arranmore thought that relief had come at last. But the expected gift of barley seed and turnip seed was offered with animus by the greedy and opportunistic administrators. They insisted on a price considerably higher than the market, and the islanders watched in disbelief as the ships sailed away without leaving its contents; not one had the money to purchase even a pound of seed. The islanders later were told that the "lazy dogs" were offered the seed, but refused it, not willing to take the trouble to sow it.

> "The winter passed, but the spring brought no fresh hopes; onward was the fearful march—many faces that were ruddy, and limbs that were robust, and hearts that had scarcely had a fear that the wolf would enter their dwelling, now began to fade, stumble, and finally sink under the pursuer."[27]

By spring of 1847, the island's residents were completely malnourished and fell easy victims to the onslaught of disease. Pestilence, dysentery, scurvy, and fever, the usual concomitants of famine, spread across the island, reaching epidemic proportions. *An Fiabhr Dubh* (black fever), *agus án Fiabhr ás Ballach* (typhoid fever), and spotted fever, known locally as relapsing fever, were common in the region.[28] Entire families were decimated as the fevers spread amongst many or all the members of a household. The islanders, already ravaged by two crop failures were at their lowest level of resistance to the virulent fevers, which tightened their grip on many of the humble homesteads.

Father James Horgan, "a fat and surly-looking man,"[29] had been transferred to the island prior to the onset of the Famine. When needled by a local curate from the mainland that his people were in a bad state, he responded "bad enough, they give me nothing. Why should they? You cannot expect or ask anything of the poor starving creatures.[30] Generations of islanders relate stories of his heroic work maintaining the spirits of his parishioners—even lashing the corpses of the victims to his back with reed-rope and carrying them up the slope to the seaside graveyard to bury them himself.

So desperate and moving were the anguished cries of the starving and sick women and children that the men of the island set out in boats and waylaid cargo ships, which plied along the northwest of Ireland. In June, 1847, the vessel *LARNE* of Belfast was making for Westport, Mayo, with a cargo of wheat meal. The islanders becalmed her near Owey Sound and boarded her, armed with hatchets and hammers. They broke the hatchway and took twelve bags of meal. Before the *LARNE* could escape, another party of islanders came aboard and took three tons of meal with them. A few days later police arrived on Arranmore and searched the island. They confiscated fifteen bags of meal buried in sand on the west side of the island. Members of a starving island family were tried and convicted for the attack on the *LARNE* and sentenced to stiff jail terms. Those who informed on them, islanders also, had done so with the false expectation that they would be rewarded with food. They were forced to leave Arranmore and it was necessary to keep them in Lifford jail to protect them from retribution from the *Clann Mhaláidh* (*clan molly*), or Molly Maguire's, a secret society of Irish vigilantes, who wished to wreak their own form of corporeal justice. The depot at the neighboring town of Burtonport on the mainland was also frequently raided by men in boats, and it was surmised that the culprits must be from Arranmore.[31]

Reporting on her arrival to Arranmore Island during the summer of 1847, Mrs. Nicholson writes:

> "The next day we were to visit Arranmore, a pretty sunny island, where peace and comfort had ever reigned. The peasantry here were about 1500 in number, occupying a green spot three miles in length, and had always maintained a good character for morality and industry. They kept cows, which supplied them with milk, sheep with wool, geese with beds, fowls with eggs; and grew oats, potatoes, and barley; they wore shoes and stockings, which none of the female peasantry can do in the country places; they likewise spun and made their own wearing apparel, and as the difficulty of crossing the channel of the sea, which was three miles, was considerable, they seldom visited the main land. When they saw the potato was gone, they ate their fowls, sheep, and cows, and then began to cross the sea to Templecrone for relief. What could they find there? One man could do but little to stay the desolation. Hundreds had died before this, and though I knew that painful scenes were in waiting, yet, if possible, the half was not told me. Six men, beside Mr. Griffith, crossed with me in an open boat, and we landed, not buoyantly, upon the once pretty island. The first that called my attention was the death-like stillness—nothing of life was seen or heard, excepting occasionally a dog. These looked so unlike all others I had seen among the poor. I unwittingly said—'How can the dogs look so fat and shining here, where there is no food for the people?' 'Shall I tell her?' said the pilot to Mr. Griffith, not supposing that I heard him.

This was enough: if anything were wanting to make the horrors of a famine complete, this supplied the deficiency. Reader, I leave you to your thoughts, and only add that the sleek dogs of Arranmore were my horror, if not my hatred, and have stamped on my mind images which can never be effaced."[32]

Sheep herding dogs were numerous on the island and relied upon extensively by the locals for maintaining their flocks. As the Famine progressed the dogs resorted to their basic survival instincts to keep from starvation. Mrs. Nicholson explains:

"A famine burying-ground on the sea-coast has some peculiarities belonging to itself. First, it often lies on the borders of the sea, without any wall, and the dead are put into the earth without a coffin, so many piles on piles that the top one often can be seen through the thin covering; loose stones are placed over, but the dogs can easily put these aside, and tear away the loose dirt . . . This was the burial-place of Arranmore, and here, at the foot, was the old roaring ocean, dashing its proud waves, embracing in its broad arms this trembling green gem, while the spray was continually sprinkling its salt tears upon its once fair cheek, as if weeping over a desolation that it could not repair."[33]

I have known the people of Arranmore to be fiercely independent, proud, honest, and resourceful. I have discerned this through my father's stories and have witnessed the same on many occasions. So, when Mrs. Nicholson relates her astonishment at the sight of such a poor and miserable community, it comes as no surprise to me how warmly they greeted her and how congenial they were toward her.

"We went from cabin to cabin, till I begged the curate to show me no more. Not in a solitary instance did one beg. When we entered their dark, smoky, floor-less abodes, made darker by the glaring of a bright sun, which had been shining upon us, they stood up before us in a speechless, vacant, staring, yet most eloquent posture, mutely graphically saying, 'Here we are, your bone and your flesh, made in God's image, like you. Look at us! What brought us here?' Let darkness and the shadow of death stain that day when first the potato was planted in this green isle of the sea.

In every cabin we visited, some were so weak that they could neither stand nor sit, and when we entered they saluted us, by crawling on all fours toward us, and trying to give some token of welcome. Never, never was the ruling passion stronger in death. That heart-felt greeting which they give the stranger, had not in the least died within them; it was not asking charity, for the curate answered my inquiries afterward, concerning the self-control, which was the wonder of all, [said] that he had sent a man previously through the island, to say that a stranger, from across the sea, was coming to visit them, but she had no money or food to give, and they must not trouble her.

A decently clad woman, with shoes and stockings, and blue petticoat (that was the kind the peasants always wore in their days of comfort), very pleasantly offered me a bowl of milk. Astonished at the sight of such a luxury, I refused, from the principle that it would be robbing the starving. 'I regret,' said the curate, as we turned away, 'that you did not take it, her feelings were deeply injured: a shadow of disappointment,' he said, 'came over her face', as she answered in Irish: 'The stranger looks weary and her heart is drooping for the nourishment.'"[34]

Mrs. Nicholson was unaware of her social gaffe. The generous practice of accepting a drink when offered by the people of this locality is a tradition that has continued down through the centuries from the time of Red Hugh O'Donnell.

The story goes that Aodh Roe (Red Hugh) O'Donnell spent the day hunting in the Bluestack Mountains. He and his party of huntsmen were returning to Donegal town when they stopped at an inn in *The Rosses* for refreshment. O'Donnell called for a gallon of drink but the innkeeper, being so excited at his noble company, produced instead four gallons, one pint and one glass. On seeing his mistake the innkeeper was about to pour the excess back but O'Donnell wouldn't allow it and paid for the lot. He declared it *"Galún Uí Dhomhnaill"* (the O'Donnell Gallon) and invited his men to drink their fill. The remainder was to be left for travelers passing that way.[35]

Today when food and drink are offered in abundance on Arranmore and elsewhere in *The Rosses*, it is still referred to as Galún Uí Dhomhnaill. The practice was something my father was very keen on teaching me. "Always remember," he said, "it is considered an insult of the highest degree to refuse such an offer from the island people." Regardless of their means, such a sharing gesture is common among them. Reciprocation is generally a good indication that you have been accepted by that individual. It is a subtle dance, and only one of many important cultural nuances among the island people passed down through the centuries.

Shortly after Mrs. Nicholson's visit, in 1848, the island came under the management of a new, spurious landlord from Belfast, John Stoup Charley. The islanders called him Charley *Beag* (*beg*), meaning little Charley, a diminutive term owing more to his nature than to his physical stature. Charley bought the island for £1,500 from the Marquis Conyngham who sold it due to "the unruly nature of the people."[36] The twenty-four-year-old solicitor, Charley Beag, earned his wealth in the textile industry. He had a new plan for the use of his property, and it didn't include the islanders. He wanted to convert nearly the whole of it to cattle grazing. He concluded that the island, seriously over-populated, was more than the land could sustain and that alone exacerbated the situation. He conveniently decided to cut the population in half. Only families who could show proper title to their land as rent-payers were allowed to stay. He suspended the Rundale system of land division and consolidated the farms of those who could still pay their rent. The rest, the sub-tenants and squatters, he systematically evicted. This included several members of my ancestral family, although Charles and Meave Conaghan were among those allowed to stay as rent-abiding tenants.

The fear of eviction hung over the islanders like the Sword of Damocles, and they were powerless to stop it. Eviction came without warning. A party of local officials knocked at the door, read the Eviction Order and the Riot Act, often while the tenant's goods were confiscated.[37] The panicking people scrambled to secure as many possessions as they could before the house was set ablaze and burned to the ground so that they could not return. They were banished from the island and in many cases Charley had them deported out of the country.

Those too old, too weak, or unable to find passage out of Ireland were landed on the headland. Most made their way to the already over-crowded workhouse in the town of Glenties on the mainland.

Slowly and fearfully they made their way on foot over the Bluestack Mountains for the grim, grey world of the workhouse, without any rights or privileges, as poor, starved, homeless specimens of humanity.[38]

The Glenties workhouse was a workhouse in name only. It was a place to come to die. It was grossly overcrowded, which made the living conditions appalling for the inmates. Fevers spread quickly and a large proportion succumbed to sickness and disease shortly after arriving. The death rate at Glenties was among the highest in the country. This was understandable since the ground on which the workhouse stood was swampy. The building was lower than the surrounding ground and frequently flooded. The conditions were filthy. Cholera claimed most of the half-starved and barely clothed inmates.

> "They had one meal daily which consisted of oatmeal and water. The beds of dirty straw were laid in rows on the floor. Six or seven persons crowded together under one rag. There were no blankets. The rooms were hardly bearable for the filth. The living and dying were stretched side-by-side under the same filthy covering. No wonder that disease and pestilence were filling the infirmary and that the pale, haggard countenances of the poor boys and girls told of suffering impossible to comprehend."[39]

> "There was a most offensive smell in every part of the house, but, especially in the dormitories. The floors were not properly cleansed and it was apparent that the necessities of nature were performed without due regard to decency or cleanliness. The straw beds are old and musty and ventilation is non-existent"[40]

Conditions were so bad that authorities were compelled to dismiss the matron who ran the house for gross dereliction of duty.

Salvation came to those who remained on Arranmore thanks entirely to an organization called "The Religious Society of Friends," the Quakers. They hired two government steamers, the ALBERT and the SCOURGE, in Liverpool in 1847 to bring a cargo of peas, rice, meal, biscuits, and beef to Arranmore and the most distressed areas of the Donegal coast. They also shipped to Donegal the big *coire* (*choir*, caldron), in which they prepared broth for the poor at their soup kitchens. Officials of the Society visited Arranmore from time to time during the famine years and a passage from elder William Bennett to the headquarters of the Society in March, 1847, includes the following:

> "Throughout the island there was remarkable equality, one mass of deep, sunk poverty, disease and degradation. There were the same gaunt looks in men, and peculiar, worn-out expressions of premature old age in the countenance of women and children, with the latter still clutched, with an eagerness I shall never forget, at some biscuit I had brought with me when offered to eat with their seaweed; very different from the vacant stare with which the sight of food was regarded by those in whom the very desire and volition for food were past."

The following year, a malnourished Meave Eoin Conaghan miraculously gave birth to her third child, a tiny and frail daughter, whom she named Brigid (my great-grandmother). She would be called Biddy Charlie among the islanders and despite the fact that nearly her entire family immigrated to America, Brigid never left Arranmore.

By the spring of 1849, Arranmore began to recover from the Famine. Under the careful management of the Society of Friends, the islanders voluntarily saved as much for seed as they could. For those of us whose families were among the victims of the Great Hunger, we owe a sincere and perpetual debt of gratitude to the Quakers for the comfort they brought to the people of Arranmore in the black years of famine when our forefathers' distress was so acute and salvation seemed so hopelessly distant.

As Charles and Meave Eoin celebrated the miraculous birth of another child, a daughter, Madgie, they mourned with the rest of the islanders the loss of five hundred who died from famine—one third the island's population. An equal number were banished by Charley Beag to the mainland and untold numbers died in the Glenties workhouse. But the plight of the Arranmore people was far from over.

As life began to return to normal, the island's new landlord, John Charley, built himself a large two-story house overlooking the main pier in Leabgarrow (today the Glen Hotel). He grew increasingly impatient with the slow progress of his plan to rid the island of its inhabitants, and in one fell-swoop evicted more than thirty families from the island. As a magnanimous gesture of good will to those he banished, he promised to hire a ship to bring them to America. The suddenly dispossessed islanders abruptly left Arranmore for good in April, 1851. Their houses razed and their meager possessions confiscated, the islanders were put out into a world completely foreign to them, far from the remote and closed community they had known all their lives. They were, by and large, an illiterate people, unable to speak or understand English, and they possessed very limited skills. What was to become of them?

Their families and neighbors came down to the pier on that cold and rainy April morning to bid them goodbye. As the boats set off for the mainland, screams of anguish, wailing, and caioning drifted over the grey water as if death had befallen them. Indeed it was very much like death. Never again would they be allowed to return to their island or see or be seen by their families and loved ones—at least, not in this world.

The exiled left in the wake of the worst winter in living memory. Most winters saw little or no snowfall. But blizzard after blizzard had swept mercilessly over the mountains and glens of Donegal in the preceding months, depositing heavy, drifting snows. One hundred and sixty-six gaunt individuals made their way from Burtonport with little more than rags lashed to their feet, trudging through the snow-laden passes of the Bluestack Mountains for Donegal Town, forty miles away. It took them nearly a week to make the journey on foot under those conditions. Six of the islanders died along the way, succumbing to the cold, hunger, and disease. When the islanders arrived in Donegal town there was no ship waiting for them as John Charley had promised. They had nowhere to turn.

> "These poor Arranmore islanders were plunged into such terrible misery and destitution, that, had not the charitable inhabitants of Donegal Town come to their aid many would have perished of sickness and starvation."[41]

Eventually, the one hundred and sixty souls who survived the journey through the mountains found passage to Quebec, Canada, aboard the

COUNTESS OF ARAN. John Charley reluctantly paid £201 Sterling for their passage,[42] just to be rid of them.

With their extensive knowledge of the sea, the Arranmore people knew the vessel was not seaworthy but had no choice but to board her. She was leaky, ill-fitted, and lice-infested. Conditions were appalling. It would be the last voyage of human cargo for the *COUNTESS OF ARAN*. Manifests from the time recorded only the names, ages, occupations, and nationalities of the countless emigrants. They make no mention of the death rate during the crossing (which was as high as thirty percent), or how the bodies of the dead were ripped from the dark and filthy cargo holds, sewn into canvas bags, lashed with ballast stone, and unceremoniously thrown overboard to be swallowed up by the Atlantic Ocean. On her return voyage to Ireland from Quebec, the *COUNTESS OF ARAN* sank, with all hands lost.

Many of the islanders who managed to survive the long and arduous sea voyage made their way to Toronto, New York, and the coal mines of Pennsylvania, places where the need for menial labor was greatest. The surviving islanders in many cases faced just as much racism and persecution in the New World as they were forced to leave behind in the old one. Their lack of education, their inability to speak English, and their belief in a religion most other immigrants did not share made them feared and despised. The Irish in those days were considered a sub-race.[43] It was not uncommon to see "No Irish Need Apply" in storefront windows and among businesses. The Irish were relegated to the poorest ghettos and held what were considered at the time to be the most menial jobs in the cities: policemen, firemen, gangers on the railways, and navvies on canal and tunnel projects, where they earned an average of 4 shillings a day (approximately 40 cents in 2008 money).[44] An oft quoted outburst of bigotry during this period appeared in the Chicago Tribune in 1855: "the most depraved, debased, worthless and irredeemable drunkards and sots which curse the community, are the Irish Catholics."[45]

The Famine Memorial on Customs House Quay, along the River Liffey Dublin. Dedicated in 1997. Sculptor Rowan Gillespie's evocative figures are a palpable reminder of Ireland's tragic past. Cast in iron, they represent the strength and resiliency of the Irish race. I cannot describe how haunting and disturbing it is to walk among these lost souls.—*Photo by author*

CHAPTER 4

✦

THE NEW WORLD

WHILE THE SEVENTH CENTURY HEIRS of Niall of the Nine Hostages were conquering local Irish chieftains and expanding their dynasties, three thousand miles to the west of *The Lagan* lay a world unknown to Europe. It would be another thousand years before white men first set eyes on the verdant hardwood forest and giant blue-stem grass prairie that became my boyhood village. The inhabitants of this pre-Columbian land during that time were called Mound Builders, after the way they buried their dead. The burial mounds consisted of surface soil found along the many inland rivers and fresh-water lakes. These tombs contained tools and weapons, but the people left little else before moving on.[46]

By 1650, as the descendants of Seán Mac Mánus Óg O'Donnell were beginning to settle on Arranmore, mission records indicate that Native Americans in the area of the lower Great Lakes led a semi-mobile lifestyle, growing corn, hunting small game, fishing, making maple syrup, and gathering wild rice and other plant foods. They also engaged in fur trade with the French.[47] These native peoples were among the central Algonquian Indians. The predominant tribes in the region at the time Europeans first arrived were the Miami, Mascouten, Fox, and Potawatomi. These were the observations of French-born Jesuit missionary, Father Jacques Marquette, and his companion Louis Joliet, a former philosophy student turned Canadian explorer, fur trapper, and map maker. The intrepid explorers visited the northeast region of Illinois between 1673-75, and canoed the waters of the Des Plaines River, claiming the land for France.

The Indians traded with French fur trappers in present day Lake County Illinois, north of what is now Mundelein, at a spot the first European settlers called Fort Hill. The large alluvial mound of glacial till rose out of the prairie immediately northwest of the present day intersection of Peterson and Alleghany Roads. Its elevation was seventeen feet higher than the next highest location in the county. Its commanding view in all directions provided a convenient gathering place and look-out point.[48] It was a familiar stop along what was later referred to as The Hiawatha Trail. This footpath, or trace, was well-used by the Indians connecting the place of "wild garlic," or what the Miami called *shikaakwa* (and the French referred to as Chicago), to the glacial remnant outwash fifty miles to the northwest, the Chain O'Lakes. As a child, I saw round commemorative signs denoting the historic Hiawatha Trail along Route 176 north and west of town. I often looked for Indians out the window of my father's car as we sped past. I always hoped to see one who may have become lost or who never relocated to the Wisconsin Dells, where my family vacationed when I was five years old, and where, I mistakenly thought, all Indians moved to work in the amusement park and entertain tourists. As a boy I imagined what it must have been like to live in the frontier days among the Indians who hunted and camped and walked the woods and the fields that I walked. I couldn't comprehend that these native peoples hadn't actually occupied this area for more than one hundred and twenty-five years.

When the French were defeated by the British in the Seven Year's War, they lost their bid for an empire in the New World and surrendered their lands east of the Mississippi River (then called the Illinois Country of Upper Louisiana) in the Treaty of Paris in 1763. The Illinois territory became part of the United States as a result of America's claim of independence from Britain in 1776. The area of northeast Illinois was of little strategic importance during this period and was prone to marauding bands of Indians; thus, it remained mostly unsettled except for a fort built in 1802 at the edge of a dismal swamp at the mouth of the Chicago River and Lake Michigan. It was called Fort Dearborn. The nearest fur trading post was forty miles up the north shore called "Little Fort," or *Wauk-e-gan* in Potawatomi. These frontier stockades were utilized as military outposts to defend against Britain's unsuccessful attempt in 1812 to regain control over its previously acquired spoils from the French by providing military support to Indians who were hostile to the United States.

In the aftermath of the Black Hawk War of 1832, Native Americans reluctantly ceded all lands east of the Mississippi River to the United States Government. On the advent of the antebellum period of American history, the first European to settle in the area that eventually became my town was Peter Shaddle. He arrived in Illinois in 1835 from upstate New York.[49] It is likely that he traveled by canoe and paddled his way up the north branch of the Chicago River. Then, portaging to the Des Plaines River, he passed the cabin of Captain Daniel Wright and the small settlement of an Aptikisic Indian chief named Hafda (later becoming Half Day). When he came to the trace he portaged west for a few miles and built his log cabin in an oak grove on the banks of a long, shallow lake in an area now occupied by the University of St. Mary of the Lake Mundelein Seminary. He was among a handful of area homesteaders who staked his claim before the 1836 federal expiration treaty agreement with the Indians. By 1839, Shaddle had neighbors—tradesmen fleeing England's industrial depression. They paid $1.25 per acre to the U.S. government and turned the trace into a wagon trail and turned the prairie soil to farming. They named the place Mechanic's Grove, in honor of their former professions back home.

When newspaperman John L. Sullivan coined the term "manifest destiny" to describe America's mission to "overspread the continent allotted [to us] by Providence," homesteaders began streaming across the fertile lands of northern Illinois. In 1833 the town of Chicago had a population of about 300; by 1837 it was more than 4,000. Forty miles north of Chicago, near Shaddle's Mud Lake cabin, the area around the one hundred and twenty-five acre Diamond Lake began to experience its share of growth. The first to build there was William Fenwick, who arrived in 1835. Fenwick's descendants owned a shoe store on the northeast corner of Lake Street and Park Avenue. Their front window advertised, *"you're never too late, we're open 'til eight."* My parents always took us to Mr. Fenwick's for new shoes at the beginning of each school year. Joe Fenwick, a bright student and talented athlete, was a teammate of mine on "The Vikings" little league football team. Joe caught the decisive touchdown when we won the little league championship in 1968.

Two years after the Fenwicks homesteaded, David Whitney found the remains of an Indian village when he built his modest home on the west side of Diamond Lake,[50] in what is now West Shore Park. It is just a few blocks from where our house at 409 South Prairie was eventually built in the middle of forty acres of land along the lake's north shore, first purchased by Alexander Bellinski in 1840. Bellinski also built one of the first stores and rooming houses on the east side of the lake. By the early 1900's it was called Hackett's Place. When I was a kid, that store and hotel was a tavern called the "Happy Hollow," operated by George and Irene Okon. My father often took us there to swim at its small beach below the tavern while he sat at the bar above, sipping on glasses of beer and chatting with his cronies.

A one-room clapboard schoolhouse stood near the south end of the lake where Route 60 joins Route 83, east of Diamond Lake Road. Its second incarnation built in 1881 was still standing, but just barely, a few hundred yards from Ed's Highland Gas Station, where my brother Rodger and I worked during our high school years beginning in 1970.

The original Diamond Lake School was established in 1848, the same year, a half a world away, Charles and Meave Conaghan narrowly survived the ravages of The Great Famine, and Meave gave birth to my great-great-grandmother, Biddy Charlie.

The family of Ira B. Ray, a Rhode Island-born carpenter, figured prominently in the growth of Diamond Lake. Their local family history and contributions to the community over the last century and a half are well documented. Many members still live in the area. Gregarious and energetic, the Rays have continued their well-known reputation as a family who works hard and plays hard. Ira's grand-daughter, Vivian (*née* Ray) Johnson, has long been a friend of our family. A kind and amiable woman, she ran a beauty parlor out of her home on Maple Street near Route 45, and often cut my hair when I was old enough to escape my father's sheers. Sometimes she saw my brothers and me walking to school on bitterly cold winter mornings and offered us a ride. I also worked with her at Marshall Field's Department Store at Hawthorn Center Mall when it opened in August, 1973.

The Rays all seemed to have large families. It used to be that you couldn't walk from one end of town to the other without running into a Ray. I suppose it was inevitable then, that my family would one day marry into theirs. In June, 1980, my sister, Tisha (Patricia), wed Vivian's youngest son, Mark (Ira's great-grandson). I think Ira would be pleased to know that his fourth generation grandson, Adam, my nephew, is also a carpenter.

By the end of the 19th century Diamond Lake began to come into its own as a resort area, and catered to the Chicago crowd with seven popular hotels dotting the beaches and many small cottages surrounding the lake.[51] By the time my family moved to the area in 1959, the few resorts that survived the Great Depression era of the 1930's had gone from dowdy to derelict. They were subsequently razed or burned down, and many of the get-away cottages on the east side of the lake became occupied by low-income migrant workers from Mexico.

Another founding family that took root, grew the village, and branched out in the generations to follow was the Rouse family. John and Matilda Rouse arrived from England in the 1840's, raised nine children, and purchased more than five hundred acres of land in the center and south end of town—including most of Diamond Lake. Their family history is both engaging and tragic. My father and I crossed paths with the grandson and great-grandsons of the founding family and those events would prove to figure prominently in my childhood, youth, and young adulthood, inexorably changing the course of my life.

CHAPTER 5

⌇

AMERICA'S EMERALD ISLE

B Y THE 1850'S, THE GROWING farm community of Mechanics
Grove changed its name to Holcomb, in honor of John Holcomb, a
local civic-minded and spiritual community leader. The bounty for wolves
in the township at that time was $8, and pioneer William Fenwick donated
land to build the area's first church. The Diamond Lake Free Church
Society came into existence at a cost of $969. The building is still there, its
original foundation still intact, making it the oldest surviving structure in
Mundelein. It was a stop along the Underground Railroad where abolitionist
members of the church temporarily harbored runaway slaves in the rafters
before and during the Civil War.[52]

Also during the 1850's, many of the deported Arranmore islanders,
rebuilding their lives in America and Canada, were about to find a new
and permanent home. In 1856, Charlie Strac O'Donnell, originally from
Arranmore's neighboring island, Rutland, was a ganger on the rapidly
expanding Canadian Pacific Railway. He got into a "dispute" with some of
his co-workers in Toronto and absconded with the crew's payroll. He fled
across the border to Detroit. From there he sailed up Lake Huron. While on
the lam, he passed through the Straits of Mackinac and stopped at Beaver
Island in Lake Michigan where he was hired on as a laborer constructing the
lighthouse at Whiskey Point. The island had recently been "swept clean of
Mormons" who colonized it in 1847 under the rogue Mormon prophet and

self-proclaimed king, James Jesse Strang. When Strang was shot dead by a couple of his followers, it put an end to America's last monarchy and left the colony of 2,600 Mormons leaderless and vulnerable. A mob of eighty men from the surrounding islands, most of whom were Irish fishermen and some of them Arranmore men, invaded the kingdom of St. James, expelled the colony, moved in on their farms, and took over their houses and businesses. The opportunistic Charlie Strac O'Donnell was so enamored by it all that he wrote to his wife to come, saying, "this place looks just like Ireland, only better!"

Word among the displaced Arranmore people quickly spread and they flocked to Beaver Island where O'Donnell convinced them "the fishing is excellent, land cheap and plentiful, and timber for houses abundant."[53]

The remote island was still on the American wilderness and the Arranmore islanders quickly established a parallel island community to their homeland, far from the racism and persecution they endured on the mainland. They had become distrustful of centralized government and remained wary of outsiders. The island provided them the opportunity once again to interact, work, and fish independently in the most bountiful waters of the Great Lakes. They held strong to their own language and customs. The fish-based economy of the region was booming and the availability of cheap or even free land and abandoned Mormon houses allowed the first wave of Arranmore settlers to save enough money to send for their families and friends. Experienced sailors from Arranmore chartered ships bringing several families at a time. By 1863 there were 52 families from Arranmore living on Beaver Island. The 1880 census lists 123 Boyles, 121 Gallaghers, and 90 O'Donnells, nearly all of them from Arranmore.

In 1871 Charles Conaghan was a stout seventy-one years old. He and his wife, Meave Eoin, made a surprising decision to leave Arranmore and the constant reminders of the Famine and brutal landlordism to undertake the perilous journey to Beaver Island. The elderly couple took their two youngest children with them: Mary, 17, and John, 13. They fearlessly made their way, booking passage in steerage aboard one of the many steamboat packets criss-crossing the Atlantic. They arrived in New York and traveled by scow up the Erie Canal from Albany to Buffalo. From there they sailed to their new home, Beaver Island, renewing friendships with other Arranmore (as they called themselves) who had been banished twenty years earlier by the now bankrupt Charley Beag.

On the evening of October 8th in the year of the Conaghans' arrival, they and the rest of the Beaver Islanders speculated over the bright orange glow they observed in the skies to the west and on the horizon to the south. Billows of smoke streaked across the starry sky and a snow of fine grey ash fell from the heavens and dusted the ground. Soon boatloads of people began arriving in St. James harbor from various towns along the western shores of Lake Michigan. They were fleeing from what they thought was the Apocalypse. They described in horrible detail how a fire of unimaginable magnitude and fury burst out of the darkness, with leaping large firewhirls that twisted off the tree tops and raced ahead of the wall of flame toward the waters of Lake Michigan. Fireballs shot into the sky like lightning as the trees exploded and wind showered the landscape with fire brands, cinders, and hot sand. The fire became a great convection feeding itself, drawing in oxygen and fuel and creating hurricane force winds that ripped the roofs off of houses, blew over barns, uprooted trees, and tossed rail cars around like tumbleweed. The flames moved so rapidly people found themselves surrounded with no means of escape. Families fled amid a barrage of falling embers and hot ash which set their clothes and hair on fire. The heat was so intense that it raised large blisters on the backs, arms, and faces of the fleeing, panic-stricken people. Attempting to find refuge some fled into cellars, only to die of asphyxiation. Others seeking safety jumped into wells and shallow marshes to escape the 1,800° heat, only to be boiled alive. The roaring tempest engulfed the entire Sugar Bush region of northeast Wisconsin and Upper Michigan, consuming everything in its path. It completely destroyed twelve towns, at the center of which was the lumber mill town of Peshtigo. The lurid flames, propelled by their own winds, jumped the waters of the Green Bay, touching off another firestorm in the Door County peninsula.[54] Those lucky enough to escape the devil's breath waded in the chilly waters of Lake Michigan or ran to the wharves and climbed onto boats not set ablaze by the shower of red-hot cinders and made their way out to the open waters of the Great Lake.

The conflagration raged for several days until the wind changed direction and the firestorms were extinguished by a combination of heavy rains and a lack of fuel.

It left a black, smoldering scar as far as the eye could see—more than 2,400 square miles. Nearly a million and a half acres of woodland, farms, factories, sawmills, harbors, and towns were leveled to char and ash. An estimated two billion trees burned and more than two thousand people were killed. It remains the largest and most destructive fire in American history.

While the residents of Beaver Island watched the eerie orange, smoke-filled sky to the west, the distant light on the horizon to the south arose from yet another fire, in the great Midwestern city of Chicago, three hundred miles away. For three days the urban fire raged out of control and the labor of years was devoured by flame within hours, destroying over 17,000 buildings across 2,600 acres of city streets, killing an estimated 300 citizens and leaving more than 100,000 people homeless.[55] It's true, the Great Peshtigo Fire and the Great Chicago Fire happened on the same night. But for whatever reasons—an irresistibly charming legend about a cow and a lantern among them—the Great Chicago Fire became part of the national consciousness while the Peshtigo Fire went virtually unnoticed.

Growing up in the Chicago area, no one that I knew had ever heard of the Peshtigo Fire, but every schoolchild was familiar with the history of The Great Chicago Fire. We used to sing a camp round about it:

> *Late last night when we were all in bed*
> *Mrs. O'Leary hung a lantern in the shed*
> *And when her cow kicked it over, she winked her eye and said*
> *"There's gonna be a hot time in the old town tonight. Fire! Fire! Fire!"*

When I was twelve years old, my family's summer vacation involved visiting distant relations—what my father called his "shirt-tail relatives"—in Marinette, Wisconsin. On the way we stopped in the sleepy little paper mill town of Peshtigo. We toured the Fire Museum, burial mound, and memorial. I was fascinated by the museum's artifacts and impressed with the murals depicting scenes from the tragic event. I have returned to that museum several times over the years and remain equally intrigued by the area's history and confounded by its relative obscurity. The Peshtigo Fire has come to be known as America's "forgotten fire."

Shortly after the Great Fires, the Conaghan's eldest son, Owen, and his newlywed bride, Isabella Elizabeth McCauley, left Arranmore and headed west to America. They arrived on the banks of the Schuylkill River in Pottsville, Pennsylvania, where Owen worked for a time in the area's coal mines. But by 1878 he and his young, growing family made their way to Beaver Island to join the rest of his expatriate family. Later, when fishing began to wane, Owen and Isabella moved their family—all ten children—to the mainland. In 1900 they were living at 309 Sarah Street (now called 14th Street) in Escanaba, Michigan, according to the county's census records.

Charles and Meave's oldest daughter, Nellie Charlie, her husband, Paddy Melaghlin Gallagher, and their four children arrived on Beaver Island in 1874, but not in time to attend the marriage of Nellie's youngest sister, Mary, to John S. Boyle. His family had been deported from Arranmore in 1851 when he was nine, by Charley Beag.

Paddy Melaghlin had to flee Ireland because of his involvement with "The Ribbon Men," a recalcitrant secret society that flouted the law and sought vengeance against area landlords. Beaver Island provided him just the remote refuge he needed. Nellie died a few years after they arrived, at age thirty-five. What became of Paddy is not certain. The 1880 Beaver Island census shows the Gallaghers' two youngest children living with their grandparents, Charles and Meave Eoin Conaghan (or Margaret Marjorie, as she was known on Beaver Island).

The elderly Conaghan's remaining daughters, Brigid Biddy Charlie and Madge Madgie Charlie, both young brides and raising families of their own, stayed behind on Arranmore. When Charles left Ireland he bequeathed his homestead to his daughter, Madgie, and her new husband, Tom Rua Coll.

Brigid Biddy Charlie was twenty years old when she was "matched" with an island boy she knew all her life, Bryan Oge O'Donnell. They married in 1868. As was common among the poor Irish Catholics of that time, couples had enormous families. Bryan Oge and Biddy Charlie raised ten children, keeping pace with the families of Biddy's brother, Owen, and her sister, Mary, in America, each of whom had ten children. Many of Biddy's children and those of her sister Madgie, followed their grandparents, Charles and Meave, to America. Most preferred to be near their kin in Escanaba, Marinette, Beaver Island, and Chicago, and worked as domestics or laborers. Others landed in New York and settled across the Hudson River in Bayonne, New Jersey, among other Irish from *The Rosses*, including my maternal grandparents, Edward and Celia Boyle. They arrived in the spring of 1925.

Like so many of that generation, and as celebrated tearfully in countless Irish songs, young Brigid and Madgie never saw their parents, siblings, or children again once they sailed off to America.

Charles and Meave Eoin spent sixteen years on Beaver Island where Charles continued his trade as a carpenter. In 1887 they moved to the rebuilt town of Marinette, Wisconsin, destroyed by the Great Peshtigo Fire, and each lived into their nineties. They were survived by more than forty grandchildren and are buried in the Catholic section of Woodlawn Cemetery in Marinette, along with their daughter, Mary.

In 1884 the last great wave of Arranmore immigrants arrived at "America's Emerald Isle," Beaver Island, with the help of the local priest, Father Peter Gallagher.[56] Over forty families boarded a steamer in Buffalo, New York, that took them to St. James. Several generations of Arranmore followed periodically until the turn of the century. They were a maritime people with an affinity for the cities, port towns, and islands of Lake Michigan, where their forefathers exiled by the Famine had settled before them. Here they prospered and raised families, and dozens of their descendants to whom I can claim kinship still reside.

When the succeeding years saw Great Lakes fishing and Irish immigration gradually decline, the Arranmore people established themselves in a new frontier, Chicago.

Charles and Meave Eoin Conaghan, my great-great-grandparents. Taken shortly after they immigrated to the United States from Arranmore Island, Co. Donegal, Ireland. Circa 1871, Beaver Island, Michigan.

—*Photo courtesy of Peter O'Donnell*

CHAPTER 6

❧

THE STAGE IS SET

BY 1902, ARRANMORE'S POPULATION HAD exceeded its pre-famine numbers: 2,000. Hugh Stokes Rodgers, a Gaelic speaking "spirit grocer" who could neither read nor write lived in Ballintra, near the middle of the island, at the foot of *Cnoc an Lolair* (*nock'n lo 'lar*, Eagle Mountain).[55] Apparently he did his best to increase the island population all on his own and eventually fathered twenty-two children, leaving little wonder what his island name "Stokes" implied. His eldest daughter, Mary (who would become my grandmother), was "the fairest girl on all of Arran. She had a quiet, pleasant manner and raven hair that fell over her shoulders like waves upon the strand."[57]

More than three thousand miles away, the town of Holcomb, carved from the hardwood forest in northeast Illinois, was a hotbed of prosperity. In 1909 the town incorporated and changed its name to Rockefeller in homage to William Rockefeller, a major stockholder in his brother's railroad. John D. Rockefeller laid his steel rails through town in 1885 and added a train station. Local folklore recounts how William Rockefeller rode on the inaugural train through the village and requested that it stop so he could admire the town named in his honor. When he climbed down from the train he took a quick look up and down Seymour Street, climbed back on the train, and was not heard from in these parts again.

The name Rockefeller was nearly as short-lived as its namesake's visit, for in July 1909 the name was changed, yet again, to Area, at the request of a local charismatic educational entrepreneur named Arthur Sheldon. Sheldon bought 600 acres near town and built a correspondence school on it. The school taught sales techniques, including the philosophy of "AREA," which stood for "Ability, Reliability, Endurance, and Action." At one time the school boasted a staff of 200 and more than 10,000 correspondence students, many of them women (which was unusual for 1909). However, after several successive years of decline during World War I, the school closed.[58]

Beginning in 1918, the slightly eccentric and megalomaniacal Archbishop George (and later Cardinal) Mundelein, from the Archdiocese of Chicago, quietly began purchasing 1,000 acres of property around the lake where Peter Shaddle built his cabin eighty-three years earlier. His spending spree included the shallow Mud Lake, as it was known then, and the acreage formerly owned by Sheldon's school. At the astronomical cost of about 12 million dollars (that's 12 million 1921 dollars), Mundelein constructed the world's largest and most opulent theological seminary, St. Mary of the Lake, now called the University of St. Mary of the Lake Mundelein Seminary.

Although the seminary was on the opposite end of town from where we lived, it repeatedly played an integral part in my youth. It was a rare and special treat as a child when my father piled the family into the car and took a leisurely drive around St. Mary's Lake. He made a point to stagger our tours as the seasons changed throughout the year. It remains among my favorite childhood memories.

Rockefeller (later Mundelein), Illinois, 1909. Seymour Street looking north from Park Avenue.—*Photo courtesy Fort Hill Heritage Museum.*

Mundelein, Illinois, 2008. Same view as above. The building at far left was the former Rexall Drug. Lad & Helen's Tavern was the tall gabled roof building near the end of the block.—*Photo by author.*

CHAPTER 7

✧

A MAN OF ARAN

THERE ARE SEVERAL LEGENDARY STORIES of triumph and tragedy of Arranmore islanders who settled in America, told and retold by those left behind. One such story was first related to me by my cousin, Bernard Byrne, when we were aboard the ferry *South Shore* enroute from Charlevoix to Beaver Island, Michigan, in 1986. The tale has survived nearly a century's worth of retelling by the islanders and has gained much exaggeration and romance through the years. Although no one denies that the character in the story, Peter Neily Boyle, from Aphort, was a hero, it is a wonderful example of how the distance of miles and the passage of time can obscure the facts and invoke legend among the proud island people. A version of this story appears on the Arranmore Island website. I have taken the liberty of paraphrasing certain passages and providing some additional background to Bernard's essay for purposes of clarity. These statements are enclosed in brackets. Bernard calls the story "Man of Aran."

"The 24th of July, 1915, was a drizzly but otherwise pleasant morning in Chicago. Clusters of elderberry blossoms dangled like woolly tassels from the shrubbery lining the estuary of the great Chicago River as it deposited its muddy torrent into the clear waters of Lake Michigan. The narrow streets along the river were clogged with electric street cars, automobiles, and horse-drawn wagons piled high with swollen sacks of wheat and corn and other commercial goods headed for the wharves along the lakefront. There, steamers had their hatches open ready to receive whatever cargo was for export, linking Chicago to the rest of the world. [Adding to the chaos on this particular Saturday morning were nearly seven thousand revelers, employees of the Western Electric Company, and their families. They converged along the south side of the river, between the Clark and LaSalle Street bridges, dressed in their finest attire, to board one of five chartered boats headed for an all-day company picnic across the lake in Michigan City, Indiana. One of those boats was the *SS Eastland*, a rusting Lake Michigan steamer owned by the Chicago-South Haven Line. She was a large vessel, able to accommodate as many as 2,500 passengers but with a notorious reputation for being top-heavy and unstable.]

Arriving in the city that day was Peter Neily Boyle. [Like Bernard Byrne, Peter was a distant cousin of mine from Arranmore.] He, like all island men, had been a son of the sea all his life, as had been his forbearers. The sea was in his blood and he was not afraid of it. Fourteen years earlier his older brother Dan had drowned on the Wicklow coast when the *Exile*, on which he was a deck hand, foundered on a reef during a gale. But Arranmore islanders are no strangers to such tragedies and accept them as a way of life. When the time came for Peter to make his way in the world he had to consider emigrating, as most of his contemporaries on Arranmore had already done. He knew right where to go, and what career to follow. Many of his friends who had gone abroad, like true island men, secured positions as crewmen on vessels plying the Great Lakes in the American mid-west. Most of those Peter knew had settled on Beaver Island and it was there he decided to go. It did not take him long to get a job as a trimmer aboard a schooner and he felt he was now set to make his fortune in America, with Arranmore just a memory.

As he ambled along the wharves of the city in the early morning, he was as happy as any man in Chicago. His ship being two days on the journey and having but little rest, Peter was feeling bedraggled for the lack of sleep, and being still young (in his mid-twenties), he was conscious of his smuttiness as well. He longed for a tub of steamy hot water in some local saloon and a trip to the barber shop to have his beard trimmed and his bushy locks shortened to his taste. He selected a barber's parlor along the river's north promenade. The barber was busy and Peter had to wait his turn. He settled into a cozy arm-chair close to a window overlooking the river [and the flood of excited picnickers making their way up the gangplanks of the *Theodore Roosevelt*, the *Petoskey*, and the *Eastland* on the opposite side.] After a brief spell he heard a ship's klaxon sounding close at hand and on looking out, beheld a medium-sized pleasure-boat backing away from the dock, with a multitude of passengers lined up on her starboard rail waving pennants and cheering while a rag-time orchestra belted out a tune from the ballroom on the forward poop deck. As Peter sat there taking in this scene the thought struck him that the vessel was off her center of gravity and listing dangerously.

'She must have no ballast at all,' he thought as the barber nudged him that his chair was now vacant. As he walked across the floor, there was a tumult of shouting and screaming coming from the street. Rushing back to the window, Peter went rigid as he beheld the pleasure-boat's gunwale disappear under the edge of the wharf and her passengers being toppled into the swirling current. There was an outburst of yelling and screaming with street pedestrians running in all directions wondering if what they were seeing was real. The ship tried to right herself but continued past her center and gently rolled over onto her starboard side. A geyser of water belched into the air as the funnels disappeared below the waterline [taking the estimated 3,200 passengers on board with it]. Many trapped below deck were crushed and suffocated. Those topside were thrown into the water and were thrashing about with others hanging on to them in their panic. One of the ship's lifeboats had been dislodged from its davits and was now being carried away down stream. Peter instantly bounded through the open door and without hesitation jumped into the turbulent water. Many hands reached out to him, so many that he saw he was in danger of being swamped. He disregarded all pleas for help and being a strong swimmer headed out after the capsized life-boat. He knew the drill in such procedures and in very little time he was safely aboard and rowing desperately back to where the helpless people were trying to keep afloat. With the energy of a giant he began hauling them aboard one by one, while others clung desperately to the sides. In less than ten minutes the life-boat was clogged with dripping women and children and knowing that they at least were safe he began to swim out into the depths again searching for others. He could see none and coming to the conclusion that many had already drowned he guided the rescued gang back to the slipway. Just as the last of them was on dry ground, a piercing cry came from far down the estuary. In that direction he saw what seemed to be a teen-age girl being carried toward the lake. Why he did not resort to the boat he had just emptied remains a mystery to this day but he jumped in instead and swam strongly towards the distressed girl while dozens of spectators watched but offered no help.

With powerful strokes he closed in fast and in spite of her exhaustion she swam to meet him. He managed to get her turned on her back and adopting the same position himself, grasped her firmly between his thighs and swam towards the shore. With her soaking clothes and inability to offer him any help at all, she began to drag him down. With mighty strokes he ploughed his course backwards while his torso sank lower and lower into the roiling river. Eventually he shouted for help and although there was an empty boat lying by the slip-way no one thought of going to his aid. When the girl seemed to have died the load on his body became unbearable. He was exhausted and enhancing his buoyancy was not any longer in his power. With one final gasp, he flung up his hands and disappeared below the waters of the river. He was far from home."

There is no question that Peter Boyle was but one of many heroes that July morning, and one of 844 souls who perished in the Eastland Disaster. The bodies of the victims were taken to a temporary morgue at the 2nd Regiment Armory at 1058 West Washington Boulevard, currently the home of HARPO Studios where the Oprah Winfrey Show is filmed. He laid in a row among hundreds of others who had drowned or who had suffocated in the crush of the crowd and debris below decks. They were all waiting for a relative to reach down, lift the sheet, and identify their bodies.

Bernard went on to say, "I have been told that some friendly society or another erected a monument to commemorate his heroic feat and that it can be seen there to this day." I did not have the heart to tell Bernard that in all probability, no such monument existed. Seventy-four years passed before the city of Chicago officially recognized the Eastland Disaster. The Illinois Mathematics and Science Academy, along with the Illinois State Historical Society, first placed a commemorative plaque in 1989 at the foot of the LaSalle Street Bridge at Wacker Drive—a solemn and obscure reminder of one of the most tragic maritime disasters in American history.

In the spring of 2008, the City of Chicago began construction on an $80 million Chicago Riverwalk development project. The plan calls for a new, permanent exhibit called *At The River's Edge*, which will include six steel frames containing twelve panels telling the story of the Eastland Disaster.

For the record, Peter Boyle was born about 1892 in Aphort, Arranmore. In 1901 he was recorded as an eight-year-old in the Aphort Census, in the household of his grandmother Margaret, along with his parents and seven siblings. At age nineteen he emigrated, sailing to Quebec on the *SS Scandinavian*, which he boarded in Glasgow on June 29, 1912. His brother, Daniel, who was living at 123 E Illinois Street, Chicago, Illinois, paid his passage. By 1915, Peter was living at 110 E Illinois Street in Chicago and on the day of the Eastland Disaster, he was employed as a Lookout on the steamer *Petoskey*. According to Captain Petrosky and the crew of the *Petoskey*, Peter was attempting to rescue a woman who had been thrown from the capsized *Eastland*. He dove into the river from a lifeboat, while it was still about fifteen feet above the water and he drowned among the throngs of people in the river. Peter Neily Boyle is buried in Mount Carmel Catholic Cemetery, in Hillside, Illinois.[59]

CHAPTER 8

✧

THE YOUNGEST SON

A S HOLCOMB FLOURISHED ON THE vast prairie of Illinois, the Donegal Parish of Templecrone was enjoying the mild economic success of a revived fishing industry. Bryan Oge O'Donnell and his wife, Brigid Biddy Charlie, were busy tending to their small patches of barley, turnips, and potatoes and raising their brood of ten children on the remote island of Arranmore. On April 4th, 1902, their twenty-three-year-old son (my grandfather), Cornelius Bryan Condy, a largely unambitious fisherman/farmer like his father, eagerly married Mary Rodgers, the beautiful eldest daughter of the prodigious Hugh Stokes Rodgers and the by-now weary Grace Coll. Fair Mary with the raven hair had just turned eighteen. She, like most islanders of her generation, was illiterate. My father's original birth registration document contains an "x" where the mother's name should be. The recorder testified that it was "her mark." Mary left her father's house and pub and her nine siblings in Ballintra and moved with Condy to a cottage in Aphort, a mile west along the road, where they wasted no time establishing a family of their own.

Soon after they were married, Mary's mother, Grace Coll, died during childbirth, leaving poor Hugh alone to raise the children. He soon remarried another islander, Kate Molloy, twenty-three years his junior.

Condy and Mary's first child was a girl, born within ten months of their wedding. Mary named her daughter after her recently departed mother, Grace. According to the 1910 census, Condy's mother, Brigid Biddy Charlie, was now a sixty-six-year-old widow living alone in Ballintra. Most of her children had emigrated to America.

Business at the spirit grocer was either terribly slow or remarkably successful, for Hugh continued his multiplicity—and he and Kate had eleven more children. This unusual twist of progeny led Hugh to have children younger than his own grandchildren, and for me continues to be a constant source of confusion in understanding my family genealogy.

Condy and Mary eventually had eight children. Their youngest child, my father, was born John Cornelius O'Donnell (John Mary Hughie), on August 1st, 1920, in their humble, two room thatched cottage in the townland of Aphort. To the closest of relatives, my father was affectionately known as John Condy.

Like so many generations of islanders before him, John Condy's existence was difficult and impoverished, without luxury of electricity or running water. As a very young lad he enjoyed a pleasant life and like all island children his feet were strangers to the encumbrances of *brogues* (shoes) until he was "a brave lump of a lad," and made off with the tattie-hoking squads at age twelve.

"I skipped over rill and mountain, ran along the strand and hopped over the jagged *Tora Dubh* (black bull, a tidal outcrop of rock in Aphort) in my bare feet with ease. I was sure-footed as a goat, and twice as good lookin'," he told me, "my soles were thick as leather; at home, at school, at Mass, it didn't matter, we were always barefoot."

My father's seven sisters and brothers were, in chronological order: Grace, Bridget, Hugh, Mary, Annie, Bernard, and James. Grace, the eldest, is the person for whom the nationally cherished song "The Rose of Arranmore" was allegedly written. Grace married Anthon Frank Gallagher. They lived in Torries, Arranmore. Bridget, who became the authoritative one after her mother, Mary, died, was my godmother. She married a mainlander, Manus O'Donnell, and they immigrated to America and lived in Bayonne, New Jersey. My father's oldest brother, Hugh, drowned off the Jersey Shore when he was only in his early twenties. Mary married Patrick Boyle and moved to Glasgow, Scotland. Annie (my cousin Brian Fisher's mother), married a northerner, James Fisher, and moved to Antrim. Bernard (Barney) never married and lived his entire life in his father's house in Aphort. He and I became great pen pals. James died at the age of eleven ostensibly from spinal meningitis.

As a peasant farm boy, my father did the work required of him: he assisted with the *ware* (spring planting) and the harvest, and worked side-by-side with his father late into the summer night, as the sun rode the horizon until well after ten o'clock. They continuously wrestled with the rocky soil in their efforts to force subsistence from it. He manured the potato ridges behind the house, planted seed, broke the soil, weeded the crops, skillfully cut hay with a scythe, cut and stacked the turf, and gathered the potatoes. Other than sailing to the mainland on a few occasions, he was isolated on the peaceful, emerald shores of the island. The extent of his world was limited to as far as he could see across to the mainland on clear days. It was then he wondered, what lies beyond *The Lagan?*

My father's school photo, spring 1926, Arranmore School #2, Arranmore Island, Co. Donegal, Ireland. *l to r:* Dad (5), his sister, Annie (10), and his brother, Barney (8). School photos were taken in family groups and students dressed in their best clothes for the occasion. Note Barney's darned jumper (sweater), my father's hemmed shirt—formerly his sister's dress—the dirt floor, and the shoeless, smile-less pose.

CHAPTER 9

⌀

FROM PRAIRIE TO PROMINENCE

CONDY, MARY, AND THEIR EIGHT children struggled to survive in their two room cottage on Arranmore. Islanders who could afford to immigrate, more often than not, made their way beyond *The Lagan* to the bustling city of Chicago, where they were no strangers to the newly appointed Archbishop George Mundelein. He rose quickly through the church hierarchy and was, at forty-three, the youngest archbishop in America.[60] Eight years later, he was elevated to cardinal. He was a popular and influential man, a tireless worker and a beloved pastoral leader of more than a million and a half Roman Catholics. Among his thoughtfully organized accomplishments during his tenure in Chicago were: unifying the ethnic Catholic churches, establishing the St. Vincent De Paul Society, the Associated Catholic Charities, the Misericordia Maternity Hospital for charity cases, and reorganizing the House of The Good Shepard, founded for the care of wayward girls. "I would rather lift up the poor and despairing to a better and happier life than rear the greatest cathedral in the world," Mundelein said.[61]

He led several of his American born contemporaries, which included Cardinals Spellman of New York, O'Connell of Boston, Glennon of Saint Louis, and Dougherty of Philadelphia, in a shared vision to revitalize Catholicism in America and bring respect and status to the church. They operated their diocese on a set of five principles: giantism, going first-class, business-like administration, gaining political influence, and promoting Americanism.[62]

This did not sit well with their boss, Pope Benedict XV, who saw Americanism of the church as a threat to the Vatican. Benedict's successor, Pope Pius XI, continued the policies of his predecessor as a hardliner on modernism. Pius was thoroughly orthodox theologically and had no sympathy with modernist ideas that revitalized fundamental Catholic teaching. However, it was hard to argue the fact that the bishops had not only succeeded in raising a previously disorganized mission church to a respected American institution, but in doing so, the American Church had become the Vatican's greatest financial asset.[63]

Mundelein took skillful advantage of the privilege and entitlement bestowed upon him by the church and used his popularity and adroit influence among the society of Chicago to generate interest and raise funds for his seminary project in the town of Area, forty miles north of the city. He intended to build a "Catholic University of the West" and oversaw every last detail of its construction. In the grand tradition of the Papal Roman Cardinals before him, Mundelein treated the project like it was his own personal estate. His plan called for the campus to be outwardly American and inwardly Roman, blending his love for his country with his zeal for the church. He petitioned Pope Benedict XV to contribute some works and statuary from the Vatican and elsewhere in Rome to adorn the new campus. But the ultra-orthodox pope was skeptical of Mundelein.

I was told by a former seminary student at the school that Mundelein long envisioned having Rome's famous Colonna dell'Immacolata (column of the Immaculate Conception of the Virgin Mary) as the centerpiece for his new seminary. The ancient Roman column, topped with a Gian Lorenzo Bernini statue of the Virgin Mary, stands near the foot of the Piazza di Spagna (the Spanish Steps). Mundelein used to admire the original, located in front of the old Propaganda Fide College, where he lived as a seminary student.[64] His request was rebuffed by the Vatican, citing that it was neither theirs to give, nor his to take. The cardinal was not discouraged. In a wry and subtle display of one-upmanship, Mundelein had a replica column erected—and at sixty-seven feet, it stands taller than the one in Rome (legend has it by eight inches). He didn't stop there; he added his own personal adornments and legacy repeatedly throughout the campus.

His Grace began the institution with a $500,000 gift from the family of Chicago lumber magnate, Edward Hines, in honor of their son, Edward Hines, Jr., who died of exposure in the trenches of France during WWI. The soldier was interred on the campus in a small mausoleum at the base of the central ceremonial pier east of Mundelein's replica Colonna dell'Immacolata. The soldier's remains were moved to the family's gravesite in Chicago in 1971 when rumors briefly circulated that the Archdiocese considered closing the seminary and selling the property.

Mundelein, among his many talents and interests, was a student of architecture. He instructed his chief architect, Joseph McCarthy, to make each of the seminary's buildings unique but similar. They were all to be built of red brick and Bedford Limestone, in a complement of early American Renaissance, neo-classical, Colonial, Georgian, and American Revival, to symbolize the "Americanness" of the Catholic Church. " . . . [A]nd since we have a great archdiocese and must provide for the future, we must erect a great institution. It will take years to complete it . . . but if we do it, we ought to do it well," the cardinal stated when laying out his plan in 1919.[65]

McCarthy, who studied under famed Chicago architect and visionary Daniel Burnham, followed Burnham's philosophy, "Make no little plans. They have no magic to stir men's blood and probably will not themselves be realized."

Mundelein and McCarthy shared a grandiose dream for a university to rival that of Catholic University in Washington, D.C., but administrators there saw Mundelein's vision as a threat to their institution, lobbied against it in Rome, and won. The university plan was scaled back and the cardinal instead built Saint Mary of the Lake into the largest and most modern and opulent seminary in the country.

They began by dredging Mud Lake. Crews of European immigrants came down by train from Wisconsin farms. Other neighboring farmers brought their wagons and draft animals to help clear the land. It was dangerous work. A local farm boy, G. Hardin Rouse, the Mayor's son (and grandson of the area's first settlers), worked a team of horses clearing the land and moving dirt and boulders from around Mud Lake. While heading down an embankment, the young Hardin lost control of the team and the wagon, and they tumbled down the hill. He was nearly killed, his leg crushed and broken in the accident.[66]

Campus construction began with the Philosophy Building but Mundelein and McCarthy soon turned their focus to the design of the main chapel set on the highest point along Principle Boulevard. Mundelein spent most of the Hines' endowment (today worth an estimated $6 million), on the chapel's construction.[67] Its form is curiously Protestant, modeled after the First Congregational Meeting House in Old Lyme, Connecticut, which Mundelein recalled from his boyhood vacations in New England.[68] Contemporary theologians dryly referred to it as "Mundelein's meeting house." The interior is Greco-Roman. Adorning its Adamesque ceiling is a pair of elaborate Bohemian crystal chandeliers. They are replicas of those originally designed for the White House in Washington, D.C. Mundelein used his significant political muscle to get an Act of Congress passed in order to have the presidential glass lighting fixtures duplicated.

The sublime interior of the seminary's Feehan Memorial Library is a replica of the 16th century Palazzo Barberini in Rome, the same villa occupied by Cardinal Antonio Barberini when he received the letter from Mary Stuart O'Donnell in the 1640's, seeking assistance from his uncle the pope. The library contains over 180,000 volumes, some dating back to the 12th century. Additionally, its rare first editions include the beautifully illustrated Douai-Rheims Bible,[69] created the same year Rory O'Donnell, the First Earl of Tyrconnell, died and was buried in Rome.

The library's central court is surrounded by three stories of arcades that give way to an ornate coffered ceiling—complete with the Archbishop's self-designed coat of arms. His thoughtful insignia includes elements of the Barberini family's heraldry, namely its distinctive bees, a classic symbol of industriousness. Years earlier, the papal Barberini family generously sponsored the prelate's education in Rome, and Mundelein, who always admired the Palazzo for its architecture, could now have a replica palace to call his own. Each of the solid walnut reading tables within the library contains the Archbishop's coat of arms, and the bee motif is repeated along the ceiling beams. In fact, his coat of arms, bearing symbols of the Blessed Virgin Mary along with three bees (in the lower left quadrant), is ubiquitous throughout the seminary. It was cast into a mold from which solid bronze doorknobs were made and used in the residence halls. Seminarians jokingly stated that every time they placed their hand upon the coat of arms on the doorknobs, they felt "the sting" of Cardinal Mundelein.

Further down Principle Boulevard, the Administration Building, an adaptation of Independence Hall in Philadelphia, houses an extensive collection of artwork, a ten thousand piece coin collection (including rare ancient Roman and Greek coins), and an assortment of the cardinal's personal ephemera. He was a frugal but avid collector of Americana memorabilia, negotiating astute deals with various collectors. He acquired the autographs of all the signers of the Declaration of Independence, all the U.S. Presidents and Chief Justices of the Supreme Court, and a letter from Mary Todd Lincoln in her own hand.

The two dormitory buildings straddling the main campus are Dutch Colonial, [70] each built in the shape of the capital letter "M". An aerial view of the campus clearly suggests a clever integration of the initials of the two principal architects, Mundelein and McCarthy. The marbled dormitory hallways lead to 186 spacious 17' x 14' ensuite rooms. In Rome, and across the United States, people were shocked to learn each seminarian had his own private room and bath. This was unheard of in its day and drew the scandalized ire of critics who viewed it as wasteful and ostentatious. But Mundelein stood fast to his belief of providing the best and then demanding much in return, insisting that strict training and first-class facilities would produce high quality priests. He constantly reminded the seminarians that he wanted them to be giants—mentally, physically, and morally.[71]

Mundelein's own palatial villa, built on a hill north of the lake, is fashioned after George Washington's Mount Vernon home, with a separate coach house for the cardinal's butler and chauffeur. A grand view of the lake lies beyond the central fountain and formal European gardens. The fourteen-room mansion had on its first floor a "throne room" to hold a papal audience, which Mundelein thought was a possibility, though it never came to be. (No seated pope ever came to the seminary, but four future popes did.) The dining room within the cardinal's residence can accommodate sixteen guests around a twenty-four foot table carved from a single piece of solid mahogany. Two custom Wedgewood chandeliers are suspended from above, and dual sets of specially made Wedgewood China and silverware service are adorned with the cardinal's coat of arms. The villa's halls are lined with original 17th century artwork, including etchings by Rembrandt and Rubens. The cardinal's second story bedroom suite contains an office, a black marble bath, and a separate shower enclosure which originally contained nine shower heads.[72] There was a 35 mm movie projector and theatre in the attic where His Grace entertained guests with first run movies.

In 1924, during the height of the seminary's construction, representatives of the Soo Line Railroad suggested to village officials that they change the name of the town to Mundelein as a gesture of gratitude for the cardinal's sponsorship of the seminary, which was beginning to bring economic prosperity and recognition to the tiny village. Both the railroad and the village trustees were well aware of the marketing potential of riding on the tails of the prelate's mitre. The cardinal, at first, opposed the notion. But when he saw the impact this would have on his popularity and his status among the church's elite, not to mention the pope, he capitulated, and discretely sent a messenger to the village trustees voicing his flattery and giving his modest approval. The mostly Lutheran village trustees quickly voted in favor of the name change—the third such change in fifteen years; overnight, Area became Mundelein. In return, the benevolent cardinal, who became aware that the only piece of firefighting equipment in town was a modified horse-drawn hose cart, shrewdly donated to the village its first fire truck.

The seminary opened its doors to students in 1921, but construction wasn't fully completed in time for its official debut, the 28th International Eucharistic Congress in June of 1926. Mundelein insisted that all building materials and construction debris be cleared from the grounds in time for the global event. He ordered that the train siding along the southwest corner of the property, which was used to deliver building materials, be diverted into the recently dredged Mud Lake, now renamed St. Mary's Lake. Construction crews hastily filled empty boxcars with all the unsightly construction materials and scuttled them. When they were finished, the workers tore up the tracks and threw them into the lake, too.

In 1926, the population of the Village of Mundelein had just topped five hundred. It had a couple of grain elevators, a shoe factory, a fairly substantial milk production, and one policeman, Clayton Tiffany. But the eyes of the world would soon be focused on the sleepy little community and Cardinal Mundelein would be at center stage. The cardinal's crowning glory and the village's global notoriety came when his Eminence hosted the closing ceremonies of the 28th International Eucharistic Congress (the first such event held in the United States) on the grounds of his beloved seminary. On the evening of June 23rd, after the Congress had celebrated a series of Masses at Soldier Field in Chicago, which more than 650,000 people attended, the faithful began to make their way to Mundelein. Some walked the forty miles from Chicago, others came by automobile, but most came by train.[73]

Cardinal Mundelein succeeded in having the Pullman Company of Chicago build seven special palace cars funded by the largesse of wealthy Chicago parishioners. The exteriors were painted in Cardinal red and emblazoned with the papal coat of arms. The interiors were luxuriously appointed and upholstered in rich red leather. The famous Cardinal train transported the procession of European church dignitaries from New York to Chicago. Thousands of spectators in the cities and towns along the route cheered and waved as the bright red train containing the Vatican emissaries eventually made its way to the mid-west masterpiece of Catholic learning in the village named after its genius creator.

For a day, all roads leading into the village were turned into one-way streets. Transportation arrangements by the railroads were made a year in advance and brought more than 350,000 people to the prairie village. In addition to the tens of thousands of lay pilgrims who journeyed from all parts of the world to participate in the Eucharistic Congress, came 12 Cardinals, including Patrick Joseph Cardinal O'Donnell, the Primate of Ireland, who hailed from *The Rosses* townland of Glenties. There were 64 Archbishops, 390 Bishops, 500 Monsignors, 8,000 priests and 10,000 nuns. Attendance estimates vary, but the number was said to be between 400,000 and 1,000,000 people. The Archdiocese of Chicago officially puts the number at a conservative half-million.[74]

Ninety-year-old Stanley Rouse, John and Matilda Rouse's grandson and life-long Mundelein resident, was eight years old when the Eucharistic Congress came to town. He remembers the day clearly: "It's what put Mundelein on the map." He and his family and members of the Congregational Church had a fundraiser serving lunches to the hordes of visitors.

The drama, pomp and pageantry of the one-day spectacle at St. Mary of the Lake Seminary was witnessed by journalist James O'Donnell-Bennett and reported in the Chicago Tribune the day after the event:

> "The most colossal prayer meeting and song service in the authentic annals of Christendom has brought to a close the 28th International Eucharistic congress of the Catholic Church. The world's records for throngs of that character have been broken."

> "... a solemn pontifical high Mass was followed by a glittering processional that wound its way through the consecrated glades and beside the still waters of this spacious seat of Catholic learning ..."[75]

He goes on to describe how the faithful "knelt in pools of water" as the procession passed in the torrential rain.

"During part of the three-mile processional in which the Sacrament
was borne by Cardinal Legate Bonzano in a kind of Roman car or
chariot between ranks upon ranks of men, women and children, the
rain and hail of a receding tempest continued to fall, and the lawns,
groves and avenues of Mundelein were streaming with water. But
at the sight of the ostensorium containing the consecrated particles
which are to Catholics the very body of their 'Eucharistic Lord and
King' the multitude sank upon its knees and the murmur of prayers
mingled with the voices of the wind and rain. The cardinals and
archbishops were as steadfast in their homage as were their people.
No venerable man faltered or turned back, and when pages and
officers stationed on the bridges and in the glades hurried toward
the prelates with umbrellas they were gently motioned back."

The cardinal hired motion picture directors and crews and had the entire
Eucharistic Congress recorded for posterity. He was well known for documenting
the details and was himself rarely without his full-time personal photographer.

Tradition holds that Cardinal Mundelein and his entourage made their
exit at the conclusion of the festivities aboard a giant gondola awaiting
them in the boathouse located directly beneath the ceremonial altar jutting
out into the lake. Oarsmen, I was told, ferried the cardinals perched on
"thrones," and festooned in full red regalia. They glided between the twin
belvederes which flank the boathouse as if embracing them on the placid
waters of St. Mary's Lake. As the passing showers gave way to brilliant
sunshine, the boatload of bishops made their way toward the Cardinal's villa,
while a half-million rain-soaked faithful waved from the shore. Although
unsubstantiated, it certainly would not have been out of character for the
cardinal, and it sure makes for a good story. And it's an exit that even his
equally ego-driven nemesis, the pope, could not have upstaged.

When the Eucharistic Congress closed, a half-million people exited at
once, leaving the seminary and the village trampled and muddy. "It was one
holy mess. People stuck everywhere and they left the town with a whole lot
of garbage to pick up."[76] Within eighteen hours after the world converged
on my village, Mundelein returned to its familiar and unassuming little
self. The village grew modestly over the next few decades and its character
remained mostly unchanged with local real estate developers inexplicably
promoting it as "the Athens of America."

June 24, 1926. Thousands wait to board trains on the corner of Adams and Wabash in Chicago bound for Mundelein to attend the closing ceremonies of the 28th International Eucharistic Congress at St. Mary of the Lake Seminary.

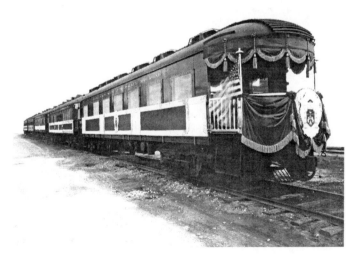

The famous Cardinal Train built by the Pullman Company of Chicago.

Ariel view of St. Mary of the Lake Seminary main campus, with attendees congregating on the final day of the Eucharistic Congress. An estimated half-million faithful were present. The large "M" shaped building in the upper right is one of two dormitories that bookend the campus and suggest the initials of the architects, Mundelein & McCarthy.—*Photos courtesy of the Fort Hill Heritage Museum.*

The original Colonna dell'Immacolata (column of the Immaculate Conception of the Virgin Mary) in Rome that Pope Benedict XV would not part with.

Cardinal Mundelein's replica on the grounds of Saint Mary of the Lake Mundelein Seminary. The original, while more ornate, appears shorter.

Santa Maria del Popolo Church, Rome, completed in 1477. Its blend of architectural styles resulted from two centuries of additions and modifications. The original Italian Renaissance architecture was later modernized by Gian Lorenzo Bernini beginning in 1655 in the style of the Baroque. The dome's interior is decorated with mosaics by Raffael and the Cerasi side chapel contains two Caravaggio canvases.—*Photos by author.*

CHAPTER 10

c✓ɔ

BEYOND *THE LAGAN*

I N 1926 THERE WAS NO cause for celebration on Arranmore. My father's carefree childhood came to an abrupt end when his mother, Mary, fell sick with fever and died of consumption (Tuberculosis). She was only forty-three. My father, far younger than his other siblings, was left to be cared for by his sisters, Annie and Mary, who tried to protect him from their fiercely stern and often mean-spirited father.

Shortly after my grandmother, Mary, died, my grandfather presented my father with a donkey whom he named "Jack." Dad became very attached to the animal, as much as a boy would a dog. Beginning in May year after year, my father led Jack over *Cur na Garn* (the heap of stones), the barren mountain behind his home in Aphort, to *an chescan* (*chess keen*), the family's peat bog on the craggy and windswept far side of the island. He spent many long, lonely hours there cutting and stacking the winter's firing. It was a centuries-old and tedious process though somewhat a luxury, for it provided a nearly inexhaustible source of heat and cooking fuel on the depressingly poor island.

Every morning before setting out over the mountain, my father's sister put a wedge of stout oat bread or soda bread in his pocket to protect him from hunger-weakness, *"feur gortach"* (*fear gortock*), they called it. Hunger-weakness was not uncommon in the Donegal Mountains. It was traditional for local travelers to leave a morsel for a passing poor person, or for the fairies. Failure to leave food for the hungry would infuriate the fairies into casting a spell upon the spot. Anyone who walked the cursed ground afterwards would suddenly be stricken by the feur gortach and sink into exhaustion. It was believed to be very risky to walk the mountains without carrying something edible. "Often," my father said, "I would be overcome by the feur gortach, although one minute before I felt no hunger a 'tall."

My father dug the soft, water-logged black turf with a double-bladed spade called a *sláan* (*schlan*)—the blades set at right angles twelve inches deep and four inches wide. Layer after layer had been cut off the turf bank for countless generations. Good bogs are often ten or twelve feet deep. Each succeeding layer is blacker and denser and makes a better turf than the previous layer. With one thrust of his double-bladed spade my father cut a clean turf, like a knife through butter, and then another and the pair fell from the bank. He repeated this process over and over and laid the fresh turfs singly to dry, for at least two-thirds of the weight of new turf is water. My father took frequent rests. Alone on the hillside he sprinkled bread crumbs for the fairies, cried when he thought about his mother without fear of retribution from his father, and sang in his native Gaelic to Jack. He played his fiddle to entertain them both and to pass the time on the nearly four mile round-trip journey from his home to the bogside.

After the cutting, my father and Jack returned daily to the bog to "foot" the turf, that is, to place them on end, three or four of them leaning together. A few weeks later, when the turf was fairly dry, he built them into turf clamps—long little stacks. He then pared them, covering them with a header called a scraw, the top layer of turf which contained grass or moss. After several weeks of exposure to the unrelenting winds that race over the bogs, the water within the turf evaporated. My father removed the scraw and loaded the bricks of the dried sod into large wicker *creedles* (baskets) strapped to the donkey's back. From there they toted them home over the mountain and my father stacked them beside the *byre* (a barn or shed) for the daily hearth fires.

My grandfather, Cornelius, had a reputation for harshness and cruelty. My father never admitted as much, but several island relatives who knew them both confessed to me that Condy was hard on all of his children and on my father in particular. He didn't want to see my father succeed and he often took pleasure in killing my father's joy. I suspect that was because my father displayed considerable intelligence and ambition, and my grandfather, Condy, was both petty-jealous and resentful, not an uncommon trait of the island men of his generation.

Nowhere was my grandfather's heartlessness more evidently related to me than the time my father and his burro, Jack, while returning home from the mountain with a load of peat, stumbled on the rocky ground and fell into a ditch. Jack injured his leg and couldn't get up. My father ran home for help. He returned with my grandfather, who knew immediately that Jack's leg was broken, and the animal could not be saved. Without explanation, Condy shot the animal in the head and uncompassionately ordered his son to bury Jack then and there under a cairn of stones. Grandfather returned home and left his young son alone on the barren mountainside to do as he was told. For the second time in his young life, the closest thing to my father had been taken from him.

I believe that was a watershed moment—the catalyst that solidified the boy's decision to leave his despot father and the depressingly poor rural Irish life forever.

My father never took to the sea as a fisherman like his father and his father's father, and he left home at the first opportunity. He was twelve years old. He had the extent of a sixth grade education and sought work in Scotland. He went with other children from the island as part of a "tattie-hoking" squad. Tattie-hokers were gangs of migrant children, usually from the same village, twelve to eighteen years old, who traveled in groups, or squads, to the fertile fields of Scotland and England in search of work. They rotated from farm to farm as demand required, cultivating and harvesting potatoes and cabbage. In exchange for their work they were paid a few pence, maybe given a meal, and allowed to sleep in the farmer's *bothy* (shed). The Arranmore squads left the island in June and did not return until early November. My father spent three summers with the squads, long enough to know that he wanted something better.

If you were a few years older, averse to tattie-hoking, and were a bit more ambitious, you might find work and better pay as a *navvy*—digging ditches, building roads or working down in the "pits" (mines).

The term navvy stems from the nineteenth century laborers who built navigations—canals, tunnels, and railroads throughout Britain. They came to be called navigators, or *navvies* for short. They were generally of low social standing, poor, uneducated gangs of itinerants—known as much for their hard drinking and unruly behavior as they were for their ability to endure hard physical labor. The tools of their trade were shovels, pickaxes, and wheelbarrows. They came from throughout the British Isles, but the overwhelming majority were Irish. Many eventually made their way to North America to build the canals, railroads, and tunnels of a growing nation, and where, as the years passed, the definition of navvy became more diluted. By the mid-twentieth century, a navvy came to mean anyone employed as a laborer on a civil engineering project.

If you were young, Irish, and uneducated, you were more or less relegated to this type of menial labor abroad. My father, realizing this, did all he could to shed his "Irishness." He learned to speak English; up to this point he only spoke Irish. He became a voracious reader, polished his manners, and worked hard at losing his brogue, all in an effort to improve his station.

CHAPTER 11

✺

THE GREAT ARRANMORE DISASTER

UPON RETURNING FROM THE UK with the Arranmore tattie-hoking squads in the autumn of his 15th year, my father's group met-up with several other islanders in the Northern town of Derry. He was traveling with Tony and Ned Gallagher, brothers who lived nearby on Arranmore. Along with them were John, Eddie, Charlie, Hannah, and Madgie Gallagher, who lived just below the road from my father, along with their cousin, also named Johnny Gallagher. Aboard the ferry from Scotland, they met with other islanders: Paddy O'Donnell from Plohogue, and his sister, Kitty, and Mickey Mhór Gallagher's two boys, Donal and Manus, and their sister, Hannah. My father wasn't related to any of them, strange as it may seem, but he knew them all. There were fourteen of them, including my father, returning to Arranmore that day. The date was November 9th, 1935. As they walked through town awaiting the train that would take them to Burtonport, my father became separated from the rest of his gang. As he searched for the familiar faces down the narrow streets and in the little shops of the bustling border town, he lost track of the time. In the distance he heard the pitiful cry of the train whistle blow, and he ran back to the railway station to catch the Swilly Train, the final leg on the long journey home. But by the time he reached the station the train and his traveling companions were well down the track. My father was now forced to find a local hostel to spend the night and wait for the next train to Burtonport the following day. His friends on the other hand, would reach the port by evening, cross over to Arranmore, reunite with their families, and sleep in their own beds that night.

When my father arrived at the port the following evening, he was shaken by the news of what had happened to the others on their return to the island the night before. When the squads arrived by train to Burtonport, Edward Gallagher, his two sons, Mickey, and Paddy, sailed across to the mainland to meet them. Along with them were four of their neighbors: young John Gallagher, John Bow O'Donnell, Johnny Rodgers, and Eamon Ward.

It had rained earlier that day and the tide was exceptionally high.

"Ye know, I never since have seen it rain as hard as on *that* day," my Uncle Anthon Frank Gallagher told me, recalling the events in a 1985 interview.

The island welcoming party made the crossing from Arranmore in Edward's yawl without incident, although four of the men had to take to the oars, the wind dead against them and a terrifying darkness enveloping them from the west. They had seen a darkening sky before, but this one was different and it made them all take notice. By the time they had crossed the three miles of open ocean, the sea went extraordinarily calm. Edward Gallagher was one of the island's most experienced sailors. He studied the sea and the sky carefully while the others loaded the boat with the returning tattie-hoker's trunks and cases. He thought about waiting until morning to return to the island. But the hour was late and there was no place for the twenty of them to stay on the mainland. He decided to make for Arranmore before the weather turned once again. It was a tight fit. There were thirteen waiting on the pier when the boat arrived, more than Edward and the others expected. Somehow, they managed to cram everyone and all their belongings into the tiny yawl. The boat sat low in the water as Edward sailed out of the harbor and slipped into the darkness past the Isle of Iniscoo.

The giddy banter of the tattie-hokers drifted out over the black water. They were relieved to be so near home and happy to see the glow of their island's cottage lights twinkling through the gloaming. Edward's son Paddy, who returned from the squads earlier in the season due to a severe bout of rheumatic fever, listened intently to the recounting of the stories and adventures he had missed while his brothers, sisters, and the others were abroad. Paddy told them there would be a "welcome home" dance on the island the following night in Neily Phil's hall—the Ballroom of Romance, as it was known in those days.

They had cleared Rutland Island by this time and leaned toward the treacherous open waters of "Arran Roads." A threatening shower was fast

approaching from the east but with Edward at the helm, no one felt any
danger. A light shower began to fall, then a barrage of hail. The passengers
laughed and tried to cover as best they could. The boat sent up an icy spray
as it skipped along at a terrific pace driven by the wind which accompanied
the shower. Edward brought the boat about, as he had countless times
before, in front of *Bailé na Eilin* (*bal a kneel yin*, "a clutch of chickens" in local
dialect), a scattering of rocks stretching out from the island at Cloughcorr
(*clo car*, odd stone). From there Edward would tack west, past na Rannagh
to Aphort pier. But the unusually high, murky tide had concealed the rocks
of Bailé na Eilin. Visibility was poor and the storm had caused Edward to
misjudge his location. He was closer to the island than he thought. Johnny
Rodgers, also an experienced sailor, sat in the forward look-out. Suddenly,
Johnny cried out a warning and four or five of the men quickly tore the
sail from the mast, but it was too late. The agile boat bumped one of the
submerged rocks. An ensuing wave lifted the top-heavy vessel half-way
up the rock. When the wave passed, the boat fell backwards and capsized,
spilling all of its cargo and twenty tangled bodies into the sea. Some were
struck by the falling debris. Others became caught within the rigging and
under the sails and struggled to free themselves, but were dragged down
as the boat heeled over. Nine of them scrambled onto the upturned keel,
but a moment later the yawl flipped over again and threw them off. Their
heavy winter clothing acted as a fetter and the frigid water paralyzed them.
Young Paddy Edward Gallagher, the only one among them unable to swim,
grabbed the gunwale and pulled himself onto the upturned hull. He heard
the desperate cries of his brothers and sisters along with the others. Then
he heard nothing. He screamed and shouted and whistled in hopes that
someone would hear him. No one did. His father and his brother, Johnny,
managed to stay with the boat but unable to remain conscious, they soon
succumbed to exposure. Before Paddy could tie them both to the boat, his
father slipped beneath the waves.

The shower had passed, the skies had cleared, and a full moon rose over
Errigal Mountain, bathing Paddy and the red-bellied boat in a pale blue
light. They drifted closer to the Island of Innishkeeragh, then westwards
toward Rutland. If they drifted beyond the islands, they would be carried
out to sea. Paddy shouted until he could shout no more. One by one he
watched the lights go out on Arranmore and Innishkeeragh. When the last
light went out, at Paddy McGill's in Ballintra, Paddy was alone. He clung
steadfastly to his dead brother with one hand and to the keel of the boat

with the other. Battling freezing temperatures and pounding waves, he fought to stay awake.

It wasn't until 8:30 the next morning that Paddy and the up-turned boat were seen adrift, perilously close to the breakwaters called *Tonn Shalach* (*ton hallah*). A rescue party was launched at once and they pulled Paddy from the icy waters. The frail, sickly boy, unable to swim, miraculously survived fourteen grueling hours in the bone-chilling ocean. But he was the *only* one. The other nineteen islanders aboard the boat perished, including Paddy's father, his four brothers and two sisters.

The lifeboat crew, along with every available craft from Arranmore, began a hopeful search for possible survivors and the grim task of recovering the victims. They examined *Carraic Bheal a 'tStrotha* (*carrick veal a stroch*, rock at the mouth of the inlet) at first, a large cluster of rocks halfway between Arran and Rutland, but found nothing. They proceeded to Bailé na Eilin. There they discovered traces of red paint on a rock. They also found a pair of rubber Wellingtons which were identified as belonging to John Rodgers, one of the neighbors who sailed with Edward from the island to collect the returning party. He apparently took them off to swim after the drifting boat. They remained where he left them undisturbed by the waves. Had he stayed on the rocks he could have walked ashore within a few hours with the ebbing tide. But he must have mistakenly thought they had capsized further out at Carraic Bheal a 'tShrotha. They all misjudged the speed at which the boat was traveling in the darkness; in reality, they were only a few hundred feet from home.

Everyone now concentrated their search efforts at Bailé na Eilin. Mickey Mhór Gallagher of Aphort, a neighbor of Edward Gallagher, said to one of the islanders beside him as they made their way to the site, "God, wasn't I lucky that *my* three children weren't coming in last night. Hannah wrote me the other day and said they wouldn't be finished on the farm for another week."

But poor Mickey Mhór was in for a terrible shock. He hadn't come along the rocks very far when he saw his two sons, Donal and Manus, wet and covered with sand and draped in seaweed. They were sitting side-by-side, their backs up against a boulder. Their eyes were wide open and fixed. He was sure they were alive. He knelt beside them. "We didn't expect ye boys. Where's Hannah? Where's your sister?" he asked.

When he realized the boys were dead he ran down towards the sea. He fell to his knees and began shouting at the cruel waves, "Give me back my child, my only daughter! Haven't you done enough to rob me of my two sons?"

His island neighbors gathered around to console him and they brought him home.

Hannah was a tall, fair-haired twenty-one-year-old girl with aspirations of becoming a good wife and homemaker for a worthy island boy. When her trunk was found among the rocks it contained new curtains, blinds and bed linens. Her body was one of two that were never recovered from the bitter ocean.

Seven bodies were taken off the rocks at Bailé na Eilin that horrible day. Paddy Edward had lashed the body of his brother, John, to the boat before he died and the body of bootless Johnny Rodgers was discovered when they up-righted the ill-fated craft. He swam to the boat as he intended and tied himself off when he realized that he was too weak to withstand the night in the frigid water. He was an experienced fisherman and knew to make certain that his corpse would be recovered.

The nine bodies were laid out in the Lifeboat House at na Rannagh—eight fine young men, the eldest among them only twenty-nine, and Madgie Edward Gallagher, Paddy's sister, whose long black hair was entwined with seashells and sand that hung in wet strands about her demure face; her lips wan. She was found still gripping to the partially eaten apple she took from her coat pocket just before the boat capsized.

Over the next several weeks the bodies of the remaining victims washed ashore on the nearby islands. It wasn't until nine months after the tragedy that the body of Paddy's father, Edward Gallagher, was found on Iniscoo near the mouth of Burtonport harbor. His intact and fully-clothed body was partially buried in the sand, having returned to within a few hundred yards of the pier where he set sail on his last, fateful voyage.

The seventeen bodies that were eventually recovered (two were never found), were buried in a communal grave and are marked by a tall Celtic cross in a corner of the church graveyard.

For months afterward, Mickey Mhór Gallagher was seen walking the shores of the island still calling for his only daughter, Hannah, to come home. The sea refused to relinquish her and free Mickey from his grief.

Paddy Edward lived his remaining years peacefully on Arranmore. He came to own and operate a little grocer in Torries, along with his younger brother Anthony, directly across the road from my Uncle Barney's house.

On my visits to Arranmore, I frequently ducked into his shop for a candy bar or ice cream. I didn't know that the short, quiet man behind the counter was the sole survivor of the Arranmore Disaster of 1935.

Out of respect, no one on the island speaks of the tragic day that remains the greatest domestic sea tragedy in Irish history. Paddy never spoke of it either—choosing instead to keep his grief private. I heard only vague references of the event from my father during my childhood. When he, my sister, Sheila, and I visited Arranmore in 1985, we sat in Uncle Barney's parlor and from the window could see Paddy below the road in front of his shop. Only then did my father tell me how he had traveled with the group and that he missed the train in Derry and the events that followed.

He warned me in a whisper, "Don't go talkin' about it neither. And don't be askin' any questions, of anyone!"

Later that day I went for a walk in a vain search for the Cave of the Slaughter, where in 1649 one of Oliver Cromwell's garrisons is said to have massacred seventy island people. On my return I saw Paddy sitting on the stone wall along the road outside his store. He was just watching the world go by. He followed me into his shop where I bought a can of Coke and a Bounty candy bar. I went back outside in the warm sunshine and sat on the wall to enjoy my snack. Paddy came out and picked up a fishing net he'd been mending.

"How's your Da?" he asked. (Well, he knew who I was.)

"Fine." I replied. "He's up at Barney Condy's."

"Aye, I heard ye's were here. How's he been keepin' since your mother died last year?" She actually died nearly two years prior in 1983, but I wasn't going to correct him.

"You know," I shrugged.

"Aye," he said.

The minutes passed.

"Paddy Edward, right?" I asked.

"Aye."

Another minute or two of silence.

"Lovely weather," he commented.

"Yeah, a beautiful day," I said cheerfully.

He scanned the sea. A couple of half-deckers plied their way from Aphort pier southeast down Gweebara Bay.

"The salmon will be running close to shore tonight, so they will," he said.

I nodded in agreement, as if *I* knew. I waited a few moments searching for a way to delicately broach the subject.

"I saw in the paper that it's been fifty years since the disaster."

"Aye, this November the ninth," he stated.

"No one talks about it," I said.

"No. No one will."

"Has anyone asked you about it, reporters or . . . "

"Some," he muttered.

"Would you tell *me*?" I asked sheepishly.

"Tell you what?"

"About the disaster, what happened?" I lit a cigarette. I offered Paddy one. He declined.

"They all died, so they did. What is it you want to know?" he asked.

"The facts," I said. "I've heard so many stories from people that . . . I just want to know what happened, that's all."

He hesitated.

"I'm sorry if I've offended you. I didn't mean to pry . . . "

"You're alright," he interrupted.

He put down the fishing net. Calm came over him. He looked . . . relieved. Perhaps he felt it was time as there was much discussion of it in the local press during the week of our visit.

"It was just there, ye see," he began, pointing to the rocks of Bailé na Eilin.

I didn't ask anymore questions. I patiently let him tell me what he wanted to tell me, and what he didn't, he didn't. The shy, private and unassuming man rarely looked at me when he spoke, and there were plenty of long pauses and staccato responses. Mostly, we sat enjoying the rare beautiful weather, the view, and for me, his company. After thirty minutes or so, I reasoned that he told me all that he was going to tell me, and I changed the subject.

'We're staying over at the Glen," I told him.

"I have to go now," he said. "Be sure and tell your Da that Paddy Edward says hello."

I shook his hand and thanked him. He walked into his shop. I returned to Uncle Barney's house and told my father about the discussion I had with Paddy. He was furious that I had disobeyed him. Later, he told me that he didn't think that Paddy ever told anyone what he told me. I don't know if that's true, but I am grateful to have spent the time with him. I'll never

forget what he told me, or that he felt comfortable enough to reveal to me the grief and pain he carried with him for fifty years.

When I returned to the states, I began to research the events of the disaster. I obtained a copy of the front page of the *Donegal Democrat* weekly newspaper dated November 16th, 1935. Drawn from that paper, and my experience with Paddy, I wrote a song-documentary to honor him and the victims of the disaster. I recorded the song on an album in 1986 and sent Paddy a copy of the record asking for his permission to release it. He wrote back, thanking me. In a simple statement of approval he said, "I like the song very much and have learnt to sing it."

When Paddy died in 1987, he was laid to rest in the mass grave with the other victims of the disaster. I was told by the islanders that they played my recording "The Great Arranmore Disaster of 1935" at his funeral. I can think of no greater honor.

CHAPTER 12

c✈ɔ

DIASPORA

THE SUMMER FOLLOWING THE ARRANMORE Disaster, my father and his cousin and close friend, Brian Mary Cissie Rodgers, traveled to England and worked as navvies, digging post-holes by hand for the telephone company. It was perhaps the most miserable and desperate time in my father's life. He once excavated a valuable 1st century Roman coin, "but," he said, "I was so near starvation I traded it to a fellow navvy in exchange for an apple."

In the spring of 1937 my father left England and returned briefly to Arran. He was restless and despondent. He struggled to find peace with his father and found it difficult to live under his roof. Their relationship grew progressively tense and estranged. He read with fascination about developments in the world beyond *The Lagan* and longed to be a part of it. Newspapers, when he could get his hands on them, frequently reported on an Austrian named Adolph Hitler and his alarming rise to power in Germany. My father realized that England would soon be drawn into war. News from Chicago always interested my father, for many of his island neighbors and cousins immigrated there and found well-paying jobs in city departments. He read how George Cardinal Mundelein, the Archbishop of Chicago, expressed his contempt of Adolph Hitler. In a pejorative speech delivered in Chicago in May, 1937, Cardinal Mundelein, who was himself of German ancestry, compared Hitler, who fancied himself an artist, to a wallpaper hanger—"and a poor one at that."[77] Hitler was immediately ridiculed in the international press. The temperamental dictator vowed to get even with Cardinal Mundelein and sent agents to Chicago to see if they could uncover some scandal. The only irregularity they discovered was that the will of one Fr. Netstraeter [to build a church in Wilmette] had never been executed by the cardinal, who had put all his time and resources into constructing the seminary. Supposedly, Hitler forced the relatives of Fr. Netstraeter who still lived in Germany to sue the Archdiocese in order to embarrass Cardinal Mundelein. The case was promptly thrown out of court.[78]

The cardinal's bold speech caught the attention of President Franklin Delano Roosevelt, who wrote to the cardinal asking for an exchange of autographs. The two ultimately became friends, and Mundelein served the President as emissary to the Vatican until the prelate died of a stroke at his seminary villa in 1939.

In the fall of 1937, at the age of seventeen, my father went to Dublin. On the way, he forged his Certificate of Birth, changing the year from 1920 to 1917. He had a grand vision. He would join the British Navy and see the world beyond the British Isles and raise himself up from the cruel, hard island life which he felt he could not endure and to which he did not belong. My father's original birth certificate is so blatantly and comically forged that I'm sure navy recruiters gave it only a cursory look when he applied. He was, after all, Irish. England was on the verge of entering war and would take any able-bodied young men, especially any able-bodied, expendable young *Irishmen* to fill their ranks. He was issued service number D/MX102879.

He returned to Arranmore after his basic training and a short tour of duty in 1939. He had become a wise, mature, and handsome young man who charmed many of the young ladies of the island with his dashing good looks, proper English, and worldly personality. The island men, those not jealous of his early success and exploits, admired him—if not for his prankish wit and intelligence, then for his determination to break away from the cycle of hardship and poverty to which so many were destined. I have heard corroborating tales verifying his esteem from many islanders of his generation. He left Arranmore in 1939. It would be the last time he ever saw his father and he would not return to the island again for thirty-eight years.

On December 22nd, 1939, Dad was issued a travel permit to enter the United Kingdom indefinitely, as an Irish citizen. He sailed to Liverpool on January 5th, 1940, and re-enlisted in Portsmouth on the 23rd of October, 1941. He was among the last crews to receive training aboard the *H.M.S. Victory* before it was damaged by German Luftwaffe in 1941. He served on several of Her Majesty's Ships including *H.M.S. Collingwood* and *H.M.S. Britannia II*.

Despite the bigotry and persecution he was subjected to, my father persevered and saw considerable war-time service. He spent most of his active duty time below decks in the engine room. His *Certificate of Naval Service* describes him as "an ordinary seaman, air fitter engine room mechanic, 5th class." The *Britannia II* cruised the Mediterranean when Germany occupied North Africa. Dad was injured during a gun battle on the 27th of December, 1942. His *Certificate for Wounds or Hurt* states that he "suffered a simple fracture to the base of the distal phalanx with no displacement." In other words, he broke the big toe on his left foot when he dropped a wrench on it.

He obviously enjoyed some shore leave. In Tunis, North Africa, he got a tattoo on his left upper arm—a cross with a wreath and the word "Mother," a son's loving tribute to the woman who was taken from him as a child. When his tour of duty ended, he re-enlisted in the Queen's Navy in Canada, where he took up the trade of machinist. He served aboard *H.M.C.S. Naden*. There he began to educate himself, distance himself, and assimilate into non-Irish society. He occupied his post-war free time by reading the entire library on board ship. He immersed himself in the classics, studied atlases, and read Webster's Collegiate Dictionary cover-to-cover to improve his English pronunciations and increase his vocabulary. And he memorized poetry which he loved to recite to me—especially when he was "into his cups." His favorite poem was *The Solitude of Alexander Selkirk* by British author Francis Turner Pelgrave. He taught it to me when I was a child and we recited it together. I loved the imagery and had little difficulty memorizing it for a talent show when I was in the fifth grade. Only now do I understand and appreciate my father's relationship with this poem.

The Solitude of Alexander Selkirk

I am monarch of all I survey;
My right there is none to dispute;
From the centre all round to the sea
I am lord of the fowl and the brute
O Solitude! where are the charms
That sages have seen in thy face?
Better dwell in the midst of alarms,
Than reign in this horrible place.

I am out of humanity's reach;
I must finish my journey alone;
Never hear the sweet music of speech—
I start at the sound of my own;
The beasts that roam over the plain
My form with indifference see—
They are so unacquainted with man,
Their tameness is shocking to me.

Society, Friendship, and Love
Divinely bestow'd upon man,
Oh had I the wings of a dove
How soon would I taste you again!
My sorrows I then might assuage
In the ways of religion and truth,
Might learn from the wisdom of age,
And be cheer'd by the sallies of youth.

Ye winds that have made me your sport,
Convey to this desolate shore
Some cordial endearing report
Of a land I shall visit no more.
My friends, do they now and then send
A wish or a thought after me?
O tell me I yet have a friend,
Though a friend I am never to see.

How fleet is a glance of the mind!
Compared with the speed of its flight,
The tempest itself lags behind,
And the swift-wingèd arrows of light.
When I think of my own native land,
In a moment I seem to be there;
But, alas! recollection at hand
Soon hurries me back to despair.

But the sea-fowl is gone to her nest,
The beast is laid down in his lair;
Even here is a season of rest,
And I to my cabin repair.
There's mercy in every place;
And mercy—encouraging thought!—
Gives even affliction a grace,
And reconciles man to his lot.

CHAPTER 13

✧

A SON OF THE SOIL

T RUE TO THEIR CHARACTER, THE people of Arranmore are
unpretentious, honest, and incredibly self-sufficient. They have
relied on each other for centuries, which has sustained them as a unique
culture and garnered respect and admiration from those on the mainland
opposite. To some they are a curiosity with their clannish customs and
rugged countenance. They are tolerant of tourists but wary of outsiders
whom they call "blow-ins." Disputes among them are often settled at one
of the local pubs, the social center of the island, over the exchange of fists
and one-too-many pints.

I was twenty-four years old when I first arrived on Arranmore, on June
23rd, 1979. The first night on my visit to the island was spent celebrating in
the Glen Hotel, formerly the landlord John Stoup Charley's (Charlie Beag's)
house, now owned and operated by my cousin, Mary the Glen, and her
tireless husband, Philly. The pub was packed and I enjoyed my first taste
of Smithwick's and countless games of darts with my cousins and some of
the other local men. It was well after midnight. I knew that the pubs in
Ireland had a strict policy of closing at "half-ten" (ten thirty). I asked my
cousin, Johnny the Glen, who was still a teenager and tending bar, what
time they closed. He appeared puzzled. I pointed to the clock on the bar.
He dismissed it. "Close?" He said incredulously, "October. That's when
all the tourists go home!"

There never was a policeman, or *Garda*, on the island to enforce such rules on any of my visits. It is not uncommon for the pubs to reach their capacity around mid-night, or later, and the young people can often be seen walking home from the dancehall at daybreak. Trouble on the island is rare and usually comes from nearby mainlanders or students enrolled in the summer Gaelic immersion studies. An ad-hoc advisory committee of elders doles out island justice. One night the only public phone booth on the island, located along the road in front of Tony the Post's house, had been vandalized. I asked Philly the Glen about it. "We know who is responsible," he said, "kids from Dungloe on the mainland. We'll deal with them in our own way, in our own time." Nothing more was said and I did not ask.

Philly the Glen offered to drive me over to the far side of the island to visit with my father's sister and brother. He had an old, rusted Renault sedan parked out front of the hotel for just such purposes. Entire sections of the floorboard were missing and the passenger door fell off its hinges when I opened it.

"It's the salt air," he said in response, "it eats the cars. Sure, it's only two years old. When they can't run anymore we strip them of all their parts, tow them out to the far side of the island and push them off the cliff."

"You're joking, right?" I asked skeptically.

"No. The sea reclaims them in no time," he said. "C'mon, get in."

I hesitated but got in anyway. The drive over to Torries was quite the adventure—a cross between "The Flintstones" and "Mr. Toad's Wild Ride." The shocks and springs of the French sedan were of little use. Dust came up from where the floor used to be. Philly drove like Mr. Magoo over the twisting, rock-strewn roads, dodging stray sheep and pedestrians and talking and gesturing wildly the entire time. Arriving safely, I visited with Philly's in-laws: my Aunt Grace, her husband, Anthon Frank Gallagher, and their daughter, Bella. I was familiar with Aunt Grace and Bella. They came to America in 1968 and stayed with us for a week. The two were always at the needles, knitting. They knitted as they talked, rarely looking at their work. Within a week's time they had each knitted my father an Arran sweater finer than any I have seen for sale in the best woolen shops.

The visit in Torries was wonderful. Anthon played his fiddle and Grace and Bella served tea and biscuits. As the night progressed, Aunt Grace seemed increasingly agitated as she furiously knitted in the corner of the room. I asked her if everything was alright. She complained about the noise outside. A rooster in their yard was constantly crowing. I barely noticed it, but it clearly angered her every time he made his presence known. Standing at the door to say our good-byes at the end of a very satisfying evening Aunt Grace alternately admonished the rooster in Gaelic and English and insisted that I come by for tea on Sunday after Mass.

I met up with Uncle Barney on the road to Mass on Sunday. He was dressed in clean trousers, a tweed jacket and cap, his best white shirt, and a narrow necktie. Everyone wore their best to Mass I observed, and nearly everyone walked to the modest chapel on the *strand* (beach).

"Are you coming to Grace and Anthon Frank's today for tea, Uncle Barney?"

"Aye," he said.

I was pleased to know that he would be there. He and I had cultivated a distant but warm correspondence over the years and now that I was on the island, I was eager to spend more time with him and get to know him better. When we reached the church, Barney veered off and congregated with the men outside the chapel, most of whom casually leaned against the wall, smoked cigarettes and chatted. All the women and children gathered along the wall on the other side of the Chapel. Moments before the start of service, they met at the front door and filed in together.

Father Eugene McDermott slowly negotiated his way through Mass in a mix of Irish, English, and Latin. The poor, elderly priest wore a pair of glasses that contained only one lens and he was so arthritic that the altar boys had to help him back to his feet whenever he genuflected. He made an announcement after Communion, "a roll of money in the amount of 500 pounds was dropped along the road in Leabgarrow near Paddy Patsy's house yesterday and brought to me; if the owner would please collect it after Mass."

I expected a rush of people to come forward and claim the cash. I later learned that it was dropped by one of the fisherman returning home after selling his catch in Burtonport. Five hundred pounds (about $800.00) represented a month's wages, maybe more. I watched with interest to see what would happen after Mass. To my astonishment, only one person came forward. The priest reached into his pocket from under his vestments and handed the roll of bills to the grateful fisherman.

After Mass, I walked with Barney back to Aphort—most of it uphill. Barney, nearly three times my age, was short and stout like a fire hydrant but had incredible stamina and walked the hills with ease. I had to ask him to stop a few times so that I could sit and rest on the ditches (stone walls) that lined the steep road to Aphort.

When we reached his cottage, Barney stood on the front stoop with his hands on his hips. He stared intently at the sea. He carefully observed the patterns of the wind on the surface of the water from the shore to the horizon and from east to west. The view was spectacular all the way across Gweebara Bay to the town of Portnoo some thirty miles distant.

"There will be no rain today," he said, "it'll be fair all day."

"How do you know that?" I asked, still out of breath from our climb.

"The sea tells me that," he said, and I followed him inside.

The parlor, to the left of the front entrance, was the largest room in his house, measuring about ten feet wide and about twelve feet deep. Along the outside wall was a modest peat fireplace which provided heat for the entire house. Barney immediately added a few pieces of turf and stoked the fire. I eased my tired frame into the sofa. This was the same house where my father grew up and I felt compelled to ask Barney to show me how to properly stoke a peat fire as I'm sure my father must have done countless times. He laughed. We sat in the parlor speaking very little. It wasn't awkward as you might suspect. I was just grateful to spend quiet time with him and I think he felt the same way, too.

"Would you like a cup o'tea, Uncle Barney?" I asked.

"Aye," he said, and started to get up.

"No, no, no," I said, "sit there, I'll make it." I jumped up from the sofa.

"You know how?" He asked.

"I can't cook but I can make a proper cuppa," I said.

His narrow kitchen was added on to the back of the original house. He had a few feet of countertop with a sink, a stove, a small dining table and two chairs. He had no refrigerator. An electric kettle sat on the counter. I filled it with water from the tap and plugged it in. I looked through the presses (cupboards) for some cups and found a few odd dishes. One press contained an egg and two potatoes—his dinner. The rest of the cabinets were bare. Barney came into the kitchen to supervise. We returned to the parlor with our tea and sat by the fire.

Every time Barney heard someone along the road, he leaned forward in his chair and peered through the lace curtains. There were built-in bookshelves on either side of the fireplace. A set of binoculars hung by its lanyard on a nail near the front window and looked as though they were well-worn from frequent use. My father brought them over for Barney when he visited two years before in 1977, his first trip back to the island in nearly forty years. Dad told me when he returned that the island had changed very little, noting that he slept in the same room, and the same bed he had as a young man. Even the same sparse decorations were unchanged.

On the shelf next to the binoculars was a large, ancient, short-wave radio, capable of pulling in stations from all across Europe. There were also three clocks in the span of twelve feet along the outside wall of the parlor: one on the shelf next to the radio, one on the fireplace mantle, and one hanging on the wall to the right. None of them were working. When I asked Barney about them he replied thoughtfully, "Well, if I look at the one, the other two get jealous, ye see, and then," he said with a wave of his hand, "they all quit."

Clocks, I came to learn, were of little relevance to the islanders. They kept their time by the turn of the tide. Every aspect of their daily lives was governed by the rhythm of the ocean.

When it was time for dinner we walked down the road to Aunt Grace's house in Torries and sat down to eat shortly after we arrived. Grace and Bella set the table with their good china and glassware. Aunt Grace brought out a chicken on a platter and began carving it as we passed around the potatoes, vegetables, and bread. Steeped in conversation, we leisurely feasted on a superbly prepared meal. I noticed that the rooster that had been such an annoyance to Aunt Grace a couple of days before was nowhere to be heard.

"It's pretty quiet outside, Aunt Grace. What did you do, put a muzzle on your rooster for the evening?"

As I filled my plate with the freshly carved chicken, she casually mentioned, "I was so upset the other night when ye's were here that after ye's left I went out with the hatchet and put an end to his crowing altogether, so I did."

I put my silverware down and stared at my plate.

Uncle Barney smiled at me from across the table. "I'll bet he had no idea he was invited to dinner too," he chuckled.

Barney was proud of the highland bagpipes he purchased "from a local plowboy" while working as a migrant in Scotland in the years leading up to Ireland's independence in 1921. He played them often and taught my father to play when he was just seven years old. Both became members of the island's Donegal Pipe Band. Before I left the island on my inaugural visit, I stopped at Barney's house to say good-bye. He handed me a battered, black lacquered wooden box and told me to take it with me. It contained his bagpipes, music books, reeds, and chanter. I gratefully accepted them, returned to Chicago, and had them refurbished. Committed to learning how to play them, I drove eighty miles round trip once a week for several months to take private lessons. I practiced with the Chicago Highlander's Pipe Band at the old VFW Hall in Elmhurst, and was elected an active member of the band for a few years during the mid-1980's. I participated in parades, political events, and competitions. Although I no longer play, I will always cherish Barney's pipes.

CHAPTER 14

❧

CONDY COOK

I ENJOYED GOOD *CRAIC* (PARTYING) DOWN at Phil Bánn's Pub a few days into my visit on Arranmore, and arose late the following morning. I nursed through the previous night's indulgences by casually dining on a superb breakfast prepared by my cousin, Mary the Glen, and her painfully shy ten-year-old daughter, Angela. While I was at at Phil Bánn's I asked what would be the best way to get to the mainland in the morning. (This was a few years prior to the opening of the ferry service.) I was told that for fifty pence I could board one of the many fishing boats and be dropped off at the Burtonport pier.

By the time I strolled down the steep and narrow lane from The Glen to Leabgarrow pier, all the fishing boats were gone. I was stranded. I paced along the sand and gazed longingly across the straights to the port and tried to cobble together some alternate plans for the remainder of the day.

"The boats ha' been away with the tide," I heard in a raspy, matter-of-fact voice from behind me.

I turned and watched the slight old man walk past me. He didn't look up. He lifted and inspected a few strands of kale left behind on the strand by the ebbing tide.

"Pardon me?" I replied.

"If ye want t'go across te the mainlan' ye have to git here before the tide goes out," he said. He looked me over. He threw down the kale and brushed the sand from his hands against his baggy pants.

"There will be no boats now, so there won't" he said. He grimaced as he read the water from shore to the horizon.

He wasn't a big man. He was lean and cagey looking—red faced with wispy white hair, large protruding ears, and an impish grin. His face bore a great knowledge and wisdom of the sea. His eyes were clear and bright, full of honesty and mischief. The sleeves of his ragged jumper (sweater) were pulled up nearly to his elbows, revealing forearms massive for a man of his size. Like most fishermen of the region, the hand-knit jumper he wore comprised a series of elaborate stitches and patterns unique to his family, like a signature. That way, if his body was to be recovered from an accident at sea (an all-too-frequent occurrence since most island men can't swim—the result of a deep-seated superstition that it brings bad luck), the pattern in his jumper would be used to identify who he was and from where he came. The patterns have been handed down for centuries—the jumpers made by the wife or mother of those who wear them. They are knitted in their cottages of yarn spun from wool sheared from their own sheep. He, like all the island men, wore a tweed cap, the brim worn and dirty from where his sea-worthy hands frequently pulled it down about his twinkling eyes.

He then blurted out my father's island name in a half declarative—half interrogative melodic island tone.

"You're John Mary Hughie's son from Chee-cago are ye not?"

"Yes! I am," I said cheerfully, "how'd you know?"

"The whole of the island knows yer here," he said. "I'm Condy. Condy Cook they call me, ye know. Sure, we're related, so we are, and I'm married to yer cousin, Annie as well." He looked at me quizzically. "Annie Johnnie Ban Byrne? Do ye follow? Her grandmother, Madgie was Biddy Charlie's daughter."

I smiled and shrugged. "Condy the cook?" I asked.

"That's right, that's right," he said with a powerful grasp of my hand.

"Jesus, it's Popeye," I whispered under my breath, "it's nice to meet you," I said.

"Aye," he said.

"Half the people on this island seem to be my cousins," I laughed.

He looked back at me, and thought about it pensively for a few seconds.

"Aye," he said with a quick tilt of his head.

He was born Cornelius O'Donnell of the Bryan Óg O'Donnell clan, same as me, and as best as I can tell, married a second or third cousin of mine once or twice removed. Due to my great-grandfather, Hugh Stokes Rodgers', unusual progeny, I have so many cousins a generation or two older than I that I never have been able to make complete sense of my lineage on my father's side—regardless of repeated explanation. When I returned to the States, I asked my father about Condy Cook. He knew him when they were youths, said his nickname was well earned. "They call him Condy Cook as in *Coo-koo*," my father said twirling his index finger next to his temple. "He was rakish and free spirited, jabbered to himself, delighted in his own shenanigans and had a reputation for performing outrageous feats of foolishness. Would you believe he once slid down a guy wire from atop the Arranmore lighthouse with his bare hands, skinning them down to the bone?" My father laughed and shook his head. "He often set off by himself in a skiff just to row around the island or out on the open sea, sometimes disappearing for days at a time," he added.

As Condy and I talked on the water's edge, I told him of my foiled plans. "I wanted to go across to the mainland today to go shopping at the Cope (the local women's knitting retail co-op) in Dungloe to buy some sweaters and stuff. Looks like I missed the boat," I said with tongue-in-cheek sarcasm.

"Aye, the Cope is only open on Tuesdays. You'll have to wait 'til next week now, so ye will," he informed me.

"Yeah, well, I'm only here until Friday," I sighed.

"Well, there will be no boats now," he repeated, pointing to the fleet out at sea. There was a long, awkward pause. "But I'm goin' to the mainland, so I am. I can take ye in my boat if ye are wantin' to go. That's my flat bottom there," he said, pointing in the general direction of a couple of derelict half-deckers and what looked to be an overturned skiff about ten or twelve feet long. He began to walk away.

"I must go back up to the house to get me oars," he said, "these kids see the oars and they're off with me boat no tellin' where they'll leave it, the cheeky wee bastards. I *must* get me oars. Wait right there now. I'll get me oars an' we'll be off. I'll take ye to the mainlan', no bother. There's a woman in the port. You can get the taxi to Dungloe from there," he shouted as he hurried back to his cottage.

Several children were playing around the pier and on the nearby strand—chasing each other and throwing dead jellyfish at one another. They wandered near to me as they played, laughing and teasing each other and speaking in Irish when they didn't want me to hear them. When I turned to look at them, they darted off, like a school of skipjacks, only to approach again.

I looked to the horizon and took in the simple beauty of the place, grateful that after so many years of promises, I had finally made the journey to my father's island. The sky was fair and the sea, calm. It was an unusually warm and sunny day, which I estimated to be 21degrees (70° F).

The children scattered when they noticed Condy returning with a pair of battered oars over his shoulder. They were mocking me for the risky venture I was about to undertake, one that would soon be broadcast and known to everyone on the island and talked about for years to come.

Condy made straight for the skiff, a small rowboat the islanders refer to as a punt. He flipped the boat upright, threw in the oars, and wasted no time wrestling the boat to the water's edge. He motioned me over. I carefully placed in the bow my shoulder bag containing an 8mm movie camera and a tape recorder. The boat was well-worn, but by all appearances it seemed sturdy enough.

I helped Condy shove off, careful not to get my shoes wet. He made no such effort. I sat on the forward seat. Condy hopped into the middle seat, placed the oars into their locks, and immediately began rowing. After a few vigorous strokes he stopped and looked over his shoulder at me.

"Sit there," he said, pointing aft. I clumsily made my way.

Condy resumed rowing, heaving his small frame as far forward as he could to grab as much of the sea as possible. Bracing his feet against my seat he finished each stroke leaning back with the oar handle held tight against his chest. I moved my legs aside to accommodate him.

"Ach, you're alright," he said, "you're alright."

His frenetic cadence was as precise as a metronome. His efforts seemed tireless. In less than a minute we were too far from shore to successfully swim back if we were to capsize, I thought. I looked back at the pier. The children were standing on the end of it watching us with a curious look of disbelief. I took the small tape recorder out of my bag, turned it on and placed it on the seat beside me.

"So, Condy, do you row to the mainland often?"

"Aye, all the time," he said, "all the time. I've rowed around the island three times, so I have," he boasted.

"Three times?"

"Aye, three times," he said, "the one time I was just rowin' up through there, ye see." He paused to point along the south shore of the island and then quickly continued at his task. "Just there now, rowin', so I was, an' a gale come up from there, ye see," pointing in the opposite direction, "and right through there and down through there and it blowed me down there and down by there, and all the way right down through there, so it did," he said gleefully, pointing wildly in all directions. "I was rowing for four or five hours maybe, tryin'so I was, to row with the gale. An' I come up along the mainland thirty miles down the coast, so I did. And it was dark, ye know. Aye, dark as pitch, so it was. An' I pulled me boat up on the shore at this wee village down through there, ye see, and it was a lashin' rain by that time, ye know. And I saw a light in your man's pub there. Well, I walked up to your man's pub there in desperate need of a pint, so I was. And I had myself a pint too, so I did. And yer man at the bar was lookin' at me, funny like.

He said, 'you're not from here.'

'No,' I said, 'I'm not,' I said.

'Where is it you're from?' he said.

'Arranmore,' I said.

'Arranmore?' he said.

'Aye,' I said.

'And what are you doin' out on a night like this . . . Arranmore?' he said.

'Well it wasn't my intention to be out on a night like this,' I said, 'but the wind had other ideas,' I said.

'An' how did you get here then?' he said.

'I rowed,' I said.

'Ach! Ye did not!' he said. 'And he slapped his hand on the bar like that, ye see.'

'I did,' I said.

Ye know, I bet him a pint that I did! An' he had to walk down to the boat in the lashin' rain 'til he believed me a'tall."

Condy threw back his head and laughed wildly, "I paid for no pints that night a' tall. Not a one, so I didn't"

He paused for a moment, a far away look filled his bright eyes as he relished in his own tale. The punt slowly turned and began drifting with the tide. Coming back to the present he confidently nodded, "aye, three times," and resumed rowing.

We were well out on the open sea by this time. The waves were slapping at the hull and a fresh breeze blew across the boat. Condy looked over his shoulder to adjust his course.

"Your father was a reckless one as a child, ye know. He an' Brian Mary Cissie always together, so they were. Aye," he said smartly.

"So, I've heard," I replied, "Dad and Brian are still close friends. They see each other often, back home," I added.

"Is that right? Good God that's bloody marvelous!" Condy said.

The old salt regaled me with one tale after another as we crossed the few miles of open ocean—never once did he stop to rest or even slow his pace. The rhythmic clacking of the oars in their locks was hypnotic. We were nearing the outer islets of the port, a cluster of green, treeless archipelagoes with scattered ruins of homesteads that echoed of the Famine. Condy pointed out the names of each island as we glided past: Rutland, Inishfree, Owey, Inishmere, and Iniscoo. I noticed that a couple inches of water had seeped into the punt. Not as sturdy as I first thought. Preoccupied with positioning my feet so as not to get my shoes wet, I didn't notice the look of concern come over Condy. We were still a few hundred yards from the channel entrance.

"I'll have to let ye off here," he said, "I can't make it through the channel with the tide comin' out, ye see. You can walk up that way. Ye see that ruin there? Walk up that way an' over an' down an' around the other side. I'll meet ye there, so I will. I can't row us through there now. The tide is too strong, so it 'tis."

Condy made for the shore. I stepped out of the leaky flat-bottom onto a beautiful white strand. Condy got out and tilted the boat on to its gunwale to empty the water, then quickly got back in and began rowing toward the channel.

"Up that way, there," he pointed.

I looked to see no road, no footpath, only soft bog and knee-deep heather.

"That's right, head for that house up there!" Condy shouted, "I'll come around and get ye."

And there I was—suddenly alone on an abandoned island with no escape—and no one knew where I was. An unsettled feeling came over me. What did I get myself into?

I trekked as quickly as I could up the side of the hill toward the top. But the heather was thick and the scattered boulders and spongy ground made the walk difficult.

The morning sun had warmed the hills and I peeled off my jacket and sweater as I proceeded up the hill. From down below, the summit seemed so close to the strand. The walk became increasingly difficult and I was soon fatigued. At last, I made it to the top and dropped exhausted on the damp, mossy ground. The warm sun and cool Atlantic breeze was of great comfort. The air was fresh and the view, spectacular. There was no sound but for my own breath and the soft whisper of the constant breeze through the sweetly scented heather. Far below, I could see Condy struggling against the tide. He appeared to make no progress for all of his frantic effort. He looked so small—one man in a tiny white boat against all that water. I wondered if he would make it.

It was a gloriously clear day and I saw the jagged coastline from The Bloody Foreland clear down to Glencolumbkille. These were the sun-swamped hills of *The Rosses* in all of its magic. I could see the town of Dungloe some seven miles to the east—deceptively close from this vantage point. Distracted by the panoramic view, I lost sight of Condy. Several minutes passed. I began to think of a contingency plan only to realize there was no contingency plan! After about twenty minutes, and just before panic had settled in, I jumped to my feet. "There he is!" I exclaimed.

Condy had struggled through the narrows and was making fast for the shore below.

I shouted to him as I awkwardly raced down the steep hillside to the strand. Condy giggled. "Did ye think I would leave ye here?" he asked. "I wouldn't leave ye here."

I scampered into the boat, breathless and sweaty. My legs were weak and trembling as Condy continued with yet another story. I gazed back over my shoulder for one final look at my temporary prison.

By the time we reached Burtonport, the tide was nearly at full ebb. Condy moored his boat at the end of the pier and we walked the long incline to the shore. Relieved that we had made it, I asked Condy if I could buy him a pint in return.

"Aye, that would be grand," he said. "We can go in there. They know me there."

Condy led me into Boyle's pub on the quay. I had been there a few days before while waiting for a boat to get to the island. The room was dim and empty. The proprietor appeared from behind the curtain doorway that led to her living quarters. She shuffled behind the bar in her house slippers and slowly dragged on a cigarette. She looked as though she didn't recognize me and cringed whenever Condy spoke. She seemed quite put-out by the whole ordeal.

Condy whispered in Irish what I believed to be a drink order. Mrs. Boyle lazily served up a pint of Guinness for Condy and a half pint of Smithwick's for me. It was not quite 11:00 AM, too early for me to start drinking but I didn't want to insult Condy. He guzzled down his pint quicker than anyone I had ever seen do so before. He nodded to Mrs. Boyle for another. She responded leisurely. Condy tried to buy me another drink but I declined. When he coyly realized that he had no money to pay for his pint, I tendered a five-pound note to Mrs. Boyle. She walked back to the cash register with it—shaking her head.

Condy grabbed me by my arm and pulled me close.

"Listen, 'cuz," he said in an Irish whisper, "might I ask you for five pounds until later to buy m'self a few pints ye see?"

"No problem, 'cuz," I replied, and offered it to him discretely under the bar.

I never expected to see it (or him) again. He snatched the crumpled note from my fingers without hesitation. It was then I saw that he had a badly scarred and disfigured hand.

"That's right, that's right," he insisted, "I can pay ye later. Condy always pays his debts, ye know."

A likely story, I thought.

I thanked Condy profusely for taking me to the mainland under the nosey suspicion of Mrs. Boyle, of course. We said our good-byes as Condy made love to his pint and I left Boyle's in search of the house where the woman provided a taxi service.

I had not walked far when I heard Condy's voice behind me.

"I can show ye the woman's house now," he slurred. "It's up this way. Just to the right here now."

Not content with staying in the port, he decided to tag along. I began to wonder how, and if, I was going to be able to separate myself from him. He walked briskly, almost desperately, ahead of me. About a quarter mile up the road from the port he veered off to the right. As I approached, Condy pounded furiously on the door of a small, unkempt cottage. A woman appeared with several children clinging to her side. Condy explained to the woman that "we" would like a lift into Dungloe. The woman disappeared from the door for a moment and returned fumbling with a baby in her arms, along with a baby bottle, a purse, and a set of car keys. With three or four children scurrying at her feet, she walked quickly to her Volkswagen minibus. We all piled in. As I was closing the door, Condy thrust himself inside. When we reached the little village of Dungloe, the woman pulled over to the side of the steeply pitched main street. It was only about a half mile long and lined with various shops and several pubs. I paid and graciously thanked our driver. Condy tumbled out of the van. He brushed himself off and grabbed hold of my jacket, insisting that I join him for one last drink. My God, he was strong. I agreed to join him for one drink only. I went into great detail about all the shopping I had to do and he recoiled with disdain. This, I thought, would be my salvation from the man. I paid for the round, as Condy was deliberately too slow in removing *my* five pound note from his twisted trousers.

I quickly made my exit from the pub when Condy was distracted by a local man playing a fiddle in a snug near the back of the room. I ducked into a draper shop several doors down and watched out the window as a few minutes later, Condy staggered past. I exited the shop and sprinted up the street in the opposite direction.

Throughout the day I kept dodging Condy as I saw him stagger into and out of various pubs—evermore oblivious to the world around him. He must have insulted one burly publican as I saw a man burst through the door with Condy by the scruff of the neck and the back of his trousers. He literally threw Condy down the concrete steps and onto the pavement. The pedestrians paid no attention and simply walked around him. I felt embarrassed for the old drunken fool.

I entered a local café and purchased a bus ticket for the journey back to Burtonport. I was told the bus would be along in about a half an hour, give-or-take.

The room was filled with women and children, many of whom I recognized from the island. They all kept their distance. They were talking in Irish. I understood enough to realize they were gossiping about me. I saw my cousin, Bella, and walked over to talk to her. Bella is a cross-looking woman, short, and broad across the beam. Perpetually hawk-browed, she is as stern looking a woman as ever I met, which is completely contrary to her good-natured disposition. She talked through her teeth, stiff-jawed, with a whistling "s."

"What's this I hear ye came across with Condy Cook in the flat bottom?" She asked quietly.

Before I had a chance to respond she gave me "the look."

"Are ye bloody mad? Do ye know how dangerous that was? He's not right in the head ye know? He's an *'amathan'* (fool) half dotent and crazy drunk all the time, so he is! You were crazy to get in that boat with him. They're all talkin' about it, so they are. Jaysus, Kevin, have ye no sense a'tall?"

With that she turned and hurriedly walked away. I felt embarrassed and quietly sat down. I tried not to look around. I walked up to the counter and ordered a cup of tea and a Swiss roll pastry. No sooner had the young girl behind the counter brought it over to the table, then everyone rose and made for the door. The bus had arrived twenty minutes early. There was a mad scramble as women with parcels of every shape and size tried to get onto the bus. They had jericans of gasoline, live chickens, bags of cement, a bed frame, compressed gas, and bags and bags of groceries. I squeezed into the bus just as it left the station located behind the café. I saw Condy staggering wildly down the road—arms flailing, chasing after us. The bus driver never hesitated. The women and children were all talking about Condy, tisking, shaking their heads in disgust. The comments rose throughout the bus: *"gobshite,"* *"eejit,"* *"poor crachur,"* I heard them say. Then they turned and leered at me. I smiled back. It was a long and bumpy seven-mile ride back to Burtonport.

When we arrived, the harbor was empty of boats and there was no activity around the pier. The tide was coming in. Soon the fleet would be returning with their daily catch and the islanders, as they had for centuries, would find room on the boats where they could in order to get themselves and their meager provisions back to their island. I waited with them. I waited for hours—still, no sign of the fleet. I grew impatient. The locals seemed to take it all in stride. At last I heard the familiar knocking of a half-decker's engine as it lazily made its way through the channel—then another, and another.

I watched as the iron men in their wooden boats landed their day's catch upon the pier. Some had twenty or thirty salmon; others had only a few.

Their fishing strategy is to line their boats bow-to-stern and form a blockade about eight miles off Rinrowos Point, on the far side of Arranmore in their locally made twenty-eight foot half-decker boats. They keep a crew of two or three men and little in the way of sophisticated navigation. They remain within sight of the island but as far from shore as they can reasonably get where the salmon might run.

Farther out, the huge trawlers and factory ships from Spain, Portugal, Finland, and Norway take most of the fish. The salmon season lasts only a few weeks but constitutes most of the islanders' annual income.

The fishermen are wary of strangers in the port. Many of them, out of sheer necessity, are involved in the illegal practice of commercial fishing while collecting the government dole.

A loud discussion among the fishermen erupted as I walked along the pier taking 8 mm movies of the vessels, the bay, and the seagulls that came scavenging for any scraps they could steal. I noticed that at the center of the argument was young Phillip the Glen, Mary and Philly's son. After a few minutes Phillip walked over toward me pulling a net behind him. He began to unravel the net on the pier.

"They want to throw you in the drink," he said sharply, motioning his head in the direction of the argument. He moved in closer, still pulling at the nets. "They *ash't* me who's the feckin' Yank pullin' pictures. I telled them who you were—that you were me cousin, that ye meant no harm. But ye should put the camera away. They really don't give a shite who ye are," he insisted. "Put the feckin' camera in your bag and walk away. Do it now or they will, they'll throw you inte the feckin' harbor, so they will."

I did as I was told and nodded an apology. I got no response. Phillip deftly untangled the net and pulled it back onto the boat.

I later learned that government agents spy on the local fisherman to keep them from using illegal, monofilament nets at night when the salmon run closest to shore.

Each boat captain carries a shotgun on board. They shoot the seals that chase after the salmon. The seals often get tangled in the nets, destroying them. Nets are their single biggest expense. Seals take a terrible toll on the catch. A "marked" salmon is worth far less than a "pristine" fish.

Lobstering and other fishing is limited and highly regulated. So the fishermen here are dependent on a few weeks' income a year and, understandably, are very protective of their livelihood.

Some of the women began loading their supplies from town onto a half-decker captained by Phil Bánn. I observed an established priority to this procedure: provisions first, then passengers. Bella scouted me out among the crowd and guided me onto Phil's boat. I sat where I could find room.

As we were about to cast off, I heard Bella say under her breath, "ach, Jaysus, Mary and Saint Joseph, would you look at himself."

I looked up to see Condy racing down the hill to the foot of the pier. He had found his way back to the port from Dungloe. He staggered the seven miles and it only took him four and a half hours to do so. Judging by his inebriated condition, I'd say he staggered at least twice that distance. We cast off from the pier as everyone watched Condy strip down to his skivvies and dive into the filthy harbor. The neap tide had put his punt, tied to the end of the pier, about fifty yards off shore. He swam quite well considering the state he was in. We glided past, within reach of him, in Phil Bánn's half-decker and sat in silence as this pathetic man tried repeatedly to throw his leg over the gunwale and pull himself into his little flat-bottomed boat.

I did not see Condy Cook again during my remaining stay on Arranmore. I could only assume he eventually made it back safely.

ᐧᴧᴐ

I returned to Arranmore four years later, in the summer of 1983. On the last day of my visit, as I was walking up the incline in Leabgarrow that leads to the Glen Hotel, I saw the familiar form of a staggering old man trying unsuccessfully to negotiate a straight line down the steep hill. It was Condy Cook. I tried to ignore him as I passed but he veered over to me, blocking my way. He looked into my eyes. His were not the bright blue, mischievous eyes that I recalled from when last we met. But they were honest eyes just the same although red, weary, and glazed over. A quizzical look came over his face. While clinging to my sweater with one hand he looked down and unsteadily reached into his pants pocket with the other.

He looked up at me and said, "I don't remember who it 'tis that you are . . . but I remember that I owe ye five pounds."

With that, he peeled the soiled note from out of his pocket and slapped it to my chest. I put my hand over his, and he deftly slid his crippled hand out from under mine, leaving the bill in its place. He looked beyond me down the hill and sighed, "Condy always pays his debts, so he does."

He continued on his way. I was stunned and stood silent, my hand holding the money against my chest in utter disbelief. I watched as Condy rounded the bend below Andrew Early's Pub.

I never saw him again.

Arranmore postcard circa 1910

My father, his donkey, Jack, and my grandfather on their way to *an chescan*, the peat bog, to collect turf, circa 1928.

My Grandfather, Condy Bryan Oge O'Donnell, looking proud and intimidating dressed in his finest. Date unknown.

Good friends and first cousins, Brian Mary Cissie Rodgers (left) and my father, both age 16, sharing a lighter moment during a difficult time as navvies together in Ainsley, England, 1936.

Arranmore Island bagpipe band, circa 1935. Uncle Barney standing back row far right with the bagpipes he entrusted to me in 1979. Directly to Uncle Barney's right is Condy Cook O'Donnell.

Arranmore Islanders mourning the death of the recovered victims of the Great Arranmore Disaster, November, 1935.

The sun gleams off the nine coffins as the funeral cortege makes its way from the Aphort boathouse to St. Crone's Church. This remains Ireland's worst domestic sea tragedy. A total of nineteen perished. Two were never found. The recovered victims are all buried in a common grave in a corner of the island cemetery. Paddy Edward Gallagher, the sole survivor, was buried with them when he died in 1987.

Aphort Strand, Arranmore. Island men inspecting Edward Gallagher's fateful yawl a few days following the disaster. My father is the fifth man from the right. The boat was never put to sea again. The islanders burned it on the spot shortly after the tragedy. The charred hull lay undisturbed on the strand until an Atlantic storm carried the pieces out to sea.—*Photos Courtesy of Philly The Glen Boyle*

PART TWO

❧

"And in the end it's not the years in your life that count.
It's the life in your years."

—Abraham Lincoln

CHAPTER 15

༄

AFTER THE WAR

M Y FATHER WAS HONORABLY DISCHARGED from the Royal Canadian Navy on the 19th of March, 1946, in Montreal, Quebec. His life after the war found him traversing Canada twice, each time by way of the Canadian National Railway. While in Vancouver, he and a couple of former British shipmates made their way through the city and came upon a street vendor with a pushcart selling fresh steamed corn on the cob. They each purchased an ear of corn, added salt and butter before indulging in the ritual of nibbling the rows of kernels from the cob. My father—never having seen corn cooked in its original state—innocently put the entire end of the cob into his mouth and tried to bite off a piece. His friends mocked him as they roared with laughter at his expense. Experiences such as these embarrassed my father, inspiring him to try so hard to overcome his ignorance and down-play his nationality.

Six months into his travels through Canada, my father decided to visit relatives in Chicago and he applied for residency. On October 16th, 1946, he entered the United States for the first time through Windsor, Ontario, by way of the D & C Tunnel into Detroit. From there he boarded a train and headed for the "Windy City," so named after its loquacious politicians. (It is generally believed that the turn-of-the-century term was coined by journalist James O'Donnell-Bennett of the Chicago Tribune, the same reporter who so eloquently described the 28th Eucharistic Congress from the grounds of St. Mary of the Lake Seminary in 1926.)

Father lived for several months with relatives Hughie and Tess Rodgers from Arranmore. They had a flat in the DePaul neighborhood at 3630 Magnolia, near Lincoln and Fullerton Avenues. Several of his relations lived in that part of town, especially the Rodgers clan; his first cousins. Jimmy Malta (Brian Mary Cissie's brother) came to Chicago a number of years before my father and had sailed the Great Lakes. He rose through the ranks to captain a tug out of Calumet Harbor on the south side, guiding fresh water and salty freighters, including the legendary Edmond Fitzgerald, into and out of Lake Calumet.

"Uncle Jimmy" was a gregarious man, very tall and thin as a rake. I liked him. Kind and engaging, he drew me into conversation whenever I saw him. He played the bagpipes. His wife, Nellie Peadar Gallagher, from Gortgarra, Arranmore, was an imposing and curvy woman. She had a trademark hairdo: wispy and copper-colored—always with exposed grey roots—and spun on top of her head like a bonnet of rusty cotton candy. She held her hair precariously in place with countless bobby pins and she flaunted colorful, flowery dresses, gaudy mink stoles, heavy pancake makeup, and thick, uneven eyeliner. She had a curious habit of shaving her eyebrows and penciling in new ones high onto her forehead, which gave her a perpetual look of surprise. Her voice was deep and throaty, her Donegal brogue luxuriously thick and staccato. She always spoke in a pitiful tone. In her later years her penchant for makeup and hair color grew more and more exaggerated. Despite her unfortunate taste in personal couture, she was a wonderful, warm, and gracious woman and I was very fond of her.

She admitted to me not so many years ago, "Oh! I had a terrible crush on your father, so I did, when he and I were young. He was *gorgeous* and I wanted to marry him but he took no interest in me a 'tall. Aye, *gorgeous* so he was!"

My father? Gorgeous?

She told me many stories of the mischief he and Brian Mary Cissie got into in their youthful, innocent days on Arranmore.

In November, 1958, I was placed with Nellie and Jimmy for a few days while my mother was in hospital giving birth to my sister Maureen. I resorted to calling Nellie "mommy." When my mother found out that I had taken such a liking to her, she cried. I affectionately refer to Aunt Nellie as "mommy" to this day.

Among my father's other relatives living in Chicago were Scottie (his Aunt) and her husband Pat Cullen. They owned a tavern called Scottie's

Tap on the west side of Lincoln Avenue just north of North Avenue. Many years later, my father returned to visit that familiar neighborhood. During the early and mid-1960's, he took my brothers and me on annual trips to the city to see the Chicago Cubs play at Wrigley Field.

I vividly recall my first trip to the ballpark, probably because it has changed very little since the time I first gazed upon its ivy covered walls. We sat in the upper deck along the third base line. It was 1960 and the Cubs had a rookie third baseman, Ron Santo. I was more interested in the vendors walking up and down the aisles than I was the ballgame, and I kept asking my father if I could have whatever the vendors were hawking.

He repeatedly said, "No."

I spent most of the time out of my seat. A couple of men sat behind us and were quite entertained by my restlessness. I kept looking at them self-consciously. They smiled back politely. At one point I found a crisp dollar bill on my seat. I grabbed it and showed it to my father.

"Look what I found Daddy! Can I keep it? Can I keep it?" I exclaimed.

My father turned around and nodded in appreciation to the men behind us.

"Sure," he said, and he sat me on his lap.

At some point during the game my brother, John, took me to the men's room. I was confused and a little frightened by the chaotic swarm of people. I stood at the trough next to a young African-American kid, slightly older than me. Out of childish curiosity I glanced over at him. I remember reporting back to my father how surprised I was to see that the boy's penis was the same color as the rest of him. I really don't know what I was expecting but it was the first time I was aware of someone of another race. My father was highly entertained by my news, although I did not understand why.

After the game, as we herded out of the ballpark, I was allowed to buy a pennant with my new-found dollar at one of the souvenir booths located under the grandstands.

We piled back into the car and my father drove the few miles from Wrigley Field to his old DePaul neighborhood so that he could have a few glasses of beer with his aunt and uncle before making the long drive home. Scottie's Tap was well past its prime—long, dark, and narrow, with little ornamentation and few patrons. I learned years later from my experiences as a musician playing music in the city that it was no different than countless other Chicago neighborhood bars. Scottie's had a snooker table in the corner and my brothers and I played for free as we drank as many 7 oz.

bottles of 7 Up as we wanted. But we were soon bored and ordered to sit at a table in the corner for what seemed like an eternity. We tried not to annoy each other (or at least not get caught) while my father sat at the bar, drank his whiskey and beers, and conversed in Irish with Scottie. I looked out the front window of the tavern as the city flashed by. The sidewalks were crowded with pedestrians all in a hurry to get somewhere, seemingly oblivious to the screaming fire trucks and grumbling electric street cars that glided effortlessly up and down Lincoln Avenue.

CHAPTER 16

࿇

BAYONNE

WHEN MY FATHER LEFT THE Lincoln Park neighborhood of Chicago in 1949, he headed east to Bayonne, New Jersey, to visit his sister Bridget, her husband Manus, and their young family. Aunt Bridget introduced my father to her baby-sitter, a gorgeous twenty-three-year- old neighbor girl by the name of Teresa Boyle. Many of her friends and family said Teresa bore an uncanny resemblance to a popular screen actress of the day, Gene Tierney. Darryl F. Zanuk, founder of 20th Century Fox motion picture studios once described Tierney as, "unquestionably the most beautiful woman in movie history."

Teresa was the sixth youngest child in a family of ten. She was a stylish young woman with a model's figure who was as fond of visiting Coney Island for a day of roller coaster rides and drunken revelry with her friends as she was for helping her parents. She worked as a Bell Telephone operator and occasionally baby-sat for her neighbors, Bridget and Manus O'Donnell. My father was smitten. Teresa's parents, Edward and Celia Boyle, emigrated from Roshin Acres in *The Rosses* in 1925. Their Donegal homestead was a scant three miles distant and in clear view of Arranmore Island, where my father lived, but the two families did not know each other. This was not uncommon of that age, as the islanders seldom frequented the mainland, and mainlanders had no reason at all to go to Arranmore. Edward, Celia, and their five children (all under the age of six), boarded the *COLUMBIA* in

Londonderry on April 4th, 1925, and set sail for America.[79] Ten days later they glided past the Statue of Liberty in New York Harbor and entered the United States at Ellis Island. Edward had but fifty dollars in his pocket when the family arrived and they were met by Edward's cousin, John Ward. They settled in the Irish ghetto of Bayonne among several other family members, within view of the Statue of Liberty's backside and the rusting shipyards along the Upper Bay.

Edward Boyle, an uneducated Irish peasant, worked odd jobs when and where he could. When the Great Depression hit in October, 1929, he signed on with the WPA as a navvy. In 1934, he secured steady work constructing the Lincoln Tunnel under the Hudson River, which connected Weehawken, New Jersey, to the borough of Manhattan. Whenever I'm in New York and have to pass through the tunnel to Jersey, I gaze at the sooty tile walls and smile. I am reminded of what my cousin Kathy Kelly once remarked when she was told as a child that her grandfather constructed the tunnel, "You did a nice job, Pop-pop."

Teresa's parents saw John Condy as a good prospect for their daughter. The young couple had a short courtship and on November 25th, 1950, John and Teresa were married at St. Vincent de Paul's Catholic Church on Avenue C and 47th Street in Bayonne. Only a handful of guests attended. Few braved the rare autumn hurricane that bore down on the mid-Atlantic coast that morning, flooding the streets and knocking out the electricity to most of metro New York, including St. Vincent's church.

The newlyweds leased a two-flat nearby at 21 East 52nd Street (now an empty lot and dumping ground, practically underneath Exit 14A of the Jersey Turnpike). In typical Irish fashion, the couple immediately set to the task of starting a family. My brother, John (who we always called Jay), was born the following year. My father's navy skills as a machinist landed him a night-shift job at the sprawling Singer Sewing Machine manufacturing facility in the nearby port town of Elizabeth, New Jersey.

A few years before I was born my father lost the last two fingers on his left hand in a freak accident while working the graveyard shift at Singer.

"I got them caught between a chain and a sprocket on a press," he recalled. "I was working a double shift. It was me and another fella. He was deaf. I turned the machine off to work on it. He didn't know I was there and he turned it back on again. He couldn't hear me, the screaming ye know," he shrugged. "I had to wait a minute or so, until the chain went completely around the sprocket before I could remove my hand. I wrapped my fingers in a handkerchief and called an ambulance—but it was too late. There was nothing the doctor could do to reattach them," he said, looking at the place where his fingers used to be. "The company paid me $300 for them. Can you believe that?"

My father was out of work convalescing for a long time and understandably resentful toward the Singer Company after that. This only added to the young married couple's rocky start. My mother found it difficult to cope in the role of new wife and mother. She had forfeited her independence and carefree lifestyle, was pregnant with her third child in three years, and felt responsible for caring for her increasingly invalid mother who had suffered a series of strokes. She remained a devoted wife and doting mother even though her drinking became more frequent and much more excessive.

As my mother's pregnancies neared term, she always waited until the last possible minute to go to the hospital, delivering her babies within hours after arriving. Mother's Day, 1955, was on the 8th of May, and on *that* particular Sunday morning my mother severely miscalculated.

She pleaded for my father to hurry as he sped south down Avenue E through Bayonne, running red lights and dodging pedestrians crossing the street on their way to 6:00 AM Mass at St. Henry's. A police car was in hot pursuit and chased my father for another sixteen blocks. They screeched to a halt in front of the emergency room doors at Bayonne Hospital and Dispensary. My father carried my mother to a gurney where a nurse pushed him aside and immediately wheeled my mother into the first available elevator. By the time the elevator doors opened on the 4th floor maternity ward, John and Teresa's third consecutive son had made his dramatic entrance. There was no doctor, just a nurse, a cleaning lady, and my mother. It was an auspicious beginning to which my father quipped, "Maybe we should name him Otis?"

My mother was not amused.

When the time came to enter a name on the birth certificate, Mother insisted on Christopher. Father hated the name.

"That's a *dago* name," he said. "Christopher? Like Christopher Columbus? Forget it! Besides, it sounds too feminine," he said.

He wanted a rugged, manly name like his brother's, "Bernard."

My mother refused.

"I'll not have a *Barney* or a *Bernie* in my house," she insisted.

After considerable deliberation they compromised: Kevin.

I always assumed my middle name was Edward, after my godfather and Great Uncle, Edward Boyle. Recently, I discovered that I *have* no middle name—at least none was recorded on my birth certificate. All these years I have been using an alias.

CHAPTER 17

✧

THE MOVE TO ILLINOIS

M Y GRANDMOTHER, CELIA BOYLE, DIED of a massive
stroke a few months after I was born. My mother's method for
dealing with her grief was repeatedly found in the bottom of a bottle.
A whisky bottle, a beer bottle, it didn't really matter. Her drinking was
progressing at an alarming rate and my father, who grew up motherless,
knew first-hand the pain of neglect from a mother who was never there.
He feared for his children's physical safety and emotional abandonment.
He heard of a job prospect north of the city of Chicago from Jack
Connaghan, the husband of his cousin, Sarah O'Donnell, and saw that
moving to the Midwest could provide an opportunity for a fresh start for
his young family. He didn't know that a geographical relocation is never
a cure for alcoholism—the proof of which would be played out over the
years to follow.

Uncle Jack worked as a machinist for Goodyear Tire & Rubber Company
in North Chicago, Illinois. He knew my father's skills at that trade would
be desirable at the fast-growing Goodyear hose plant and recommended
him for employment. In January, 1956, my father boarded the Lackawanna
Railroad's No. 3 Train, The Phoebe Snow, in nearby Hoboken, NJ. His
two-day journey to Chicago was by way of Buffalo, New York, then over the
Nickel Plate Road to Union Station. Making his way to Waukegan on the
North Shore Interurban, he was met by Uncle Jack, taken to the Goodyear

employment office, and hired immediately. He settled into his new job and lived with Jack and Sarah for several weeks before he found a house to rent. He then sent for my mother, my two older brothers, and me.

We arrived from Newark aboard an American Airlines Douglas DC-6, at Midway Airport, at the time the world's busiest. Chicago's other area airport, O'Hare Field, located on the outskirts of the city, opened to commercial air traffic only two years earlier and was way out in the country and difficult to reach. There were no expressways or main highways near it at that time.

My brother, Rodger, a hyperactive and nervous child, could not sit still during the long flight to Chicago. He thrashed, and screamed, and generally annoyed everyone around him. He bounced in his seat and punctuated his antics by growling obscenities while alternately kicking the back of the seat in front of him. The man who occupied that seat never once acknowledged or admonished my brother. I'm sure he felt sorry for my poor mother, traveling alone with three raucous toddlers. At the end of the flight, the man stood up, turned around, and politely smiled through beads of perspiration and gritted teeth. My mother's embarrassment drew her to tears when she saw that the man stoically taking my brother's abuse for the past five hours was a Catholic Priest.

My father had rented a little two bedroom house in Waukegan, Illinois. It was located in the Lake County Gardens subdivision on the edge of town, north and west of McAree Road and Sunset Avenue. The ranch-style house at 2916 Shoshone Road was nearly identical to every other house in the neighborhood, where the interconnected and winding streets were named after Native American Indian tribes. Rodger was angry that we moved from New Jersey and acted out by running away from home a few days after arriving in Waukegan. My father drove through the neighborhood looking for him and found him a mile or so from the house on his tricycle, trying to negotiate traffic along busy Sunset Avenue. Rodger said he was headed back to New Jersey.

Even through the eyes of a toddler, I realized the Waukegan house was very small and cramped. It had a tiny eat-in kitchen, a front parlor, one bathroom, and two small bedrooms. My brothers and I slept in one room. John and Rodger had bunk beds (which my brother Rodger still owns). My crib was wedged into a corner of the room. There was barely enough space to maneuver between them. My parents' room contained my mother's only prized possession, her bedroom furniture. It consisted of a Queen Anne style black walnut triple dresser with a mirror and a four-poster double bed. At the foot of the bed was a bassinette, where my sister, Sheila, slept. When my sister Maureen was born, there was no room in my parent's bedroom to put another bassinette. Out of necessity, my mother partially opened one of the cedar-lined drawers of her triple dresser, padded it with a blanket and linens and tucked Maureen into the cantilevered, make-shift bassinette. Maureen slept there until both she and Sheila outgrew their bedding and were forced to sleep with my parents in their bed. They call that "Irish birth control."

Among my family relics, I have a photograph taken by my father with his old Brownie camera during the winter of my second year. The square black-and-white photo is of my brother, John, and me hanging tinsel on a scraggly Balsam Christmas tree. It is my earliest childhood memory and I distinctly recall the moment because I was wearing my favorite footed pajamas—the ones with Hop-a-Long Cassidy on them—and posing by the tree at the emphatic instructions of my mother while my father snapped the photo.

During that same winter my father and I, along with my brother, Rodger, fashioned a snowman in the front yard. My father insisted on hollowing-out the bottom of the snowman, giving him legs. I was completely delighted by my father's elegant ingenuity. To this day I have never seen another snowman with legs.

The following spring the Easter Bunny came to our house on Shoshone. He delivered baskets that were full of candy, wrapped in brightly colored cellophane and tied with a bow, each with our name on it. The centerpiece of sweets in each wicker basket was a giant milk chocolate bunny. I ate mine and confiscated my brother Rodger's. I decided to hide it and save it for later but when I returned, it had disappeared. I thought that it came to life and hopped away. Certain that my mother would not believe me, I showed her where I had placed my chocolate-y friend. She pulled the parlor couch away from the wall and roared with laughter. I had unwittingly placed the kidnapped bunny directly on top of the floor register and when the furnace kicked on, the bunny melted, and oozed into the ductwork below. For all I know it may still be there.

Later that spring, a local farmer planted corn in the field directly beyond the fence line in our back yard. The field ran the length of our block. The pasture nearby was bordered by a barbed wire fence, behind which roamed a large black bull. My brother John once strayed into the field, and my mother bravely ran through the mud and manure to rescue him.

My Great-Uncle Eddie (my mother's uncle, Edward Boyle) visited us from back east each summer. He lived and worked in New York at the Staten Island Hospital. A life-long bachelor, he relished all of his great-nephews and nieces but was particularly generous to me. I was his godson. My mother was among his favorite nieces and with no children of his own, Uncle Eddie spoiled us with constant attention and a seemingly endless roll of cash.

One August, Uncle Eddie entered the field behind the house and harvested an armful of corn and boiled it up for dinner. He nearly broke his dentures when he bit into it, not realizing that it was cattle corn, used for dairy feed and hard as a hickory knot.

He frequently walked my brothers and me a mile or so north on Mac Aree Road to Waukegan airport. I enjoyed watching the planes take off and land, a fascination that has stayed with me.

Our house was third from the end of our block. Beyond it to the west was the "little" woods. Within a clearing of the little woods was Scottie's house—a mansion compared to the houses in our neighborhood. Beyond Scottie's house stood the "big" woods, so massive and so dark that I was never brave enough to venture into it like the older boys. It took all the courage I could muster just to run the narrow path of the little woods back home when my brothers scurried from Scottie's house to Shoshone—a distance of about 200 feet.

Most of the kids in our neighborhood were my brothers' ages and I spent a great deal of time alone, either walking up and down the sidewalk in front of the house or sitting on the front porch singing. I was always singing to keep myself occupied and being alone fed my curiosity and gave me time to explore why things were the way they were.

Time alone also allowed me to get into my share of mischief. My mother kept a large, clear glass jar of peppermint pinwheel candies on the parlor table. When she wasn't looking, I squirreled the jar away in my bedroom and proceeded to eat the entire contents in one sitting. My rotting teeth throbbed in pain and I couldn't eat anything else for days. I have not been able to a eat peppermint pinwheel candy since. Even the smell of them spins me into a nauseous flashback.

I was particularly lonely when my brothers went to school. I was too young and reckless to be left to play outside by myself. My mother kept me in the house while she attended to the needs of Sheila, just over a year-old, and Maureen, a sickly infant who had recurring bouts of pneumonia. One morning shortly after my brothers left for school, I climbed up onto Rodger's top bunk. Rodger, although younger than John by a year, was a climber, getting into the most ridiculous and precarious spaces—the higher, the better. He insisted on sleeping in the top bunk. I was three and barely able to climb to the top. But once there, I pretended I was in a canoe, using the guardrail to paddle down a make believe river along with a tribe of Indians. It was a great adventure until I lost my balance and toppled from the bunk, striking the back of my head on the edge of my crib, and splitting it wide open. It required several stitches to close. I was frightened because my mother panicked at the site of all the blood. She called my father home from work while changing out several blood soaked towels until he arrived and drove me to the hospital. I protested when the doctor moved toward me with a giant syringe full of anesthetic. He eventually bribed me with a plastic toy, a monkey that swung summersaults on a trapeze.

I encountered many accidents as a child, the most painful of which came when I stuck my hand between the wringer-rollers of my mother's electric washtub—a predecessor to the automatic clothes washer. My mother was in the front yard talking with a neighbor and couldn't hear my screams in the basement until she returned to the house. I burned out the motor on the rollers and my fingers were swollen and bruised—but no broken bones this time.

How an iron was able to take the wrinkles out of clothes fascinated me as a child and I wondered if it would take the wrinkles out of my skin. To satisfy my curiosity, I picked up a hot iron and placed it directly on my bare thigh when my mother turned away to answer the phone. That required yet another trip to the hospital.

When Rodger started kindergarten, I wandered away one afternoon in search of him. I walked the half-mile to Oakdale Elementary School, toddled passed the administration office and began peering into the classrooms until I found my brother. It was naptime and each student had a small rug that they laid out onto the floor to take their rest. I simply walked in and lay down beside him. The school had to call my mother to come collect me.

My brother, John, also had his share of mishaps. Soon after moving to Waukegan he broke his right arm and spent several weeks in a cast. When the cast was removed, the doctor told him that it was "better than new." Convinced that it could not be broken again, John encouraged a friend to drop a large rock on it. It resulted in a compound fracture. His ulna protruded through his forearm and left him with a life-long scar and a "pucker" in his skin whenever he flexed his forearm. It also left him with a permanent loss in range of motion. Throughout his life thereafter he could not raise the palm of his right hand to his face.

My brother John (right) and me posing for my mother.
Christmas, 1957

CHAPTER 18

༄

THE TELEGRAM

I AWOKE ONE NIGHT IN THE Lake County Gardens house to the strange sound of someone sobbing. I climbed out of my crib and waddled into the darkened kitchen to investigate. My father sat with his head in his hands. A telegram lay on the table. I crawled onto his lap and wrapped my arms around his neck to comfort him. My mother shuffled into the room. She gently lifted me from my fathers lap and carried me back to bed. I asked her why Daddy was crying. She told me that he received word that his father died back in Ireland. My father could not afford to return home for the funeral.

CHAPTER 19

✧

WITNESS PROTECTION PROGRAM

SHORTLY BEFORE WE MOVED FROM the Lake County Garden's house in 1959 to the Village of Mundelein, I broke my leg. Wearing only a pair of underpants and with bath towel around my neck, I pretended I was a super hero and jumped off the basement stairs, third riser from the bottom. Recent rains had seeped into the basement and puddled on the concrete floor at the base of the steps. When I landed, my legs slipped from under me—my right leg went one way, my left leg went the other way. A human wishbone. I snapped the femur of my left leg above my knee. I cried in agony as my father rushed downstairs to see what was the matter. I could not explain what had happened through the pain and my hysteria. He lost patience with me, ordered me to stop crying and paddled my rear-end as he chased me up the wooden steps to the kitchen. My mother saw my leg dangling like a busted piñata and immediately realized what had happened. My father drove me to Saint Therese Hospital, where by now the emergency staff knew us by name. My mother stayed home with the four other children—ages 7 ½ years to 9 months. The doctor set my leg and placed me in a heavy plaster cast that went from my heel to the top of my hip. They wanted to keep me in overnight for observation and relegated me to the children's ward—a large open room with a hodge-podge of wheel-around cribs, parked like abandoned cars under the Jersey Turnpike.

The Catholic hospital was run by an order of Sisters. I don't recall having ever seen a Sister before. I had sisters of course, but it wasn't the same thing.

When I inquired to my father about how peculiar they looked he said, loud enough for them to hear, "Son, they are like angels from God."

I reasoned that they were called sisters because, like my sisters, they all looked the same and therefore they must be related. Oh! They were frightful-looking creatures, wrapped in yards and yards of floor-length black cloth with large white bibs and a crested white bonnet strapped tightly under their chins. A long black veil completely covered their hair and flowed behind them when they glided down the hall. Their faces oozed out of their headdresses like canned hams. They wore phony smiles and spoke in suspicious whispers to each other. They each wore thick leather belts, from which dangled long strands of black beads and a silver cross. The beads clicked and rattled as they moved about. I wondered if they had feet like real people because their garments went clear to the ground and they seemed to hover inches above the shiny floor. They were very nice to me. *Too* nice, in fact; they made me nervous. Daddy didn't seem to notice anything odd about them and his confidence carried me through the event—until he pried my arms from around his neck, held me down in the crib and told me he would be back tomorrow, a time concept which I did not yet understand. All I knew was he was going to leave me alone with "them." I panicked and wailed and begged for him to come back. I tried to get to my feet but my heavy plaster cast held me down like a boat anchor. One of the sisters cruised toward me and whirled as she pulled the drape around my crib. She tried to console me. I was terrified. She was stern and impatient and cooed insincerely. I screamed and cursed at her. Eventually, I cried myself to sleep and decided just before I drifted off—that come nightfall, I would have to make a break for it!

When I awoke, the hall was streaked with long, dark shadows and the room was quiet. They wheeled a crib beside me and I saw a familiar face, a girl about my age who lived across the street and a few houses down from us on Shoshone. Her leg and foot were heavily bandaged and she seemed sleepy—like when my mother drank from the bottle she kept in her bedroom closet. I learned that the girl lost part of her foot when her father accidentally ran over it with the gas-powered lawn mower. Even though she was asleep, I felt safer knowing she was there with me. I tossed and turned and drifted in and out of sleep, whimpering. I peered through my tear-soaked eyelashes. Through the bars of my hospital prison I saw silhouetted nuns silently floating back and forth across the room, their long veils of their habits waving behind them like black flags in a faint breeze. The only things missing, I thought, were their brooms.

Morning came and I awoke to see my father standing at a distance between two of "them." He smiled at me and nodded reassuringly. When he approached, I glommed onto his neck as tightly as I could and pleaded with him to get me out. He assured me we were leaving and since I was such a good boy, I would get to ride out of the hospital in a wheelchair. I felt special and privileged. I shot my most menacing glare at the Sisters as we passed.

"The Sisters told me you were not very cooperative last night," he said as he slowly navigated my chair down the hall. I denied all of it, of course, and tried to relate to him how awful the experience was.

It was an exceptionally long drive home. "Well," my father finally declared, "we're here." I craned my neck to see above the passenger door of our brown 1954 Ford Station Wagon. We were in the driveway of a house I did not recognize.

At some point between when I entered the hospital and when I left, my parents had moved. There was no explanation given by my father. We had just moved. I thought it was entirely my fault: the broken leg, the hospital, and the whole thing with the Sisters. I caused this and my family was in big, big trouble for it and we had to move into some sort of witness protection program for boys who terrorize "angels from God." Daddy carried me into the house. Everyone *seemed* happy to see me, and they were very sympathetic. I was really confused. But I savored the attention and kept a low profile hoping that no one would figure out what I had done.

CHAPTER 20

⌘

HOOLEY ON A SATURDAY NIGHT

MY FATHER GENTLY SHOOK ME from my sleep. I could smell whiskey on his breath.

"C'mon, *a mhac* (*a vic*, my son), wake up," he whispered. "They want to hear you sing. Can you give us a song now? That's my boy." He pulled me to my feet. My "little slugger" pajamas that looked like a uniform with a baseball motif on the front were crumpled and twisted. I straightened them as he guided me down the hallway that led from the boys' room. Walking was still a bit difficult. I had a pronounced limp. My heavy plaster cast from when I broke my leg at the old house had been cut off only a week before.

From the top of the stairs I could hear them, my father's relatives. Several had come out from the city, in addition to my Aunt Sarah and Uncle Jack from Waukegan, and Brian Mary Cissie and Madge Bennie Rodgers from Lake Forest. Everyone had drinks and cigarettes in their hands and were trying to talk over each other, some in Irish, others in English, dripping with distinctive Arranmore brogues. My father positioned me in the middle of the parlor. I looked around the room rubbing the sleep from my eyes. Another hooley.

A hooley is an Irish house party: a delicious blend of *ceili* (*kay lee*, dance) music, singing, and storytelling fueled by the copious consumption of alcohol. Hooleys were common among the Irish in the city but a rare gathering at our house—40 miles out—marking a special occasion.

Relatives began arriving earlier that evening. Most carried an instrument in one hand and a brown paper bag with their favorite adult beverage in the other, usually beer or whiskey. Children were not invited. We were sent to our rooms and expected to fall asleep among the cacophony of chatter, music, dancing, and laughter as the party progressed. Invariably, my father would come upstairs and bring me down to the parlor to sing a song he had prepared me for. From an early age I had good pitch and a knack for memorizing lyrics. He loved to show me off, and I loved the attention.

"Sing the one I taught you the other day," Father encouraged me. "Go on, Son. Surely, you remember it? Kevin Barry?"

He twirled his finger and hinted at the melody as he prompted me with the first few words, *"In Mountjoy Jail one Monday morning . . . "*

But I didn't want to sing that song. I wanted to debut another, one that I had just learned from my brother, John. I heard him and a few of the new neighbor kids singing it over and over again and I quickly picked it up.

"Daddy, can I sing another song?" I asked quietly.

His face was overcome with disappointment.

"Ah, sure now Kevin," Aunt Sarah replied.

"Jaysus, just give us somethin', lad," Uncle Brian insisted.

"Ach, go away wich-ye," Aunt Nellie (mommy) snapped, "sing whatever ye like, cracher."

My father conceded under the pressure.

"Um . . . it's called 'On Top of Old Smoky'," I said to the luke-warm reaction of my audience. I looked to my father for approval. He winked and nodded once. I rubbed my bare feet together to warm them on the cold parlor floor. Then, standing still and erect, chin up, and arms at my sides as my father had taught me, I began:

> *"On top of old smoky, where nobody goes . . . "*
> (I looked around the room. Going pretty well so far—everyone was smiling down on me.)

> *"I saw Annie Oakley without any clothes . . . "*
> (A few unappreciated snickers detected, but I still had 'em.)

"Along came Gene Autry who took off his vest . . . "
(Panic began to fill my mother's eyes now, everyone leaned in
for the clincher.)

"And when he saw Annie, he took off the rest . . . "

The room erupted in laughter. Never before had I heard such a reaction
to one of my songs. I was a smash hit! I beamed with pride and took a deep
bow. But before I could stand up my mother grabbed me firmly by the arm,
ripped me from the swarm of adulating relatives, and marched me through
the house and into the utility room.

"Where did you hear that song?" She grumbled with fire in her eyes,
"Where?!" She rapped her knuckle on the top of my head.

"Ouch, Mom!" I cried. "That hurts." I ducked and faded and covered my
head with my hands but she kept trying to land her notorious stingers.

"What? What did I do wrong?" I pleaded. "Jay, Jay, it was Jay . . . he
taught it to me!" I confessed.

"Don't you ever, ever, ever, sing that song again, you hear me?" she
yelled, punctuating each *ever* with a sharp rap of her knuckle. "Jesus, Mary,
and Joseph! And wait 'til I get hold of your brother in the mornin'. He'll be
gettin' the same thing from me!"

I managed to escape from her drunken blows. I tearfully dashed through
the parlor dodging several relatives still doubled over with laughter. I
scrambled up the stairs as fast as my gimpy leg would carry me to a crescendo
of applause from the parlor below. I hopped into my bed. The pain from my
mother's blows subsided quickly as the rush of adrenaline from my most
recent performance coursed through me.

Soon after, my relatives quieted down. They talked about their families
and relations, Arranmore, Bayonne, and someplace called Beaver Island,
and they took turns singing. Each song was more sorrowful than the one
before it. I tiptoed down the hall and sat quietly on the stairs. I peeked
through the wrought iron railing. Everyone was crying and comforting each
other, lofting words of encouragement to each singer between stanzas. I
sat unnoticed for a long time. They seemed to welcome the tears as they
spontaneously blurted out one nostalgic, wretchedly emotional, sad Irish
song after another. Some were so distraught they were unable to finish
singing and buried their faces in their hands. I thought it might be some
sort of adult game: whoever cried the loudest was the winner.

I scampered back to bed. I couldn't sleep. I was equally perplexed and amazed by what I had witnessed.

That night I had a remarkable revelation and learned of the incredible emotional power of "the song."

I have long advocated that all Irish songs fall into three basic categories: lost loves, lost wars, and lost weekends, the sadder, the better. It's true, the Irish thrive on emotional misery. There is no escaping it. It's been a constant throughout their history, an integral part of their character, a genetic marker in their DNA—my DNA.

CHAPTER 21

⌒⌒

409 SOUTH PRAIRIE AVENUE

I SPENT THE NEXT EIGHTEEN YEARS of my life at 409 South Prairie Avenue, in the village of Mundelein. Much to my relief, I came to realize that my father *voluntarily* purchased the post-war house for $14,000 in September of 1959, and not because of any witness protection program on my behalf.

With only $500 down, he secured a twenty-five year loan at 4% interest from Bill Shoemacher at the First National Bank of Mundelein. Although my father eventually paid off the note and owned the house free and clear, he toiled and scraped for most of the next twenty-five years in order to make the $110 monthly mortgage payment.

Ours was not unlike most other houses in our North Shore Park neighborhood, although it was one of the few to have a second story, added by its previous owner, a man named Handell. My father, who often criticized the poor workmanship of the previous owner, frequently referred to him as "unhandy Handell."

Soon after moving in, my mother had another baby, a girl, Patricia, or Tish. (So much for "Irish birth control.") In October, 1963, my youngest sister, Kathleen (whom Tish inexplicably nick-named Daser), was born, bringing the total to seven. My parents were through having children, much to my mother's relief. She had spent nearly half of her thirteen years of marriage pregnant.

Even with a second story, the 409 house was small, about 1,000 square feet. It was too small for a family of nine—although we learned to live with it, and each other. The siding was battleship gray in color. My brother Rodger and I relinquished nearly all of our free time during the summer of 1974 to repaint the house white under my father's close supervision. While painting the rear of the house Rodger took to teasing me about the tumultuous relationship I was having with a girlfriend at the time. He stood high above me on a ladder, haphazardly painting while listening to classic Elvis tunes blaring from the stereo of his brand new silver Chevrolet Monte Carlo in the driveway below. Tired of his teasing, I shook the ladder and muttered a few choice words. I took my brush and can of paint around to the front of the house to work alone in peace. An hour or so later, I returned to the rear of the house. Emblazoned in cheap white paint across the entire back of the house was the phrase: *"Kevin loves Diane Amann."* It was enclosed in a heart with an arrow running through it. Rodger was nowhere to be found. I was left to paint over it myself and worked furiously to cover it before any of my friends came by. Between my haste and the inferior quality of the paint, there was always a hint of my brother's graffiti that bled through until my father had the house re-clad with aluminum siding several years later. I'll bet if you peel back that siding today, you can still see my brother's handiwork.

The 409 house had a black asphalt shingled roof, a red front door, white window trim, and a white awning that ran partially across the front. It was stoic, stodgy, and utilitarian. It sat, like all other houses on our block, on a quarter acre, roughly 50' wide by 150' deep. It was at the bottom of the hill, the lowest point on the block. There were no curbs or storm drains and the yard often became flooded when it rained and when the winter snows began to melt.

The first floor contained the largest room, the parlor. It ran nearly the length of the house and half the depth. We had a small dining room approximately eight feet square, with modest "built-in" shelves on either side of the doorway that led to the kitchen.

As far back as I can remember, Father's only personal effect from his childhood, other than his fiddle, sat in humble honor on the highest shelf in the dining room—well out of reach of curious little hands. It was a miniature brass wheelbarrow, about four inches long and probably centuries old. My father cherished that piece. He saw me playing with it one day. I was perhaps six or seven years old at that time. He told me the story of how he and Jack, his burro, unearthed it from the bog. Like so many of the stories of his young life on Arranmore, I was fascinated by the clarity of the images he painted and I hung on to his every word. He explained how he managed to keep it with him throughout his journeys to England, the Middle East while in the navy, and through his trans-continental journeys across Canada, eventually bringing it with him to America. I sensed that this trinket was somehow very important to him, but I was too young to understand why. He gently took the artifact from me, spun its squeaky wheel a few times and carefully placed it back on the shelf. He quietly but firmly told me never to take it down from the shelf again.

A few weeks passed and he noticed the wheelbarrow was missing. He asked me if I had taken it or knew where it was. He wasn't angry so much as he was upset and his obvious disappointment forced me to lie. It wasn't until years later that I was able to work up the courage and confess to him that I had lost his brass wheelbarrow while playing with it in the yard. He didn't say anything. He only nodded in confirmation—as if he had known all along. Nearly a half-century has passed since that incident and the guilt and shame still washes over me every time I think about it.

Our kitchen at the 409 house was a room about the same size as the dining room with a few cupboards painted yellow, a few square feet of Formica countertop, and a peeling linoleum tile floor. A long, narrow utility room ran adjacent to the kitchen and dining room. It housed a water heater, a furnace that my father converted from oil to gas using "spare parts" he salvaged from work, and a fuse box (such as it was). The utility room served multiple purposes: a room for the dog, a place to hang winter coats, a discard pile for our boots and shoes, and, with no basement, a catch-all for most everything else. It was also the site where the original owner of the house, prior to unhandy Handell, hanged himself from the galvanized steel pipe that ran overhead.

The house had one bathroom with one small sink, a temperamental toilet, a tub—no shower—and a door, that in all the years I lived there, *never* locked.

Next to the bathroom was my parents' bedroom. It was so small my mother's beloved furniture didn't fit without pushing the bed into the corner, up against the wall. Even then, there was only an aisle about two feet wide between it and the dresser.

Off the back of the house was a screened porch which usually contained the overflow of whatever couldn't fit in the utility room. Years later, my father had the rickety old porch removed and a deck added.

The upstairs contained two bedrooms, one on the north side, "the girls' room," and one on the south, "the boys' room," as we always referred to them. Connected by a circuitous hallway that varied in width, each bedroom had dormer style ceilings and a set of windows on the gable ends. We traded rooms after my brother, John, left in 1970 for a two year self-imposed tour of Europe to avoid the Vietnam War draft. I redecorated: bright red walls with a white ceiling, all white furniture, and Zebra-print curtains and bedspreads. I painted a mural of a smiling moon on the wall next to my bed and a smiling sun on the dormer ceiling. It was a thing of beauty.

Upstairs also contained a long, narrow attic where my father put his ingenious mechanical skill to work. He made a couple of small bench-top grinding machines, mounting the semi-automated grinding wheels and the motors that turned them to an old dresser. There he earned cash on the side by sharpening knives used at the Goodyear hose plant. As my brothers and I reached "the proper age," he patiently taught us how to sharpen the knives—child labor laws and OSHA be damned. This was typically a Sunday night chore and incredibly risky work. Anytime you put a sharp knife blade in your bare hands and place it onto a grinding stone spinning at 1,100 rpm, you have the potential for serious injury. Miraculously, none of us received anything beyond a scraped knuckle or two. You had to stay focused. Occasionally, the stone grabbed the knife and ripped it from your hand, shooting it across the room where it became embedded in the wall or lost in the wool insulation. I didn't think the work was particularly dangerous back then. After all, we always wore safety glasses.

Late in the evening, the grinding completed, my father sat at the dining room table, bundled the knives in stacks of ten, and bound them together with masking tape. He returned them to the Goodyear plant the following Monday morning, a few bundles at a time, and was paid between two and ten cents for each piece. If he was feeling particularly flush with cash, he might give my brothers and me a handful of change for helping him. Otherwise, he took a portion of his earnings and purchased from the lunchroom vending machine a package of Chuckles candy, a cellophane-wrapped cardboard tray of 5 jelly gum drops, each a different color and flavor, sprinkled with sugar crystals. My father gathered us around him at the dining room table, and divvied them up among my siblings and me. The middle candy was black licorice and it always went to my brother, John. I didn't care what flavor I got, just as long as it wasn't a peppermint pinwheel.

There was no room in our house for a clothes washer and dryer. As a result, every Sunday afternoon after Mass, two of us were volunteered to spend the day uptown at Morrissey's Laundromat. The unfortunate ones selected were usually those who gave my parents the most grief during the previous week. I was an uncooperative victim more often than not.

The mountain of laundry accumulated by nine people over the course of a week was staggering. We toted pockets full of quarters and dimes and multiple baskets and pillow cases full of dirty clothes into Morrissey's. Wash, dry, fold—for hours on end, every Sunday, for eighteen years. It was punishment, especially on nice, sunny days when all my neighborhood friends were out playing baseball or soccer or were down at the lake. I hated it.

The kitchen was too small for an automatic dishwasher, even if we could afford one. The only thing automatic about a dishwasher in our house was when we were finished with dinner, we did the dishes—automatically. This was a chore relegated to my two older brothers and me. I didn't mind. In fact, I looked forward to it, for it was the only time we had permission to listen to what we wanted to on my mother's kitchen radio. She had it set to WGN, 720 AM, all day, every day. However, during "dishes" my brothers and I could tune into "The big 89" (WLS), or "Super CFL" (WCFL), the two rock and roll stations in Chicago. It was the mid-'60's, the height of the British invasion, and I loved every bit of it. We listened to Dex Card count down to the number one song on the station's Silver Dollar Survey, commenting and singing along as we cleared, washed, dried, and put away the dishes. My father did not understand our curious liking for this music and therefore could not be a part of it. That bothered him. He listened from the parlor, smoking his cigarettes and throwing in his bitter comments and ridiculing our music. We rolled our eyes and did our best to ignore him. My mother cautioned him to leave us alone. She understood what my father could not; this was our time—a time when the three of us could stop our daily bickering and enjoy the simple pleasure of music, our music. Come to think of it, it was the only thing the three of us ever had in common and could agree upon.

⤴

I lifted a handful of soapy silverware out of the dirty dishwater. "Property of Staten Island Hospital" was stamped onto the back of each piece—a "gift" from Uncle Eddie from one of his recent visits, no doubt. I'm sure the hospital procurement administrators were unaware of my uncle's generosity.

My father walked in the back door and kicked off his shoes in the utility room. He was returning from his usual pilgrimage to the tavern after dinner and heard me singing "Yesterday" along with Paul McCartney on the radio. He stomped into the kitchen, reached on top of the refrigerator where my mother kept her radio, and turned it off with a flip of his wrist. He waited a moment for my reaction. I stopped singing but knew better than to turn around and say anything. He was into his beers and easily provoked. I continued washing the dishes.

"Yesterday, humph! Two weeks from now you won't ever hear that song again," he mumbled, as he walked into the parlor. I was ten years old at the time. I stood at the kitchen sink and I cried. Why would he do that, I wondered? I was deeply hurt and confused and, for the first time, disappointed by my father. It wouldn't be the last. (I knew my father was wrong, but no one could have predicted how wrong he would be. "Yesterday" has been covered by more artists than any other song ever written. According to the Guinness Book of World Records, there are over 1,600 different recordings.)

The Mundelein house was, above all, drafty. The thermostat was in a constant state of adjustment. The battle raged between my mother and father every day the furnace ran for as many years as they lived there. She was always too cold, he was always too warm. We had a crawl space foundation, comprising dirt and discarded building materials. It wasn't heated and it wasn't insulated. In the winter, the parlor floor was so cold you couldn't stand to walk on it in bare feet or sit on it to watch television, and there certainly wasn't enough furniture to accommodate all nine of us. As a result, we relied heavily on the "no one take my place" declaration of seating protocol whenever we temporarily got off the couch or out of a chair. Not announcing that statement before anyone else took your place resulted in forfeiture. The rules were clear and well understood. You had to say "no one take my place" once you got up *but* while your hand was still touching the piece of furniture. No adlibs, no paraphrasing. Failure to say it *exactly* nullified all rights. Disputes were always arbitrated by those present at the time of the infraction. Hung juries went to parental appeal. We all used and honored this custom, though my parents were exempt. Those relegated to the floor to watch TV during the winter months did so wrapped in blankets.

Winter mornings were the worst. The house was always coldest then. My father often turned the thermostat down on his way to bed after he returned home from his second shift job at Twentieth Century Machine Shop in Rondout, or from one of his frequent late night runs to the tavern. We were all asleep when he returned, or at least pretending to be. Sometimes I heard my parents talking in muffled tones in their bedroom below. It was followed by a minute or two of silence and then a shrieking cry from my mother loud enough for the neighbors to hear, "Aaah! Jesus Christ! Get your bloody cold hands off of me! What the *hell's* the matter with you?"

My mother was always the first one up in the morning. She got out of bed every day at 5:45, no matter what. Her routine: turn up the thermostat, turn on the radio, boil a pot of tea and a cup of oatmeal for my father's breakfast, fill his thermos, and pack his lunch box. As soon as my father came out to the dining room, he turned down the thermostat and the daily tug-o-war began. So did our daily bathroom relay. Timing was of the essence as we raced each other to the top of the stairs. Rather than wait in queue, all those who didn't finish first darted back to bed and smothered themselves in blankets—then, listening for the precise moment the bathroom door opened we ran once again to the top of the stairs and the process repeated itself. We each savored the opportunity to maximize our occupancy in the bathroom. It was the only warm room in the house and the only place one could get a few minutes of privacy—if someone didn't barge through the unlockable door.

Our unheated crawl space was also responsible for the annually dreaded "freezing of the pipes." We awoke to no water on winter mornings whenever the nighttime temperature went below zero degrees Fahrenheit and someone didn't turn the kitchen faucet on a trickle the night before to keep the water running through the pipes. Sometimes we were without water for several days. My father, when he found time between working two jobs and daily visits to his favorite shot-and-a-beer joint, crawled under the house armed with a flashlight and a butane soldering torch. He gently heated the pipes that came up through the dirt and ran between the floor joists, in hopes that he could get the water running to the kitchen sink. Sometimes it worked, sometimes it didn't. When I was about fourteen years old, my father went under the house to perform his thawed pipe routine but got the butane torch too close to the floor boards and started a fire underneath the kitchen cabinet. My mother panicked and trudged out to the yard to retrieve buckets of snow to throw on the flames darting out from under the sink. I was in my bedroom and ran downstairs at the sound of my mother's screams. I reached for a broom and amid the flames, raked all the household cleaning products out from under the sink and onto the kitchen floor. I instructed my sister, Sheila, to call the fire department. I ran outside to find my father only to see a column of black, billowy smoke roll out of the 2' x 3' cellar entrance. I heard him coughing and gasping for air on the other side and without hesitation I crawled in to get him. I had only gone a few feet when he struck me repeatedly with his flailing arms. I grabbed him by his jacket, pulled him to the door and pushed him out into the snow. I followed. We were both rolling in the snow, coughing uncontrollably. We looked at each other. It was the only time I ever saw fear on my father's face. We were black as pitch, like characters in an old Al Jolson movie. All we could see were the whites of each other's eyes. Covered in soot, we staggered back into the kitchen to help calm my mother, who was horrified by our appearance. The fire department arrived but my sisters and I had put out the fire by bucket brigade by then. The kitchen was a mess, strewn with bottles of cleaners and piles of melting snow. The house was fogged with smoke and smelled like burning, wet wood. But we at least had running water.

As extreme as the winters were, the summers were equally uncomfortable. The house was not wired for the demands required of an air conditioner. Lack of insulation and the presence of a black, asphalt roof quickly heated the house during the dog days of summer. It was like a sauna, particularly upstairs. My father constructed a heavy wooden frame for a discarded fan that he retrieved from the salvage pile at Goodyear. It was an industrial fan taken from a piece of machinery and it had no guards on the rear side to protect the fan blades, and my father never installed any. It is a wonder that none of us ever lost a finger or hand to that beast. On oppressively hot and humid summer nights we stretched out on sheets across the parlor floor in front of the fan, like sardines in a can, and let the breeze drift over our bodies. The constant drone of the fan motor and the hum of the blades eventually lulled us to sleep. So powerful was this fan that on high speed, its constant running vibrated it across the parlor floor. Hot as the summer nights were, my brother, Rodger, preferred to sleep upstairs in the boys' room. It was not unusual to find him in the morning in bed under a mountain of blankets, even on the hottest of nights.

We had a detached, two-car garage at the end of our narrow, gravel driveway. It served as a receptacle for my father's collection of "junk" and a stash for bottles of cheap Meister Brau beer my father confiscated from my mother's secret hiding places within the house. The garage was built on no foundation except for a few cinder blocks in the corners. It had a dirt floor and a thick steel overhead door. The entire structure leaned precariously starboard, being out-of-plumb by several feet. I don't recall my father ever parking his car in it, probably because it looked as though it would collapse at any moment. My father eventually had it razed and replaced in 1975.

Of all the oddities the 409 house possessed, none was more odd—or more potentially dangerous—than the electric wiring. The fuse box was in the utility room, behind the door to the back porch. It was encased in a flimsy wood cabinet, precariously mounted to the wall. There were only a few confusing circuits and bare wires that led everywhere and nowhere. "What kind of fool puts electricity in a wooden cabinet?" my father asked, rhetorically, "unhandy Handell, that's who!" There were exposed wires hanging out of the parlor wall above the front door and outlets throughout the house that randomly worked. We all learned in time which ones to avoid when the iron was on or when the toaster was in use. And we had to make an announcement anytime we plugged in an appliance. We all fell victim to blowing a fuse now and again and we were responsible for knowing how to read a blown fuse and replacing it. To add to this frustration, our demand for fuses constantly exceeded my father's supply.

I once managed to kill the power to the entire house one Sunday morning shortly after we moved in when I took a penny from my brother, Rodger, and attempted to hide it in a wall socket. It knocked me clear across the room and left a scorch mark three feet up the parlor wall. The fact that no one was ever electrocuted or that the house never burned to the ground is truly astonishing.

A building inspector's nightmare, the house would probably be condemned by today's codes. But it was home, a place where my father was proud to raise his family. It was the only house he ever owned. He finally realized the childhood dream that began three decades before on a poor, cold island halfway around the world. He had U.S. citizenship, a steady job, a growing family, and now, a place of his own. No one helped him. He did it, as he had always done things—on his own. He had come a long, long way from the house of *his* childhood: dirt floors, turf fires, and thatched roof. The 409 house was a monument to his determination and hard work—a modest house for a modest man of modest means. It became as much a part of him as he became of it and on a quiet Sunday morning in August, shortly after his 67th birthday, he died there, alone, in his sleep, in the bed my mother so cherished still tucked up against the wall as it had been for twenty-eight years.

CHAPTER 22

∽

MRS. ROUSE'S BABY

I STOOD ON THE FRONT SEAT of my father's Ford. My broken leg still had not healed completely and I hobbled on the seat to get a better look at the activity going on around me. We were at Rouse's Standard Oil Station on the corner of Hawley and Lake Streets. My father chatted with the diminutive Eddie Poleska, a life-long "pump monkey" or gas station attendant, as he skillfully serviced my father's behemoth station wagon. We were new to the village but my father was already aware of the Rouses' reputation. The family was well known throughout our community. John Rouse, who settled in the middle of town more than a century before, eventually owned over 500 acres of the community's prime land and 80 acres of water (most of Diamond Lake). His son, Robert F. Rouse, became mayor. The mayor built the filling station near the northern edge of his property and turned the business over to his son, G. Hardin. The young man was no longer able to meet the physical demands of maintaining the family farm after his leg was crushed by the overturned wagon that tumbled down the hill during construction of the seminary. "And that's how my family got into the oil business," Stanley Rouse said.[80]

G. Hardin Rouse, or "the Old Man" as he came to be known, eventually owned or had an interest in several of the town's gas stations. He was an amiable and wiry man who always wore navy blue overalls and rocked with a pronounced limp when he walked. He worked hard and rightfully earned his reputation and economic status.

My father had the utmost respect for Mr. Rouse. Within days after moving to town, the Old Man came out to meet my father on the apron of the service station. Father had just eased his car off Lake Street with a flat tire and was desperate and embarrassed that he had no spare. He explained his situation to the Old Man and admitted that he could neither afford a new tire, nor did he have the $2 to pay to have the badly worn tire repaired. Mr. Rouse removed the tire from the car and repaired it anyway and said, "Welcome to town, John. Come back anytime and pay me when you can. I know you're good for it."

My father never forgot Mr. Rouse's kindness and became a life-long customer.

The Old Man had three sons, G. Hardin, Junior—or J.R., Mac, and Bruce, the youngest. Each eventually followed their father into the oil business, taking with them his prowess and acumen.

In 1960, Bruce was a twenty-four-year-old newlywed. He and his eighteen-year-old wife, Darlene, and infant son, Kurt, lived in the second story apartment of a farmhouse owned by the Old Man. The large, white, two-story building faced Hawley Street directly behind the filling station.

I hobbled along the front seat of the car and watched Eddie vigorously clean the windshield as he made small talk with my father. Suddenly, there was a great commotion. Black smoke came rolling out of the second story windows of the old farmhouse. Eddie Poleska was a Mundelein volunteer fireman. My father was a member of the volunteer fire brigade at Goodyear and had firefighting experience aboard ship in the Navy. They didn't hesitate.

"Wait there!" my father shouted as he jumped out of the car.

He and Eddie ran toward the house and up the back staircase. They entered the burning building as the heat and flames began to blow out the windows. I watched anxiously and waited as the two men emerged. Eddie was pulling Mrs. Rouse down the stairs. My father cradled what looked to be a rolled-up blanket in his arms as he carefully negotiated down the long set of stairs. They ran to the back of the yard as the fire department arrived on the scene. The house was gutted by the fire, but everyone got out safely.

When the two men returned to the car I asked, "what were you carrying, Daddy?"

My father leaned back in his seat and sighed. "The baby," he said with astonishment. "I was carrying Mrs. Rouse's baby."

CHAPTER 23

✿

MUNDELEIN, THE FIRST YEAR

A YEAR INTO OUR RELOCATION PROGRAM at the 409 house, I attended a morning kindergarten class in the basement of tiny St. Andrew's Lutheran Church on the corner of Lake and Courtland Streets. My mother was in her seventh month of a difficult pregnancy and overwhelmed with the responsibility of sending my older brothers off to school while taking care of Sheila, age three, Maureen, a year and a half, and me. My parents took an incalculable gamble and left me in the hands of the Lutherans whom I later learned are a lot like Catholics, but without the guilt. My parents reasoned that they could exorcize any post-Protestant symptoms I might exhibit from my pagan experience by following it up with eight years of Catholic education. They warned me not to tell any of our relatives that I was going to *that* school. But I was proud of the fact that I was old enough to attend school like my brothers, and I told everyone.

I walked to school in the mornings with John and Rodger who attended the Catholic school across the street. They always looked after me and every day escorted me into my classroom. I was bored with school. I felt out of place (not realizing that I was the only Catholic in the class) and I wasn't very obedient. I was much more interested in flirting with the girls. I watched the clock every day and waited impatiently for the big hand to be on the twelve and the little hand to be on the eleven, so I could go home.

I learned to tell time soon after I turned five years old. John made an analog clock out of construction paper as an assignment when he was in the second grade. The hands of the clock were fastened by a grommet in the center. He turned the hands from left to right and explained to me what the numbers meant. I grasped the concept immediately.

But learning to tie the shoelaces on my Red Ball Jets was another matter. My parents tried to teach me how but I seemed to lack the coordination required to copy them. After weeks of frustrating and unsuccessful attempts, John showed me and I quickly learned how to tie them in my own way, left-handed, like him. My parents were both "righties." Other than Sheila and Rodger, all of my siblings are left-handed. The concept of left-handedness and clock-wise motion comes very naturally to me. Anything that operates in a counter-clockwise manner, or right to left, is clumsily awkward, often confusing, and down-right uncomfortable. When I learned to play baseball, I instinctively ran to third base instead of first. I find driving in Ireland intuitive, and horse racing, annoying. Being of the "sinister persuasion," I would discover, prove to be an impediment as I grew into my teens.

I envied the other children in my kindergarten class whose mothers came to collect them after school. My mother never did and I often walked the three quarters of a mile home alone when I didn't invite myself to ride home with Billy Schafernak and his mother. Billy and I frequently fought over the attention of a blue-eyed, brunette classmate, Cheryl Peterson. I gave Cheryl a purple plastic ring that I won from the penny gumball machine at Diamond Lake Supermarket. Billy was jealous. We wrestled. I lost. I didn't ride home with him after that because he threatened to "beat me up if I didn't leave his woman alone."

When my school day ended, I played with my sisters and ate a sandwich of bologna, spam, or peanut butter and jelly for lunch. If I was on good behavior and my mother was in a particularly good mood, she might give me a Salerno Butter Cookie. I can clearly see her standing in the corner of the kitchen, listening to Mel Bellaire and "The Swap Shop" on the radio, dragging on her Pall Mall non-filtered cigarette, sipping at the bottle of beer she didn't know I knew she had hidden in the cupboard, and rubbing her hands across her protruding belly to calm the life rolling around inside of her.

Frequently, she made my sisters and me take an afternoon nap. She lay on her bed beside Sheila and me and lulled us to sleep. Sometimes I awoke to the cries of my sister, Maureen, in her crib, and my mother gone. I gave the baby a bottle of milk and put a few drops of Karo corn syrup on the nipple, like I had seen my mother do, to entice Maureen to take it, and hoped that she would stop crying. I ran up and down the street in search of my mother and knocked at the doors of the neighbors I knew, asking if they had seen her. None had. They all seemed surprised and concerned. Rather than answer their prying questions, I ran home, climbed back into my mother's bed, and waited for her to return. When she did, I pretended to be asleep as she quietly hid the brown paper bag inside her bedroom closet. Sometimes she would already be home when I returned and she scolded me for leaving my sisters alone. I felt guilty and cried.

"Whisht!" she slurred, pointing her finger in exclamation. "And not a word to your father if y'know what's good for ya."

After naptime, my mother sent me outside to play until my brothers came home. Again, I was bored. There were no other children my age on our block. Barbara Sue Kofski lived around the corner and Barbie Meyer lived across the street, but they were a whole year younger than I. Besides, they were girls. They didn't want to play Indians or army, they wanted to play with tea sets and dolls. Their doting mothers always made a big deal about how much I resembled *my* mother and they gushed over the length of my eyelashes, which were long, dark and thick. I was embarrassed being the envy of those women so I took a pair of pinking shears and to my mother's horror, cut off my eyelashes. They never grew back the same. My father often came to my defense whenever anyone suggested that I looked like my mother, "he may have his mother's features, but he's got his father's fixtures!" he insisted.

Without other boys on the block to play with, I wandered up and down the sidewalk on our side of the street, sang songs to keep myself occupied, and looked for ways to relieve my boredom. This led to an unexpected encounter with Hilda Shepard's tulip beds. Hundreds of the satiny flowers surrounded her house, bordered her driveway, and danced merrily in full bloom in the April sun. I found a broom handle in the yard. Wielding my new, make-believe sword with all the panache and precision worthy of Prince Red Hugh himself, I decapitated every last red- and yellow-headed dancing dragon that guarded Mrs. Shepard's castle. Petals scattered everywhere and tumbled across the lawns in the breeze. I didn't realize that a nosy neighbor saw me and reported to Mrs. Shepard. When my father came home, Mr. Shepard met him in the driveway. The two spoke briefly before my father hurried into the house. He asked me who cut down all of Mrs. Shepard's tulips. I told him that I didn't know. He led me upstairs and closed the door to the boys' room. In a single motion he took off his wide leather belt and doubled it over. He grabbed me by the arm, sat on the edge of the bed and bent me over his knee. Pulling down my pants, he struck me several times with the buckle end of his belt, forcing me to confess. He stormed out of the room and past my mother who was waiting on the stairs, and yelled "and *never* lie to me again!"

Mothers can distinguish the subtleties of their children's cries, and my mother knew from mine that I was in serious pain. She tiptoed into my room and cried when she saw the large red welts in the shape of my father's belt buckle on my backside. She soothed my pain with a compress of witch hazel to ease the sting, a thin layer of Noxzema to reduce the welts, and her gentle touch to dry my tears.

The days of spring, 1961, grew gradually warmer and sunnier. I took my time walking home from school, singing a few more songs along the way. One particularly mild afternoon, I ran up the steps and through the back porch and darted into the kitchen. My mother handed me a Popsicle to calm me down and chased me outside. I sat on the back step and slurped on the frozen, lemony ice. I noticed a bee fly past me. It landed on what remained of an old rocking horse given to us by Aunt Sarah. It had been ridden to abuse by my brothers and me before being carelessly discarded in the back yard. The rocking horse had a hole on either side of its head where a wooden handle once extended. The bee circled the hole and crawled inside. A few seconds later, he flew out again. Over the next few minutes I observed the bee come and go several times. I walked over to the rocking horse and after the bee buzzed off across the yard, I stuck my finger inside to see what was so interesting as to keep him returning. Suddenly, I felt an intense, crushing pain on the end of my finger. I ran into the house crying hysterically. My mother calmed me down, told me that I had been stung by a bee, and she treated my wound with an inexplicable mixture of spit and cigarette tobacco. I was afraid to go back out on to the porch. She promised me I had nothing to worry about.

"Bees can only sting one time," she said, rocking me in her lap. "They lose their stingers and die once they sting someone. That bee will never sting you again!" she insisted.

Reassuring me in a way that only a loving and devoted mother can, she guided me through the back porch and I sat once again on the rear steps with my thawing Popsicle. I looked over at the scene of my most recent trauma and saw the bee still circling around the hole in the horse's head. That's odd, I thought. Why isn't he dead? I watched him fly off and return a few more times. He seemed perfectly normal and healthy to me. What was going on here, I wondered? I cautiously approached the handleless horse. My sister, Sheila, stepped out onto the back porch with a Popsicle of her own.

"What'cha doin?" she asked.

I wanted to validate my mother's theory but was afraid to stick my finger back in the hole.

"Sheila," I said, "stick your finger in here."

She tottered over to the horse and without hesitation, obediently did as I had instructed. She screamed, quickly withdrew her finger, dropped her Popsicle into the dirt that was our backyard, and ran into the house crying.

I carefully observed what happened next. The bee appeared at the opening for a moment and then launched off into the distance.

I was completely mystified. How is it that this particular bee would not die? Was he some sort of special "super bee" my mother was not aware of? After all, my mother would never lie to me about such a thing. Mothers don't lie. Could she have been wrong? Did she just make the whole story up so I wouldn't be afraid?

About this time, Maureen waddled into the backyard. I called her over and motioned for her to stick her finger into the horse's head. She did, and immediately recoiled in pain as the tip of the intruding digit was greeted by the sting of the bee. She staggered into the house, wailing.

I was beside myself in amazement and paced warily around "old Trigger" (clock-wise, of course), watching the defiant bee come and go without so much as a hint of wooziness. Why would my mother tell me such a thing if it were not true?

As my mother tended to Maureen's wound, she didn't notice that I came into the house and plucked my seven month old sister, Tisha, off her blanket on the parlor floor. To continue my death-defying bee experiment, I held Tisha up under her arms and carried her outside to the rocking horse. As I carefully manipulated her fingers to insert them into the rocking horse's head, I heard my mother shout,

"Kevin Edward, don't you dare! Put that child *down*!"

She bolted toward me with Maureen on her hip. Crocodile tears ran down the baby's cherubic cheeks, her pink little index finger held high in the air as she screamed in pain.

"What the *hell* is wrong with you?" my mother barked.

She rapped her knuckles across the top of my head and chased me inside.

When I explained to her that the bee didn't die, her jaw dropped,

"What? Did it ever dawn on you that there just *might* be more than one bee in that thing?"

CHAPTER 24

✂

GINGER AND HER PUPPIES

A SLOW, BELCHING THUNDER TUMBLED ACROSS the evening sky. I arose from my bed and went to the window in the girls' room to watch the spring thunderstorm gather to the northwest. I forced open the window and propped it up with a wooden ruler. A soothing breeze carried the fresh smell of the oncoming rain. Ginger, our mostly Cocker Spaniel, whimpered at my feet. She was a great dog. She fit in well with the family, tolerant of our horseplay and patient when we pulled on her rust-colored ears. She took up permanent residence in a corner of the utility room. We never registered her, took her to the vet, or kept her on a leash. All those things cost money. She was always free to roam and explore the neighborhood with us. She obviously enjoyed her freedom because from the time she was about two years old, she had puppies every spring. I didn't know how this happened, of course. Every spring frogs had tadpoles, birds had chicks, dogs had puppies. When I questioned my parents about this phenomenon, I was told it was the natural order of things—the way God planned it. When I was old enough to figure out why her puppies looked amazingly similar to the other dogs in the neighborhood, I realized that my dog, Ginger, was basically a tramp.

Within days of having her litters in the utility room, my father took the pups out to our rickety old garage where my siblings and I seldom ventured. There, Ginger could mother them without any of us interfering. After a few weeks, my father took the puppies and "gave them away at work."

Ginger continued to pace and whine anxiously as I knelt on the floor anticipating the imminent arrival of rain, my arms folded across the window sill. The tops of the neighborhood elm trees rustled and swayed as the squall line approached. The wind swirled between the houses. Below the open window, I saw my father hastily place a corrugate box into the back of the station wagon. He opened an empty burlap potato sack that he had tucked under his arm. He placed a broken chunk of cinder block into it that lay on the side of the driveway. Reaching into the tailgate of the car, he opened the box. It contained Ginger's litter of puppies. He picked them up by the scruff of their necks and dropped them, one by one, into the bag. He tied a knot in the top of the sack and put it back into the box. He looked around. I ducked away from the window. I heard my father close the tailgate, get in the car and quickly back down the driveway. He returned about an hour later. No one suspected anything out of the ordinary. He frequently went out in the evenings for a shot-and-a-beer at one of the many local taverns.

Later that night, I challenged him on what I saw. He was shocked that he'd been caught. He lashed out bitterly, "what, you have little to do other than to *spy* on me?"

I flinched as he faked a backhand. He shook his head in disgust, gathered himself and crushed out his cigarette.

"C'mon," he said. "I want to talk to you upstairs for a minute."

I followed him up to the boys' room. He chased my brother and sisters downstairs, closed the door and sat on the edge of Rodger's bed. I sat across from him on my bed. He was fidgety. I could tell he was organizing his thoughts, preparing his defense.

"Look," he said, "those puppies . . . they're . . . they're just puppies. It's not fair to them to . . . they don't have . . . we can't afford to keep all those dogs, you know. Really, it's the best thing."

"What's the best thing, Dad?" I asked, suspecting the worst.

"That they don't suffer," he said.

"I don't understand, Dad?"

"You're old enough. It's time you learned about some facts of life, Son . . . I put them in the burlap bag, I drive them down to the Des Plaines River over on Rockland Road . . . at night when there's no one around . . . and throw the bag off the bridge. It's quick . . . They don't suffer . . . really." he said, trying to convince himself that it was true.

I could not believe what I was hearing. My ears began to ring, and I could feel my face become flush. I fought bravely to keep from crying in front of him.

"You drowned them? You told me you gave them away at work."

"Well? . . . It's quick. What else am I going to do?" He lit a cigarette. "And don't say anything to your Mother about it neither, and don't tell your sisters. They wouldn't understand. They're too young."

They're too young? I was eleven, too young to be his confessor. How was I supposed to make sense of what I had just heard? How could I forgive him for his cruelty, his insensitivity? I felt sick.

He stood up and hovered over me for a moment—waiting for my reaction. I sat paralyzed with fear and sadness for those innocent creatures and I was, above all, disappointed beyond explanation by my father's callousness.

He breathed a sigh of relief as his silent burden of guilt lifted. "Don't tell *anyone!*" he said. "That's it."

He eased out of the bedroom. When I heard that he was downstairs in the parlor, I buried my head in the covers and cried myself to sleep with the silhouette image of my father standing on the Rockland Road Bridge against a stormy, lightning-filled sky, watching a burlap bag full of yelping pups sink in the black, swirling waters of the river as they passed beneath him.

I have never been able to erase that horrible vision from my memory.

Had I known about spaying dogs, I would have paid for the surgery myself. Did my father not know? Was he that ignorant? Or did he just not have the resources to have it done? I'll never know. I am certain that my father convinced himself that he was doing the right thing. And it was painful for him to admit his actions to me. He managed to emotionally insulate himself from the cruelty of his crime. And on some level, I think he believed it was something his father would have done—and he not only resented that, but hated himself for it.

The following spring Ginger gave birth to her umpteenth and final litter. I couldn't bear to see the fate of those pups repeated. Without spilling my father's secret, I proposed to my parents that I raffle "the Easter puppies" at Santa Maria with all the proceeds going to foreign Missions—an honorable cause heavily promoted at our Catholic school, Santa Maria del Popolo.

Our Principal, Sister Mary Oona, liked the idea and gave me permission to organize the entire "event." I wrote a script and announced it over the PA system in the school office several times over the next couple of weeks. The raffle generated about $30 and we gave away four puppies out of the litter of five. My father could not bring himself to take the last puppy to the river, and it became a part of our family, too. He never had a proper name; we just called him "Puppy."

After my father passed away and my brothers and I were waxing nostalgic one evening, we learned from each other that he told us each the same story when we individually discovered his insidious crime. He swore us each to secrecy—one that we kept because we were too ashamed to repeat it.

CHAPTER 25

๑๖

M-7, M-11 & M-14

M Y MOTHER PERFORMED HER DAILY pre-dawn routine
beginning at 5:45. She prepared my father's oatmeal and boiled
up a pot of tea. The distinct but muffled voice of Wally Phillips blared from
her kitchen radio. The gas jet bellowed as it ignited in the lungs of the
old furnace located directly below me in the utility room. A minute or two
afterward, the blower kicked in with a shutter, and hot, dry air spilled out of
the heat register and across my room. I shivered as a chill ran through me,
and I pulled the covers tightly over my shoulders. Rodger eagerly sprang
out of bed to get dressed.

"C'mon, get up," he whined, and he raced downstairs.

I coveted the few extra minutes I had in the rickety twin bed and waited
for the room to warm up a few degrees before I staggered to my feet. I
dreaded the thought of having to face another bleak and drizzly November
morning and the bundle of newspapers that awaited me. I reluctantly
plodded down the stairs.

The scuffling outside the front door and the clinking of glass meant that
Delbert Rouse was removing the empty Gold Meadow milk bottles from
the thinly-insulated aluminum box on the front porch. Twice a week he
replaced them with full ones. The Rouse family owned, among other things,
a dairy on Lake Street at Division, on land now occupied by the Mundelein
Police Station. Rouses sold their dairy interests to Beatrice Foods in 1945
but continued daily operations until it closed in the mid-1960's.[81] My mother

held the flimsy storm door open and poured a handful of quarters left over from the Laundromat into Mr. Rouse's hand in exchange for the week's worth of milk. I peered through the doorway to see that my morning papers had arrived. I didn't like getting up at six o'clock in the morning, but I was expected to follow my brother's example. So, in 1963, at the age of eight, I took over some of Rodger's paper routes. I delivered about fifty papers on my bike every morning and around the same number right after school.

In 1961, my brother, Jay, an eleven-year-old entrepreneur, took over a morning paper route from one of the Kredjcze kids up the block. My parents were opposed. But since John didn't have to collect the monthly subscription payments and the papers were delivered from the news agency to the house (in other words, my parents didn't have to get involved), they soon gave in, and the O'Donnell brothers' paper route dynasty began. When John started high school, he passed his route down to my brother, Rodger, a tireless and conscientious worker. The Hamm brothers forfeited their morning and afternoon routes in Hawthorne Hills and West Shore Park, and Rodger gladly accepted them. These were the routes that I inherited. Combined, Rodger and I delivered more papers than any other boys in town.

Each Monday through Saturday, Leo, from the Libertyville News Agency, darted up to the house in his little red van and dropped off our bundles of papers. They were stacked flat and bound in copper wire with a blank sheet on top that read "M-7, M-11, and M-14." Leo and Mr. Rouse often greeted each other on the front walk in the morning.

Regardless of the weather, the newspapers had to be delivered every day without fail. My brothers and I were committed to the process: folding the papers, securing them with a rubber band—or wrapping them in a sleeve of waxed paper if it was raining, and delivering them by bicycle to houses all throughout our end of town. There were no holidays, no sick days, and no vacations.

My father sipped his morning tea, ate his oatmeal, and extolled upon me on the virtues of commitment and responsibility.

"It's wise to pack your own parachute," he said.

I nodded, but I didn't know what that meant. My father used a lot of expressions and I didn't know what most of them meant. He had a peculiar way of phrasing things. "I may not always be right, but I'm never wrong," he'd say. He referred to dentists as "tooth dentists" (as if there were any other kind). When my brothers and I got into mischief he said, "You three make a fine pair if there ever was one." And as my mother poured my father's tea, he often waved his hand beside his cup and warned her not to fill it too high saying, "Save some room for the cow, Teresa." And the topper: "every time I hear that phone, it's ringing."

I was particularly fond of my father's self-deprecating Irish wit. One summer evening as he observed a bright waxing moon in the eastern sky obscured behind a thin layer of clouds, he asked me in a very serious tone, "what is that light over there?"

"What light? Where?" I replied.

He pointed. "That light over there. What *is* that?" he asked. He truly was confused.

"Uh, Dad," I said condescendingly, "that's the moon."

He glared at me for a moment. Then in his own defense replied, "Now how in the *hell* am I supposed to know that? I'm not from around here."

When my father completely lost patience with one of us he shouted, "knock it off or I'll Barbados ye." This peculiar term he learned from his father. It was handed down through generations of Arranmore and dates back to the heavily whitewashed and intentionally obscure 17th century Irish slave trade. Yes, Irish slave trade. The despicable practice began after the Battle of Kinsale in 1602, when the English were faced with the nagging problem of dispositioning 30,000 military prisoners. The solution: establish an official policy to banish Irish political prisoners to colonies in the New World. Over the next few decades the involuntary exodus of Irish to the Americas grew exponentially and there were not enough military and political prisoners incarcerated on even the most menial infractions to meet demand. As a result, the Penal Laws were tweaked so that every petty crime carried with it a sentence of transportation. This was abhorrently effective but did not solve the "Irish problem" entirely. King James II subsequently encouraged selling the Irish as slaves to planters and settlers in the New World colonies. In the twelve year period during and following the Confederation revolt (1641-52), over 850,000 Irish soldiers and citizens were wasted by the sword, plague, famine, hardship, and banishment, and 300,000 were sold as slaves. Privateers flourished as trafficking human lives became Ireland's number one export and the Catholic population plummeted from 1,466,000 to 616,000. This resulted in a growing number of homeless women and children. Considered a public nuisance, they were tracked down by complicit Irish slaver gangs that combed the countryside, kidnapped them, and sold them into slavery. During the 1650's, the decade of Oliver Cromwell's Reign of Terror, over 100,000 Irish Catholic children, generally from ten to fourteen years old, who were either orphans, or simply taken from their parents, were driven like cattle to waiting ships and sold as slaves in the West Indies, Virginia, and New England. It was hoped that they might lose their faith and all knowledge of their nationality, and in most instances even their names were changed with no respect to their former station in life.[82] Some 52,000 Irish, mostly women and sturdy boys and girls, were sold to Barbados and the royal colony of Virginia alone. In 1656, Cromwell's Council of State ordered the rounding up of 1,000 Irish girls and 1,000 Irish boys. They were taken to Jamaica and sold as slaves to English planters. So lucrative was the industry that the number of "Barbadosed Irish" sold as slaves to the American colonies and sugar plantations of the West Indies between 1651 and 1660 alone was between 80,000 and 130,000. This exceeded the total "free" population of the Americas at that time. As horrendous as these numbers sound, it only reflects a small part of the immense program, as most of the slaving activity was not recorded and continued steadily for one hundred and fifty years. While African Negroes were better suited to work in the semi-tropical climates of the Caribbean than the Irish, they were considerably more expensive and infinitely more valuable. Irish Catholics were in nearly limitless supply on the other hand, expendable, and "free for the catching." And while history has rightly recorded the African slave trade as far more extensive and exploitive, from 1600 to 1699 more Irish were sold as slaves in the Americas than were Africans.[83]

Despite my father's cryptic threats and quirky expressions, I knew he was wise and I knew better than to question him, lest I be "Barbadosed." I also knew he was no stranger to hard work at an early age, and he instilled that virtue into my brothers and me. He insisted that if I wanted to get ahead and attend Catholic high school like my brothers, I had to earn and save the money myself. He couldn't afford the $700 annual tuition. Whether or not I wanted to go to Carmel High School for Boys didn't matter. It was my father's expectation and I dutifully fulfilled my obligation, first with a morning route, then later with the addition of an afternoon route.

The afternoon papers were already waiting for me when I raced home from school every day. I'd watch the last inning or two of the Cubs game on WGN TV as I folded my papers on the parlor floor in front of the television. If Billy Williams came up to bat, I rolled a newspaper up in my hand and took a sweet swing when he swung. In my best Jack Brickhouse impersonation I blurted out, "that's pretty well hit to left field . . . back she goes, back, back, back . . . hey-hey! A home run! Billy Williams has done it again folks, and the Cubs *win*! Oh brother!" With the game over, I wrapped my arms around the bundled papers stacked neatly on the floor and carried them out to my bicycle.

My Sears & Roebuck bike was retrofitted with a huge rectangular galvanized wire basket. It was secured to the front handle bars and had forks that extended down to the front axle mount. It made my bike look very *uncool*, but broadcasted to the rest of the kids at school and in the neighborhood that I had a coveted job—and somehow I was more responsible than they. The basket cost $7, nearly a month's wages, and was genuine News Agency issue. Packed correctly, it could hold about fifty newspapers on any day but Thursday. Thursday's papers were always crammed full of weekend sale advertisements and I had to make two trips.

It was best to stand the papers on-end in the basket—less likelihood of them popping out if I lost control and hit a curb or a pot hole, as was likely to happen due to the thirty extra pounds cantilevered to the front of my bike. Compensating for the weight imbalance took some getting used to.

There were three morning papers: The Chicago Tribune, by far the most popular; the Chicago Sun-Times, which always had the fewest pages so you could roll them tightly, like a baton; and The Wall Street Journal, an odd sized and expensive newspaper with only a few subscribers. We didn't have many financial types in our part of town. Folks were mostly blue collar.

The afternoon editions were The Chicago Daily News, The Chicago American, and The Waukegan News-Sun. I sorted them all by type in the basket and because they were each rolled and rubber-banded differently, I could easily identify them.

The Agency provided an ample supply of rubber bands and waxed paper. I also had a flip chart of thick manila cards marked with each subscriber's name, address, and choice of newspaper. I was supposed to mount it to my bike and every time there was a change, I was issued a new card. But after a couple of weeks on the job, I had my route memorized and the flip-cards were unnecessary.

My brothers and I became proficient at folding, creasing, rubber banding, and stacking the papers as we sat cross-legged on the parlor floor. I always took time to read the front page of each paper. As a result, I had a better understanding than most kids my age of current events. I clearly remember the details of the Kennedy assassinations, the Gemini Missions, and the 1968 Democratic National Convention in Chicago, for example, because I read about them on my parlor floor as they happened.

From beginning to end, my routes took about an hour to complete, except in winter when the roads were covered with snow. Then I walked with the papers in a canvas sack slung over my shoulder. On bitterly cold winter days, of the frozen water pipe variety, my dad often drove me on my route. But it meant that I had to be ready well before he left for work at 6:30 AM. I sat on the folded-down rear deck of the station wagon with the papers stacked in back. I ran from house to house with an armful of papers, criss-crossing the street as I made my deliveries.

The worst ice storm I can remember occurred during the winter of 1966. Several inches of ice coated everything. Trees and power lines were downed, and our water pipes frozen. Schools and shops were closed as we all tried to chisel out of the deep freeze. But for a few glorious days, Rodger and I delivered our papers wearing ice skates. We glided through the streets and across lawns and along driveways and were able to complete our routes in record time.

In January, 1967, we had a twenty-three inch snowstorm followed by long stretches of sub-zero weather and with it, more frozen water pipes. The snow stayed on the ground until April. Delivering papers that winter was especially difficult.

For all of this effort, Rodger and I each yielded between $7 and $14 a month, depending on the size of our routes. We always looked forward to Christmas when most of our subscribers gave us a tip that was generally in the range of $2-$5, $5 dollars if they knew us and liked the service, $2 if they did not.

Over time, I became deadly accurate at throwing newspapers onto people's porches. Proper technique was essential. I learned that you couldn't throw them across your body like a shot-put as you passed by the target. Lateral movement against the forward momentum of the bicycle caused a loss of control and before you could react, you were up over the curb, or in a hedge, or slamming into a parked car with your load of papers scattered everywhere. For accuracy, the projectile had to be thrown forward and overhead, like a baseball, in order to keep proper center of gravity. This also enabled better control of the release point. I liked spiking the Sun Times the most. Rolled and banded tightly, I could flick them end-over-end and "walk" the paper right up onto the front stoop.

I had my share of wild pitches, of course. My errant throws ended up under bushes, broke windows, and dented storm doors. I misplayed windage and heaved some onto rooftops, and accidentally shattered milk bottles (both empty and full). The Agency always paid for any damages.

Like a good pitcher who can put the ball where he wants it, I developed an arsenal of placement pitches. Sometimes, I intentionally threw at people I didn't like or who stiffed me out of a tip at Christmas. I called this my brush-back pitch. Other times, I slammed the paper against their aluminum storm door as hard as I could without breaking the glass (fast ball). It sounded like a gunshot! In the summer I could often hear the customers' startled reactions inside their homes. By the time they figured out what the noise was, I had coasted several houses down the street, wearing a satisfied smile.

Those who unjustifiably complained to the Agency about me often found their papers the next day just within range of their lawn sprinklers or strafed along the concrete, in a flower bed (slider), slowly rolled up under their car (change-up), or some other equally inconvenient place within their yard (curve ball).

Those who had a newspaper tube mounted to their mail box posts near the street were the most challenging. Without ever slowing down, I coasted up to the mail box and leaned forward. Just a few seconds before I reached the target, I extended my arm under the handlebar with paper in hand and completed the transaction by inserting the paper into the tube as I passed by, quickly retracting my hand behind my back before I whacked it against the mail box. If there were an Olympic category for this event, I would have been a gold medalist.

When the weather was fine on my afternoon route, I waited until the Cubs game was over before wedging a transistor radio in with the papers. I tuned in to Dick Biondi on WLS, and I sang along with the songs he played as I meandered through the canopied streets on my end of town.

My father negotiated a deal with the News Agency to provide us with an extra paper for the Sisters at Santa Maria del Popolo. On his orders, I rode my bike up to the convent when I completed my route. I rang the doorbell and cheerfully handed one of the BVM's a copy of the Daily News. My father insisted: "always save them a nice one."

On warm summer evenings, as I dawdled home from the convent, I often stopped in front of a quaint ranch house at 222 Woodlawn Drive and listened to an older couple engage in classical music in their front parlor. One played piano, the other, violin. Their sweet and delicate duets drifted out the open windows and swirled around me. It was unlike anything I had ever heard before.

By far the greatest joy I experienced delivering papers was having Ginger as company. As I loaded my papers into the basket on my bike, Ginger's tail frantically waggled back and forth as she eagerly awaited our daily run. She never strayed and often led the way. She never tired and rarely missed a day. She stopped when I stopped, waited beside my bike if I had to dismount to retrieve an errant throw, and protected me from other neighborhood dogs. Dealing with aggressive dogs was the most hazardous part of the job and over the years I was bitten a few times. Mostly, dogs were just an annoyance and I learned which ones to avoid. One particular yippy little fur ball used to chase me down Hillside Drive in West Shore Park every afternoon and chomp at my ankles. I worked up enough speed as I approached his house so that I could put my feet up on my handlebars and coast all the way down the hill while he nipped at my bike pedals. When the owners refused my repeated requests to keep the dog tethered, I took matters into my own hands. I bought a water pistol at the Ben Franklin Store in Fairhaven Plaza and filled it with Bo-Peep ammonia from the bottle my mother kept underneath her kitchen sink. One squirt directly to the dog's nose, and he never chased me again.

One afternoon as I loaded an armful of papers into my basket in front of the house, Mrs. Pfister, a curmudgeonly widow who lived one street over, was walking her two Great Danes, Duke and Duchess. They pulled her along the sidewalk like a team of wild horses. One of them broke free, and bounded toward me in full gallop. Just as the dog was about to pounce on me, Ginger cut him off, hurling herself at the attacker. She was no match for the Great Dane, who was ten times her size and weight, but she fought him fearlessly. The two of them growled and snarled and gnawed at each other viciously until the old woman got her dog under control and I was safely back inside the house. Ginger suffered the worst of the attack. It took several days until she felt healthy enough to run along side me again. From that day forward, I delivered Mrs. Pfister's newspaper everywhere but on her front porch.

Ginger had a great disposition but one very, very bad habit. She liked to chase trucks. Whether it was fear, protection, or defense I cannot say, but whenever a truck came down the street she ran along side it within inches of the wheels, barking frantically, oblivious to our calls demanding her to stop. When the truck was a few hundred feet from the house, she suddenly stopped and sauntered back home.

In August, 1968, Rodger and I were given orders from my father to trim the bushes in the front yard before he returned from work. Ginger kept us company, as always. A Skokie Valley Diaper truck (a home delivery service nearly obsolete with the advent of disposable diapers) stopped at the top of the street to make a delivery of clean cloth diapers to Mrs. Church. As the step van approached our house, Ginger ran after it. The driver yelled at Ginger to get back as he sped down the street. She trotted back into the yard when the truck was a non-threatening distance away. A few minutes later, the truck came back down the block. This time the driver sped up as Ginger barked and chased after him. I walked toward the street commanding Ginger to stop. When the truck was directly in front of the house, the driver intentionally jerked at the steering wheel and Ginger got caught under the truck's rear axle. She tumbled down the pavement over and over again and then lay motionless in the middle of the street. The driver never slowed down. He ran the stop sign at the top of the hill and squealed around the corner onto Lake Shore Drive. Rodger and I knelt down beside Ginger and called her softly. She tried to get up as she whined in pain. We cried angrily, afraid to move her. We watched the rise and fall of her chest as she struggled to breathe. After a minute or two her breathing became more labored and erratic. Then she put her head down on the blacktop and stopped breathing altogether. Rodger and I ran into the house, hysterical. My mother called the Mundelein Police Department who dispatched a streets and sanitation truck. Mother insisted we all stay in the house until after they had gone. I watched from the front window as a burly man in a flatbed utility truck stopped at the scene of the crime. He pulled on a pair of leather gloves and waddled into the street. He plucked Ginger up off the pavement by her hind legs and uncompassionately flung her into the bed of the truck. I was crushed and mortified by his insensitivity and ran from the house as he sped up the block. I jumped on my bike and raced after him, yelling and screaming at him along Lakeview Drive until he was well out of range.

When my Father arrived home from work and was told of the news, he immediately dug the phone book out of the parlor closet, slammed it down on the table, and whipped through the Yellow Pages in search of the phone number for Skokie Valley Diaper Service. I sat beside him as he yelled into the phone. The company denied any wrongdoing and I heard them hang up. But my father continued to angrily spew epithets and idle threats into the dead receiver. There was little else he could do. I sensed his futility and went along with his ruse. I was proud of him that he had made the call. But deep down I knew he had no recourse. Nothing he could do would bring Ginger back and that's all that any of us really wanted. The house was quiet and empty without her now, and my paper route was never the same. It became nothing but a tedious chore. I missed her terribly and within a few weeks I quit my paper routes, turning them back over to the News Agency.

CHAPTER 26

༺

THE NEIGHBORHOOD AND BEYOND

M Y ENDLESS SUMMERS OF IGNORANCE and hijinks extended the length of two and a half blocks of South Prairie Avenue, a four hundred yard stretch of Americana bordered by Diamond Lake at the south end and Billy Schafernak's house on the corner of Woodland Drive on the north end. A total of twenty-four cottages and post-war houses straddled both sides of our curbless street occupied mostly by young, growing, blue-collar families. We were the only Irish Catholics on the block, and, at seven children, far outnumbered all the other families. The non-Catholics were considerably more restrained when it came to procreation. The largest was Barbie Meyer's family, which, along with the Schafernaks and the Churches, had five children. The houses on our block were like rabbit warrens—kids everywhere. And like any good neighborhood, many of the kids had nick-names. There was Smitty, Dinger, Bam-bam, and most notably, Bellybutton, a scrawny, melon-headed kid with coke-bottle glasses who ran around in circles and talked to the grass. We all thought he was retarded. He grew up to be a genius mathematician.

Directly beside us on the west side of the street were the Zweifkas, beside them, the Shepards (site of the infamous tulip caper), next to them, the Guidos (later, the Beneventis, and then the Fairs occupied the house). At the top of the block were the Churches. Across Lake Shore Drive lived the Danes and next door to them, in an austere brick ranch house overlooking the lake lived the elusive "Bachelors."

The Bachelors owned and operated a little soft-serve ice cream shack on the east edge of our village called the "*Dairy Dream*." It was the most popular drive-in in town. It sat on the edge of the North Shore Train tracks between Mundelein and Libertyville. It always drew large crowds—especially on hot summer evenings.

The Bachelors lived in Florida during the winter months but were back to open their walk-up restaurant by April 1st every year without fail. The two men worked the place by themselves and come October, boarded it up again, to begin lounging in a cabana somewhere on Key West by Halloween.

What were the odds, I thought? That two strangers from the little village of Mundelein found themselves in an identical predicament—unable to find wives—and that they actually found each other, went into business together, defrayed their costs and improved their profit margin by moving in together and share living expenses. How convenient.

My father insisted that I never go to their door, but he never told me why. They were just "the Bachelors." Sure, they seemed a little odd, they always had their blinds closed and drapes drawn, but they kept to themselves and didn't bother anybody.

The adults in the neighborhood whispered about them using a different name—"the queers." I didn't really know what "queer" meant other than it was a sure way to get a knuckle on the top of my head from my mother if I called my brothers that. Most kids in the neighborhood didn't know any better, and those who did understand didn't care. We just knew that the bluff behind the Bachelors house provided the best sledding hill on Diamond Lake, "Suicide Hill!"

Through my young eyes I saw Suicide Hill as 100 feet high and a mile long. In actuality, it rose about twenty feet above the lake and the base of it flattened out onto a broad plain about fifty yards in length. A really good ride on a sled with waxed runners could make it onto the lake. And if the ice was free of snow, you could coast forever. That was my goal. I carefully positioned my sled on the precipice of the steepest section of the hill, paced five or six giant steps backwards, took a deep breath, and made a running dive onto my Red Racer. I steered my sled and shifted my weight with Olympic Bobsled precision in an attempt to avoid the other kids and obstacles on the hill. If I didn't crash or roll off and if I had enough momentum to make it onto the lake, I put my head down, closed my eyes and listened to the screams and laughter fade behind me on the hill. The hissing sound of steel rails on the frozen lake filled my senses. I slowly glided to a stop and looked between the wood slats of my sled and down through the crystal clear ice. Fish that my brothers and I were sure to catch the following spring hovered in the frigid water below unaware that their days were numbered. I listened to the ice groan and gurgle as the surface of the 125 acre lake expanded all around me. I made a mental note of the distance I traveled, hopped to my feet, pulled my blazing chariot behind me, and ran to the top of the hill to do it all over again.

Suicide Hill in the summertime was overgrown with honeysuckle and sumac, cattails and buckthorn. I once rode my bike down it on a dare. I crashed into a bramble of buckthorn near the bottom of the hill and punctured both my tires in several places. I walked up to Bud's Fix-It Bike and Mower Shop in Diamond Lake, across from the Happy Hollow, to buy a repair kit. I spent a week's worth of my Hostess Twinkie money on a can of Monkey Grip tire patch. I had to seal all the holes in my inner tubes in time for my afternoon paper route and before my father found out.

Suicide Hill is oddly incongruous to the surrounding topography and rises above the lake near where, in 1837, frontiersman David Whitney found the remains of a pre-Columbian Indian settlement. This has led some to believe that Suicide Hill is an ancient burial or ceremonial earthwork constructed by a lost race of nomadic Mound Builders, and consequently conclude the area is not only sacred—but haunted.

I can't say that I ever experienced any paranormal activity on or around Suicide Hill, unless, of course, you consider what happened to me the first time I ever kissed a girl. The rapturous event took place adjacent to the hill, where South Prairie Avenue curves sharply to the west and a pair of white stone pillars on either side of the street marks the entrance to West Shore Park.

Her name was Pam Johnson. She lived a few blocks over on the corner of North Shore Drive and Lincoln Street. I was eleven and in the 6th grade. It was a dark and blustery October afternoon. It was on a Thursday. She wasn't a Catholic but I knew her casually because she hung around with Glen Grundhofer, a kid who lived in a house next to The Bachelors at the top of Suicide Hill. She stopped me on my way home from my paper route. We talked; she flirted, and coyly led me down the sidewalk in front of Von

Dracek's house. We proceeded around the bend where she grabbed me, sat me down amongst the junipers at the base of the north pillar, clung to my jacket, and carefully planted her lips on mine. I was nervous and looked around, not knowing what to do. I couldn't for the life of me understand why she tried so hard to force *her* tongue into *my* mouth. I fought back—teeth clenched and lips pursed. I had this weird simultaneous rush of terror and toe-tingling thrill sweep over me at once. She got all squirmy and I felt things going on in my Hagars that I had never felt before. Mortified, I jumped to my feet, hopped back on my bike, and sped home. I felt that I had committed the gravest of venial sins and that God was *surely* going to punish me.

After several days and sleepless nights of guilt and torment, I approached my mother for counsel and confessed the whole, sordid affair to her. She listened to me intently, sighed, and casually crushed out her cigarette. "You're too young to be wooing the girls," she said. Then she reached for the bottle of Meister Brau she had hidden in the cupboard above the stove.

The Hamms, whose paper routes my brother, Rodger, took over, lived in the last house next to the pillars. To the north of them were the Smiths and the Von Draceks, who owned an electrical appliance store in Libertyville. Crossing Lake View Drive onto our block was the widow, Ida Brophy, whom everyone in the neighborhood affectionately called Aunt Ida. Her little house and massive yard consumed half the block and provided just the venue we needed for countless hours of neighborhood games. We filled our long summer days and after-school time with wiffle ball, bounce or fly, 500, touch and tackle football, sharks and minnows, and after dark we played kick-the-can. Next door to Aunt Ida's, to the north and directly across the street from us, were the Van Alsteins. My father sardonically referred to Mr. Van Alstein as "junk man Van," because of the assortment of old cars and appliances strewn about their yard. Diagonally, on the northwest corner lived the Meyers. Across Lake Shore Drive on our side of the street to the north were the Dreeves, Cropakowskis, Schmidts, Kredjczes, Mullers, and Schafernaks. On the west side, I can only recall the Loweckis, the Ganicks, and the Lees.

To the west, beyond Barbie Meyer's house, lay an open field. In 1961 they built a new subdivision of tidy houses with landscaped yards and curbed streets called "Hawthorn Hills." The streets and houses while under construction were a wonderful place to explore until I stepped on a nail that punctured my Red Ball Jet High Top sneaker and sank about an inch into the bottom of my left foot. I had to go see Doctor Dolan at the Libertyville Medical Group and get a tetanus shot, and my mother forbid me to play around any more construction sites. The rest of that summer was an annoyance as the dew and wet grass wicked through the hole in the bottom of my sneaker and into my sock until my father sealed the hole with Monkey Grip Tire Patch.

Beyond the cluster of new homes that comprised Hawthorn Hills were a hundred acres of open fields and wetlands. It stretched all the way to Quig's Apple Orchard on Midlothian Road—at that time, the very western edge of civilization. This one-time pasture was known by all the kids from all the bordering neighborhoods simply as "the cowpath." There were any number of paths and trails that criss-crossed these fields and fens, and there were plenty of adventures to be had. We explored them on foot or on our bikes for hours at a time. There was an old fence row of trees and shrubs that ran along the east side of the cowpath at the end of Cardinal Place. We named it "Hobo Jungle." About twenty feet wide and a hundred yards long, it contained trees of Pin Cherry, Alder, Hawthorn, Buckthorn, Honeysuckle, and Lilac. My brother, John, and his friends convinced the younger kids that hobos visited there during the night and that we were never to go in there alone—lest we get kidnapped. Evidence that the elusive hobos frequented this spot was everywhere: empty whiskey bottles, beer cans, cigarette butts, campfire ashes, and the occasional torn, rain-soaked, and mottled pages from Playboy magazines, which I was intensely curious about, but that John and his buddies always seized and hid in their secret location in the cowpath.

The rallying point for the neighborhood kids was at the edge of a swamp at a place we called "The Lightning Tree," a massive, solitary Alder on the south side of the cowpath. Charged fire from the heavens struck it so many times that the trunk was split from top to bottom, and gaping wounds oozed a sticky sap. The base of the tree was scorched black and several of its branches were split or broken, the lower ones resting against the ground. But the old Alder refused to die. Every spring as I delivered my newspapers, I noticed the Lightning Tree was among the very first to bloom.

On the high ground of the cowpath were several thickets of raspberry bushes, grape vines, and patches of rhubarb left over from when Alexander Bellinski farmed the land one hundred years earlier. We brought home armfuls of rhubarb in May and marched off with containers to fill with sweet, ripened raspberries in July—eating more berries than we ever brought home.

The wetlands were always a good place to catch tadpoles in spring, and frogs, salamanders, and crayfish throughout the summer. We often brought them home and kept them as pets until they either escaped or died. Few escaped.

A maze of narrow trails looped through the extensive cattail marshes. Riding a bicycle along them required good balance and quick reflexes. Portions of the trail were miry and just wide enough to squeeze through without catching the handlebar grips on the reeds.

A group of friends and I chased each other through an unfamiliar section far on the western edge of the cowpath, beyond the Lightning Tree. It was in late August. I sped around a bend and looked back to see if anyone was tailing me. "I lost 'em!" I said enthusiastically. Then I looked up and saw that the trail ended. Too late. Unable to react in time, I flipped over my handlebars headlong into the quagmire as my bike was sucked down into the scummy, duckweed-covered black water. I frantically tried to pull myself and my bicycle free. We were both completely encrusted in a black and green stringy scum and reeked from the putrid smell of stagnant swamp water. My riding companions skidded to a halt in time to witness me stumble out of the fen, dazed and confused, like the 1950's Richard Carlson character "Creature from the Black Lagoon." They teased me incessantly all the way home. The only thing injured was my pride. When I arrived home, I called to my mother from the back door. She shrieked at the sight of me and refused to let me in the house. She made me remove *all* my clothes in the back yard and between fits of laughter, proceeded to rinse me off with ice cold water from the garden hose.

We built a tree fort in a scraggly old Pin Cherry tree in the field behind Ray Delago's house with whatever scraps of lumber and nails we could scavenge from the construction sites of the new homes in the neighborhoods infringing on the cowpath. Our forts were vandalized and overtaken by marauding bands of kids from a few streets over, namely the Maggi brothers. We did the same to their nearby forts when they weren't around. We engaged in "pea shooter" warfare with them using hard, unripened "choke-cherries" from the Pin Cherry trees. The fruit fit perfectly down the barrel of the soda straws we collected from the Country School restaurant on Hawley Street.(Now a florist and gift shop.) Once the cherries ripened though, they made lousy ammunition and everyone became disinterested in fighting and moved on to other forms of entertainment.

In the spring that I turned nine, I fell from the top of our tree fort when a branch that I was dangling from snapped and gave way. Miraculously, I tumbled twenty feet through the branches below without striking a single one. I landed in the tall, soft prairie grass flat on my back, inches from an opened pocket knife that Billy Schafernak had dropped moments before. In addition to having the wind knocked out of me, I thought I was paralyzed. I couldn't move for several minutes. I eventually limped home after my brothers and Billy swore me to secrecy. We kept the accident from our parents for fear that we would have to abandon our tree fort.

Ironically, more than forty years later, Billy Schafernak, who now goes by Doctor Will Schafernak, is a licensed chiropractor. I am a regular patient. He still recalls the tree fort incident and attributes a great deal of my chronic back pain to my fall that day.

There was a small, shallow pond on the west side of Washington School a few hundred yards beyond our tree fort. We used to ice skate there until it was safe to go out onto the lake. Unable to afford new skates, the only hand-me-downs that fit me, were a pair of speed skates. I was the fastest kid in the neighborhood. This is my only claim to athleticism.

Most years in spring the tall grasses of the cowpath mysteriously caught fire and threatened to burn the houses along the perimeter. One year the fire swept passed our tree fort and crept into Ray Delago's backyard on Woodlawn Drive, nearly engulfing his house before it was extinguished by Eddie Poleska, Leonard Semple, Jim Carew, and other members of the Mundelein Volunteer Fire Department. Years later, my brother, John, confessed that he and his friends had started those grass fires.

I often tagged along with my brothers and some of the neighbor kids and fished Diamond Lake during the summer months. We collected worms from the backyard and scraps of stale Wonder bread from my mother and used them for bait. With our make-shift collection of bamboo poles, cheap rods and reels, and tackle thrown into old cigar boxes, we marched along Prairie Street. We crossed down to the lake at Suicide Hill. Occasionally, we stopped to eat whatever wild raspberries we could find and catch whatever grasshoppers we could outsmart along the narrow, soggy path of cattails that lined the shore. We dipped our bobbered lines in the clear water among the lily pads and spawning beds, and lifted out countless Bluegill, Sunfish, Yellow Perch, and Crappie, often hauling in more than we cared to take home, gut, or clean. We usually left the extras up on the banks. Fishing from shore on an overstocked lake doesn't require much skill or patience, which is why we engaged in it for hours nearly every day. It was a rare treat to catch Large Mouth Bass who seemed to find the grasshoppers irresistible. My brother, John, had the unofficial record for many years for a Large Mouth Bass caught on Diamond Lake, 8.5 lbs., 14". He snagged it at dusk on a silver spoon a few feet from shore while test-casting his new reel behind Danny Walker's house. It was the biggest fish I had ever seen.

In summer we often left the house in the morning and didn't return until Leo delivered our afternoon papers. When I completed my routes I'd have a little dinner, try to avoid my mother if she'd been drinking, and go back outside until the street lights came on. We rode our bikes everywhere, to Ed's beach (on the site where the Ray Brothers' Resort once stood), or uptown, or across town. No one wore bike helmets, and we didn't need to lock our bikes. We hitchhiked anywhere we wanted to go if it was too far to pedal. One day in high school, John Wegenar and I played hooky and hitch-hiked to and from the Field Museum in Chicago. We seldom checked-in at home but our parents didn't worry that they couldn't reach us all day. We drank from Aunt Ida's garden hose in between innings of our wiffle ball games, and slapped together our own lunches—sandwiches made from white bread and bologna, and chased it down with pitchers of Kool-Aid we made with heaping cupfuls of sugar. We built forts and go-karts and dared each other to jump off of garage roofs. We raced our bikes through the thick fog of mosquito insecticide that blasted out of a cannon on the back of the public works truck that rumbled down the street at twilight. We camped out in the back yard with our friends and prowled the neighborhood with flashlights in the middle of the night in search of other kids camping out, hopefully girls. No matter how close we were to the house, sleeping outside in the back yard in a tent with our friends always seemed like complete wilderness with the strumming of crickets surrounding us and the cries of the Soo Line train whistle beckoning in the distance.

In the mid-1960's cars didn't have air conditioning, most didn't have seat belts, let alone air bags, and child car seats had not yet been invented. We tried out for little league baseball and not everyone made the team.

We learned to deal with disappointment. No one cried because they didn't make the team. Medicine bottles didn't have child-resistant lids and temper-evident packaging was unnecessary. We watched one of four broadcast television stations in fuzzy black-and-white when we *had* a television. We made our own entertainment. I put on plays and variety shows (starring me, of course) in the back yard or in Mark Rohling's basement and I charged the neighborhood kids and their parents admission. In the evening we caught "lightning bugs" and put them in Mayonnaise jars. We poked holes in the metal lid (so they could breathe) and threw in a few twigs and leaves to make them feel at home. They were all dead by morning. The reeds along the lake at Suicide Hill became our cover when we decided during our teenage years to take up smoking cigarettes.

Our year was marked by four main events: the last day of school in spring; the first day of school in the fall; the carnival over the 4th of July; and Christmas, when we were thrilled to receive *one* gift each and a stocking full of fruit and nuts. There were no drug dealers, no gangs, no crime. No one was abducted (although we had a scare when Judy Crop and Karen Roy once accidentally locked themselves in the school over the weekend), and no one died. And we never, ever locked our doors at night. But over time, all this changed.

Mundelein's population nearly doubled in the eighteen years that I lived there, from 7,700 in the 1960 census to 14,400 in the mid-seventies. It was a quiet town so far on the outskirts of Chicago that it wasn't even considered a suburb. It was rural, the terminus of the North Shore Interurban Electric Train Line. It was too small to be called modest and too blue-collar to be called middle-class, and it rarely made the news.

It consisted of only a handful of predominant subdivisions: Diamond Lake and West Shore Park, both unincorporated areas that surrounded the lake on the south end of town; North Shore Park and Hawthorn Hills, my stomping ground; Uptown, Holcomb, Fairhaven, Bonniebrook, and the posh Loch Lomond, which surrounded a man-made lake by the same name on the very north end of town.

You could travel less than a mile in any direction from the center of town (Rouse's Service Station at the corner of Hawley and Lake Streets) and be among cornfields. I used to walk along Hawley Street to Gilmer Road and as far as Fairfield Road when I hitch-hiked to a girlfriend's house near the town of Wauconda during the summer of 1970. That walk to Teri Baker's house made such an impression on me that it inspired me to write my first poem. I was fifteen and have never forgotten it. Reciting it always brings me back—

> Walking on the roadside on cloudless summer days
> The air is thick, the afternoon is lost among the haze.
> Far beyond the town-line where from the fields abound
> Stalks of green their tassels seen now that August has come 'round.
> The Redwing on the wire sends a warning loud and clear
> And flashes forth his epaulettes to the stranger drawing near.
> Shadows long, late afternoon, the sky is set ablaze,
> Walking on the roadside on cloudless summer days.

The well-to-do folks lived in Loch Lomond, Fairhaven, and the north side of town. We lived on the south side and were only slightly better-off than the Mexican families of the Diamond Lake neighborhoods.

There were no such things as shopping malls in the 1960's. Any shopping we did was in town. The nearest movie theater was in Libertyville. The nearest major department store, Sears, was in Waukegan about twenty miles away. So was the nearest McDonald's. Sometimes my parents treated us to McDonald's before visiting Aunt Sarah and Uncle Jack. We each were allowed to get a hamburger for nineteen cents but had to share an order of french fries and a vanilla malt among all of us.

We shopped "uptown" at a run-down row of stores next to the fire department on Seymour Street, across from Krackelaur Park. It had just about everything you could possibly need or want. Piggly Wiggly Super Market was the largest store. It's where my mother did her weekly grocery shopping, unless my father was on strike, as he always was every four years when his union contract expired. Then we lived on food stamps. My mother, who grew up during the Great Depression, was so ashamed of having to rely on food stamps that she insisted my father drive her to a supermarket in Libertyville or Waukegan where no one knew us. That way, she did not have to suffer the indignity and embarrassment of broadcasting that we couldn't afford to buy something as essential as food. Next to "The Pig" was May's Drugstore where my mother worked briefly as a cashier when my father was on strike. Top Notch Donut Shop, The Hobby Hut, a barber shop, Morrison's Laundromat, and Grant's rounded out the businesses at the strip mall.

Grant's was a general merchandise store and in May, 1967, the scene of my one and only childhood crime. I wanted to buy a striped tee-shirt I had seen there on a recent visit with my mother. It was on sale for $1.35. I rode my bike uptown and walked into the store with my paper route money tucked into my pocket, only to discover that the sale was over. The shirt now had a price tag of $1.50. I didn't have $1.50. I saw some other shirts nearby that were marked down to $1.35. I carefully switched the price tags. A store clerk observed me and grabbed me by the back of my collar when I went to purchase it at the register. She dragged me into the backroom and called the police. Officer Madole, who lived in North Shore Park on Lincoln and Woodlawn and whose newspaper I delivered every day, escorted me out to his squad car. He put my bike in the trunk of his cruiser and drove me two blocks to the police station. He called my parents. My father came to pick me up and leered at me down the hall as I waited on a chair. He had an extended conversation with officer Madole.

I put my head down as he walked up to me. "You broke your mother's heart," he said, "now, get on your bike and get home!"

When I walked into the kitchen my mother was crying. She wouldn't even look at me. I never felt so ashamed in my life and I ran past her. I went to my room and cried into my pillow. My mother and I never spoke of the incident.

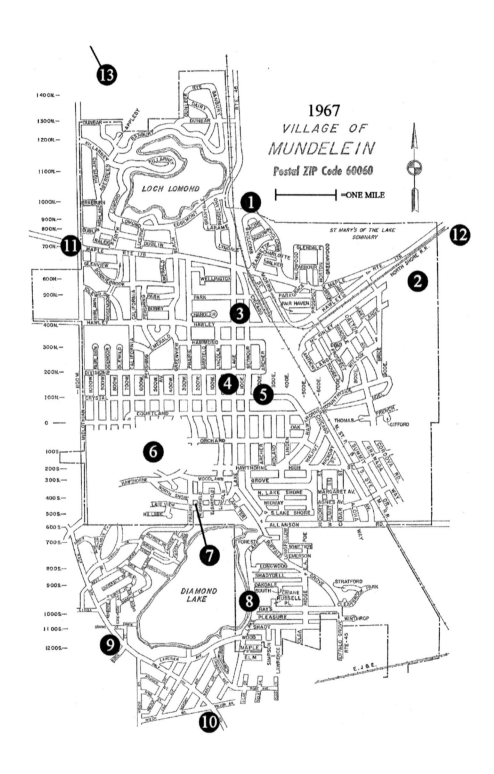

1967
VILLAGE OF
MUNDELEIN
Postal ZIP Code 60060

⊢━━━━━━⊣ =ONE MILE

1967 Mundelein Map Key:

1. Hole in the fence where we entered Saint Mary of the Lake Seminary
2. Carmel High School for Boys
3. Rouse's Standard Oil Station
4. Santa Maria del Popolo School
5. Piggly Wiggly Supermarket
6. The Cowpath
7. Our house at 409 South Prairie Avenue
8. The Happy Hollow
9. The Irish Mill
10. Ed's Highland Gas Station
11. The Hiawatha Trail (Rt. 176) site of Mechanics Grove settlement
12. The Dairy Dream
13. Fort Hill, where 18th century French fur trappers traded with the local Indians

Map from The Bell Telephone Company Yellow Pages. Published by R.R. Donnelly, Chicago Illinois, 1967.—*Courtesy of Libertyville Public Library*

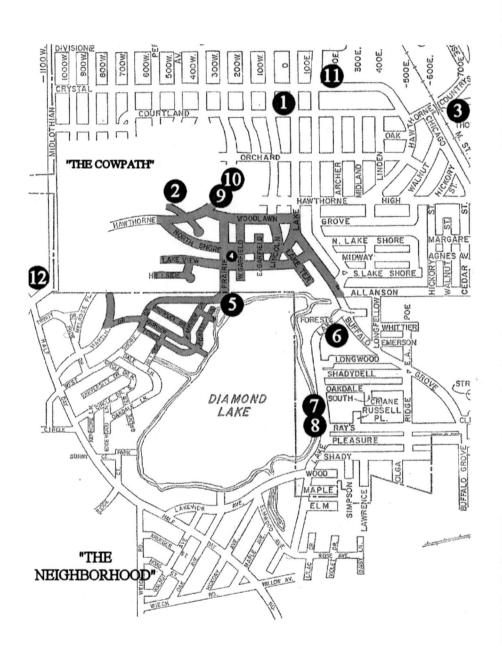

"The Neighborhood" Map Key:

1. Santa Maria del Popolo Church & School
2. Hobo Jungle
3. Little League Baseball Fields (current site of the Fort Hill Heritage Museum)
4. Our block
5. Suicide Hill
6. Diamond Lake Supermarket and Bowling Alley
7. The Happy Hollow and Bud's Bike and Mower Shop
8. Ed's Beach (formerly the Ray Brothers Resort)
9. Our tree fort
10. Skating pond and Washington Grade School
11. Strip mall containing: Morrison's Laundromat, "The Pig," May's Drug, The Hobby Hut, Top Notch Donut Shop, a barber shop, and Grants
12. Quigg's Apple Orchard (the western edge of town)

Grey Streets: extent of The O'Donnell Brothers paper route dynasty

Map from The Bell Telephone Company Yellow Pages. Published by R.R. Donnelly, Chicago Illinois, 1967.—*Courtesy of Libertyville Public Library*

CHAPTER 27

♄

MY CATHOLIC PLAYGROUND

W HEN MY VILLAGE WAS MUCH younger I used to look out my sisters' bedroom window across the two miles of village rooftops and see the seminary smokestack and Chapel steeple rise above the northern limits of town.

Cardinal Mundelein designed his institution to be a completely self-contained community. Although these self-sufficiencies began to decline in the 1960's as the student enrollment decreased, the seminary once boasted a fully functional farm with orchards, livestock, milking barns, and chicken coops. Corn, potatoes, and grain for the students and faculty were grown on land which became occupied by Carmel Catholic High School in 1963. The seminary had its own infirmary and barber shop. They drew electricity from their own power plants, and water from their own wells. They had their own garbage dump and wastewater treatment facility. Greenhouses were staffed by as many as forty-five gardeners. Groundskeepers put out some 50,000 plants each spring and tended the numerous flowerbeds, lawns, and ornamental gardens.[84] Mundelein had hand-picked famed Chicago arborist William O'Connell as his first Superintendent of Grounds. O'Connell was in charge of Lincoln Park in Chicago and was instrumental in the design and landscape construction of the city's Jackson Park for the World's Columbian Exposition in 1893. To this day, the grounds crew at the seminary excavates the occasional shoe—suctioned off the foot of some unfortunate pilgrim in the aftermath of the rains during the Eucharistic

Congress of 1926. Arrowheads and pieces of pottery discarded by the first settlers are also unearthed.

On a few occasions during my years in grade school, I accompanied some mischievous classmates from Holcomb subdivision, which bordered the seminary, and we stole onto the school grounds through a hole in a chain-link fence. We ran low along the footpaths and through the thick undergrowth among the oaks. One of us carried a crow bar. We kept a look-out for the patrolling security guard as we searched for an accessible manhole cover. Flipping one open, we scampered down the iron rails and ran through the catacomb of steam tunnels beneath the campus. We acted like secret agents embarking on a dangerous covert mission, the lead spy signaling back to the others to stop whenever we heard a noise ahead—banging pipes or the sound of a generator. We paused and held our breath before tiptoeing on. It was dark and dirty and I made sure to keep up with the others as we darted down the dimly lit corridors. My heart pounded for fear that we might get caught. We never knew where we might end up: in the basement of a building, in the woods, or on the meticulously manicured campus grounds. We never were able to navigate our way through the subterranean maze as far as the Cardinal's residence, although we tried.

In winter, the seminarians operated a toboggan run in the ravine south of the main campus. We didn't own a toboggan but some of my Lutheran friends did and I used my Catholic influence to get us in.

Curiously, there is little evidence mentioning that the Cardinal had quietly built a championship 27-hole golf course behind his villa. But I know it to be true. I had been chased across it more than once by security guards. The archdiocese has leased the links since 1985 operating under the name Pine Meadows Golf Course. A year after it opened it was voted the "best public golf course in the country."[85] Year after year it continues to rank among the top fifty public courses in the U.S.

The gymnasium located on the southeast end of Principle Boulevard was another building I became familiar with. It contained a full size basketball court and an indoor pool. While I was in the sixth grade, the use of the pool was a secret privilege shared among the altar boys of my parish. There was also a bowling alley with manual Brunswick pin-setting machines in the basement where my friends and I spent time competing against seminarians during my high school years. It is believed that those lanes are the last of their kind in existence.[86] I also stole away with my friends to the cupola atop the residence hall where we smoked cigarettes and told exaggerated tales of sexual conquests with the girls we dated.

The Benedictine Chapel of Perpetual Adoration sits on the southeast side of Cardinal Mundelein's Seminary, although apart from it. Its architecture is patterned after St. Paul Outside-of-the-Walls, the ancient Roman patriarchal basilica founded by Roman Emperor Constantine I, and the historical resting place of St. Paul the Apostle.[87] The replica contains giant stained glass windows and multiple marble pillars, each unique and imported from all over the world. Within the side chapels are religious relics Mundelein "collected," donations from various churches throughout Europe. I remember one relic in particular that I marveled at whenever I visited; encased in a small glass square, and surrounded by an opulent gold-leaf Rococo style frame, was a tiny sliver of wood said to be from Christ's Crown of Thorns.

We always referred to the Benedictine Chapel of Perpetual Adoration simply as the Benedictine Convent. A continuous vigil of prayer began there on the feast of Corpus Christi, June 7th, 1928, by 33 devoted women of the Benedictine Sisters of Perpetual Adoration. The sisters not only directed constant prayer to the elaborate ostensorium exposed on the altar, but supported themselves by making altar breads for parishes across the country and by growing their own food in their extensive gardens and orchards. Many times the demands of their work schedule meant sacrificing what little free time they had and they often worked very late into the night. Their 1950 house chronicle contains the notation, "we do not even have time to mend our clothes."[88] Their impressive liturgical adoration before the exposed Blessed Sacrament continued unbroken twenty-four hours a day for fifty years. In 1978 their dwindling numbers forced them to take their meager possessions, including the crown of thorns relic, and consolidate their ranks to a chapel in Clyde, Missouri. The Conventual Franciscan Friars took possession of the facility at that time and changed the name to Marytown, carrying on the tradition of perpetual adoration.[89]

While I attended Carmel High School for Boys, I befriended Jim Ray, a seminary student who taught class at the adjoining Carmel High School for Girls. As part of his obligation to the seminary, he was required to serve Mass at the Benedictine Convent. I remembered a few of the skills from my disastrous days as an altar boy and periodically served Sunday Mass with him. We became close friends and remained so throughout my high school years and beyond. I frequently visited him at his residence at the seminary, occasionally staying overnight in his dorm and hanging out with him and his classmates. He taught me how to play guitar. The first song he taught me was *Today While the Blossoms Still Cling to the Vine*, a venerable folkie favorite and early 60's hit by The New Christy Minstrel's. I played it over, and over, and over. *Everyone* within earshot was grateful when I eventually learned a new song. I was delighted to discover that playing guitar attracted plenty of attention from girls. I attended Father Jim's Ordination into the Priesthood at the Immaculate Conception Chapel in May of 1975, and went to his first Mass. I came to know his entire family and he eventually became good friends with mine. He con-celebrated at my wedding, baptized my son, Rory, officiated at the weddings of my sister, Sheila, and my brother, Rodger, and attended numerous family events, weddings, wakes, and funerals.

1967 Mundelein Vikings Little League Football Team. I am seated in the front row far left. Joe Fenwick seated second row, third from left. Billy Schafernak seated third row, second from left.

Three brothers. *l to r:* Rodger, me, and Jay with my godfather and great-uncle, Eddie Boyle, on the step outside the Lake County Gardens house, 1958.

My best Kenny Holtzman impersonation in the backyard of the 409 house. Still wearing my school uniform and sporting a hand-me-down 1940's "lefty" mitt—the only one in the neighborhood.

1960-1961

My kindergarten photo, St. Andrew Lutheran Church, Mundelein. My mother warned me not to smile for the Protestants. "Don't let them see your rotten teeth," she instructed.

Dad and me at home upon my graduation from 8th grade from Santa Maria del Popolo School, Mundelein. June, 1969.

Photo taken in October, 1975, in the backyard of the 409 house for my parents' surprise 25th wedding anniversary party. Front row, *l to r:* Tisha (14), Daser (12), and Sheila (18). Back row, *l to r:* me (20), Maureen (17), Rodger (22), and Jay (23).

My parents wedding photo, November 1950, Bayonne, New Jersey.

Twenty-five years later at their surprise wedding anniversary party at the 409 house in Mundelein. My father providing a rare look at his missing fingers on his left hand. Brian Mary Cissie Rodgers seated in background.

The house at 409 South Prairie, Mundelein, as it appeared in 2008.

Rodger and me outside the 409 house the winter after we moved in, January 1960. My leg cast was removed a few weeks before.

CHAPTER 28

✿

THE ATLAS & THE ISLES OF LANGERHANS

M Y FATHER'S FREQUENT, OFTEN COMICAL, and always entertaining stories of his childhood sent my imagination reeling like no adventure book ever could. We didn't have many books when I was growing up, and we had little access to them. The Fremont Township Library, such as it was, was located in an old storefront owned by the Rouses on the other end of town and too far away to walk. Certainly my parents never read adventure stories such as *Br'er Rabbit, Robinson Crusoe,* or the *Hardy Boys* series to us. We were too poor to afford to buy books and my parents were too busy to read them. I don't recall a single instance when they read to any of us. The "read to your children every day" philosophy of parental education, as far as I know, did not exist in my formative years. I do remember a few Golden Books scattered about the house, well-worn and heavily vandalized with childhood graffiti in crayon and pencil. As we grew older, we had a free daily newspaper—a perk of the job my brothers and I received for being paper route delivery boys. At about the same time we had periodic editions of *Boys Life* magazine during our Cub Scout years and read used copies of *Highlights* and *Life* Magazine, which my mother obtained second-hand from the neighbors.

In grade school, our scholastic readers through the fourth grade were a series of books called David and Ann. These were the Catholicized versions of the more popular Dick and Jane books used in the public school system. David and Ann chronicled the lives of two perfect children, their perfect parents, and their wholesome Catholic family in their all-American hometown during the 1950's. That was about the extent of my literary training.

I was given a book report assignment by my sixth grade teacher, Mrs. Hilliard. I browsed the meager school library shelves for the shortest book that was of interest to me. I selected *The Day Lincoln Was Shot* by Jim Bishop. It chronicled an hour-by-hour account of Abraham Lincoln's last day as president. I was completely absorbed by the details and the tension that built with each chapter, knowing the inevitable climax. Thus began my life-long obsession with our nation's sixteenth President. Over the decades I have read countless biographies on nearly every aspect of the man's life and have collected dozens of books, mostly first editions, by the foremost authors and authorities on the subject. I have visited many Lincoln sites, some multiple times, and continue to read everything I can about his genius. I feel that I know him like a true friend and better than I know anyone else.

Among the many attributes I inherited from my father was a love for geography. He had an over-sized Rand & McNally World Atlas that he acquired shortly after the war. It was obviously an expensive, deluxe edition with its embossed blue linen cover and pages gilded in silver along the edges. I used to wrestle it down from the shelf, lay it on the floor and kneel over it as I slowly and carefully turned the pages so as not to damage them. I spent many hours studying the colorful and amazingly detailed maps of the continents, countries, islands, and oceans. On occasion my father joined me, showing me the places he had been—complete with stories and commentary. He engaged me in a game of "can you find"—a precursor to "Where's Waldo"—where we took turns finding obscure places on different maps, determining how long it took the other to locate them. Little did I realize that it would lead to a life-long curiosity for maps. My love for maps, old maps in particular, has never waned. Whenever I see one on display in a public building, a restaurant, or in someone's home, I am immediately drawn into it. I derive great pleasure from studying them and become quickly immersed in their detail and storytelling. They offer glimpses into history that, for me, are far more vivid and more interesting than mere printed words.

In high school, I challenged my father to a round of "can you find" one evening when he returned home from work. In an effort to stump him completely, I perused the atlas thoughtfully for several minutes, concentrating on a map of the South Pacific and haughtily asked: "can you find the Isles of Langerhans?" I turned the book around and set it on my father's lap. He put on his reading glasses and began his search. He muttered under his breath as he drew the book closer. Adjusting the angle of his bifocals, he traced the map carefully with his finger. After a long, long while he sighed in frustration and handed the book back to me. "No." he said tersely. "And I never 'heared' of it neither."

I laughed. "That's because it isn't on any map. It's a cluster of cells in your pancreas that secrete insulin!" I told him. "I learned that today in biology class."

He sneered, "Oh! Aren't you the clever *amathon?*"

When I was in the seventh grade, we were given an assignment to make a map of our neighborhood. It was one of the few times I actually looked forward to—and completed—my homework. The neighborhood, I thought? That's lame. Why stop at the neighborhood? I ended up creating a street map of the entire town. It required several loose-leaf pages of notebook paper taped together. I used the street map of Mundelein that was published in the front section of the Yellow Pages of the phone directory as my guide and I labeled every street, lake, creek bed, and park. What I failed to do however, was mark where my house was located. For all of my effort, Sister Ann Dorothy gave me a C+ for not following instructions. The experience of making that map has stayed with me all these years. Although the town has more than doubled in size since I was in the fifth grade, and the newer neighborhoods with their winding streets of unfamiliar names are not part of my childhood memory, I can still make my way through the myriad of tiny, tree-lined streets that *were* on the map of my town in 1965 and recall every one by name.

CHAPTER 29

❧

THE STOCKADE

THE STAIRCASE LEADING TO THE second floor at the Mundelein house had a wrought iron railing that ran from just below the ceiling on the first floor down to the landing. It was through its grate that I sat and watched the proceedings of my parents' hooleys unfold, a window into my future as well as a portal into my past. The bars of the decorative railing contained a geometric design, the center of which was just large enough to squeeze my head through, as I was apt do on a regular basis out of boredom. Then I turned ten and suddenly the opening was no longer wide enough to squeeze my head out—my ears got in the way. I discovered this problem one sunny summer day while making my way down the stairs and gingerly rocked back and forth, tilting my head in every possible angle to extricate myself as my mother sat in the parlor chair laughing uncontrollably. This attracted the attention of several of my siblings who stood in the parlor and watched in utter fascination as I tried repeatedly to free my noggin from the self-inflicted stockade. They were all very amused by my stupidity—a predicament which only made me angrier the harder they laughed. My mother finally tried to pull me out. She stood behind me and tugged on my shoulders. But there was no room for my ears to pass back through the iron bars, and my head was now red, swollen, and tender. After several attempts, alternated with fits of her patented hoarse and whispery laugh, she finally gave up. "You'll have to wait 'til your father gets home," she resigned.

"But he won't be home for another couple of hours!" I moaned.

"Yeah, I don't know what else to do, Kev," she said. "I could call the fire department, I suppose. They can probably get you out." She paused, looked at me sympathetically, and then fell to her knees laughing.

"Don't call the fire department," I ordered. I didn't know whether to laugh with her or cry out of frustration.

"Only you could do something this idiotic. You'll just have to wait until your father gets home," she said.

She arose and went about her business. Every time she walked through the parlor she looked at me, shook her head, and giggled. I was in a very awkward and uncomfortable position—too high to sit and too crouched to stand. I had to kneel on the wooden stairs. My mother brought me a few pillows to ease my discomfort. This only added to everyone's amusement.

At long last, my father pulled into the driveway. My mother and all my siblings met him in the kitchen by the back door. I could hear her whispering to him while she tried to stifle her laughter. There was no response from my father.

He slowly walked into the dining room and sat down at the table to remove his work shoes.

I waved my hands through the bars. "Hi Dad," I said contritely. He looked up at me quizzically, tilting his head like a dog that just heard a new sound. Then he shook his head in disgust. He lit a cigarette and casually leafed through the mail my mother left for him on the dining room table. Everyone stood around him anticipating what he might do or say.

"Tea please, Teresa," he sighed. My mother stepped into the kitchen to prepare his "cuppa." A few minutes later my father went into the kitchen and returned with a large can of Crisco shortening under his arm. He stood on the stairs behind me, opened up the can of lard, and unsympathetically slathered it all over my cheeks, neck, and ears. When he felt that he had me greased up sufficiently, he leaned over the railing and pushed my head through the bars. I groaned in pain as my ears squeezed through the wrought iron. Once freed, my father looked at me with a scowl. "*Amathon*," he muttered.

CHAPTER 30

✧

CATHOLICS AND PUBLICS

UP TO THE FOURTH GRADE I thought there were only two religions: Catholic and Public. It made perfect sense; Catholic kids went to Catholic School, and I used to see all the same faces at Mass on Sunday as I did at school during the week. I never saw the Public School kids at Mass; ergo, they must be Publics. There were lots of Public Churches scattered around town, but only one Catholic Church—and it was the biggest, located on prime real estate, occupying *both* sides of the main drag, Lake Street, smack-dab in the middle of town. And we had a very impressive sounding name, too—Santa Maria del Popolo (Saint Mary of the People).

There were many distinctions, as separatist and elitist as they were, that led me to believe that we Catholics must really be special:

We wore uniforms to school. Publics did not.

We knew Latin. Publics did not.

We went to Confession. Publics did not.

We had Holy Days of Obligation. Publics did not. These were special days on the Catholic calendar when we did not have to attend school, but had to attend Mass. So, my brothers and I walked to church just like on any other day and passed Washington School enroute and taunted the kids through their classroom windows.

We ate fish on Fridays. Publics did not. Every Friday after my mother came home from the Piggly Wiggly, she fixed the same thing for dinner:

213

fish sticks and tater tots. I don't know how old I was before I realized that *Mrs. Paul's* wasn't actually a species of fish—or that tater tots were not the young offspring of full grown "adult" potatoes.

We were taught early on that as Roman Catholics we *were* special—by the Priests, by the BVM's (Sisters of the Blessed Virgin Mary), and by the few Catholic lay (non-clergy) teachers, most of whom were old and hobbled through the halls. Certainly we were more special than any non-Catholics. We were taught that Catholics practically invented religion—Christianity to be sure, and everybody else? They were Johnny-come-latelys. All the Catholic parents tolerated The Publics who, by and large, were decent enough folks. After all, God loved them too, just not as much as he loved Catholics.

There's an old joke about a man who died and met St. Peter at the Pearly Gates. St. Peter offered to show the man around heaven and pointed out that the Methodists were over on the cloud banks to the South, and the valley to the East contained the Jews, and the Muslims were all located on the plains to the West. When they came upon a great brick wall fifty feet high, St. Peter pointed out that that was where he kept the Catholics. When the man inquired why the Catholics were kept behind a fifty foot wall, St. Peter whispered, "because they like to think they are the only ones up here."

We had no African Americans in our town but there were plenty of Mexicans. They were all poor and lived in run-down little houses on the west side of Diamond Lake. They couldn't be as bad as my father made them out to be. They were, after all, Catholic. I was taught that in the order of things, race came first, then religion, then nationality.

Then there were the Jews. We didn't know any, but my father spoke of them often. I don't think there were any in our village while I was growing up. Not surprising when you think about it—a town founded largely by German immigrants, named after an imposing Roman Catholic cardinal of German ancestry, and dominated by the seminary's Catholic presence. I thought Jews existed only on television. I can't recall how many times my father saw someone on TV and said, "A Jew," and shook his head in disapproval. I didn't know what that meant but if my father disapproved, it couldn't be good. According to him, Jews owned television, controlled the

media, and ruined just about every other industry. They were the source
of all that was wrong with the world. That, and they all had noses bigger
than everybody else. He used to recite a racist little rhyme:

"The Lord called on Moses and said all Jews will have big noses
Except for Aaron, he'll have a square one
And Simon Peter will have a parking meter"

It's horrible that I even remember that—but I heard it enough
times. I never understood why my father said it, for his own nose was
his most "outstanding feature." Likewise, I don't know what caused my
father to become such a bigot and why he had such a dislike for Jews
in particular.

I was oblivious to the fact that we Catholics were a minority in our town,
scorned and ridiculed by the parents of our public friends. As I grew older I
realized that there was another name for Publics, one that my father spoke
of disparagingly—Protestants.

Catholic brainwashing began very early on. There was a very real concerted
effort to protect Catholic children from outside influences. I remember reciting
the Mass in Latin. English wasn't introduced until the 2nd Vatican Council
convened in 1962-65, when Pope John XXIII stated "it's time we opened up
the windows of the Church to let in some fresh air," and sweeping changes
were made in an effort to modernize the church and make it more meaningful
and relevant.

In 1960, within the first few days of the first grade, Sister Roberta
Clare handed out sweet-smelling mimeographed pages containing 100
questions we needed to answer correctly in preparation for receiving our
First Holy Communion, which was still two years away. It was intense. The
questions and answers were drilled into me with such regularity that I can
still remember them verbatim nearly five decades later:

Q: Who made you?
A: God made me.

Q: Why did God make you?
A: To love and serve him.

Q: How did God make you?
A: God made me in his own image and likeness.

Q: Who is Jesus Christ?
A: The only begotten Son of the Father.

Q: Why did Christ die?
A: To save man from sin and he so saved the world . . .

Most of it I didn't understand but I knew that I had better answer them correctly when the time came—or else! Or else what? I didn't know, and I surely didn't want to find out.

As we grew older, and presumably more intelligent and intuitive, the installation of Catholic morals and guilt became more subtle, but just as effective. We were not allowed to attend "mixed" parties prior to high school; we were not taught theories of evolution, or educated about sex. In fact, even uttering the word "sex" was considered taboo. When I was about twelve, and finally learned the process of procreation, I was appalled. There was no way my Catholic God invented *that*, or approved of such a disgusting thing. It took me a long time to accept the concept and even longer to erase the heinous visual of my parents engaged in such activity.

SMdP. These were the initials of our parish that appeared on every schoolboy's blue shirt and every schoolgirl's white blouse and navy blue cardigan sweater. It was embroidered in white thread onto a navy blue triangular patch just above the left breast pocket. It stood for Santa Maria del Popolo but it was widely ridiculed by the Publics as "so many dumb Pollocks," unless your name ended in "ski" or "wcz," then it stood for "so many dumb people." My family used to cleverly state that it stood for Sheila, Maureen, Daser, and Patricia.

We were required to wear our uniforms to school every day. In addition to the light blue, long-sleeved shirt (short sleeves were allowed only after April 1st), boys had to wear navy blue pants, black dress shoes, and a navy blue bow tie. Girls wore a white blouse with a Peter Pan collar, a blue plaid pleated skirt worn to the middle of the knee, white anklets (called bobby-socks), black patent-leather shoes, and a navy blue tam (for church). Females were not allowed to enter church unless they wore a dress or skirt and had their head covered. The only time you were excused from wearing the school uniform was if you belonged to the Boy Scouts or Girl Scouts. Then you were allowed to wear your scout uniform once a month.

Our school included grades 1-8, each with multiple classrooms. Class sizes ranged from forty to fifty students. We had no gymnasium, no sports of any kind, no band, no school choir, no after school intramural activities, no free bus service, and no lunchroom. We brought our lunches to school in paper bags or metal lunchboxes (mine was shaped like a school bus and had Donald Duck and his nephews, Hughie, Dewey, and Louie printed on the side, waving happily from the bus windows).

School tuition was $55 per student, per semester. Discounts were given to families with multiple students. At one point, my five siblings and I all attended Santa Maria at the same time. But that wasn't unusual; several families had that many, or more, attending at once—the Werners, the Bernards, the Weidners, the Sobons, the Cantwells, the Kristans. We *were* Catholics, after all.

Our curriculum consisted of: religion, reading, writing, and 'rithmatic; religion, spelling, geography, religion, civics, basic science, and, as I later learned through my own intensive personal pursuits, revisionist history. Did I mention religion?

Since the school had no lunchroom or cafeteria, we ate our lunches at our desks. Hundreds of small cartons of milk were brought in daily by Mr. Rouse, who stored them in stackable trays in the basement. The cost of milk, 50¢ a month for white and 55¢ a month for chocolate, was well beyond what my parents could afford, and we went without. The only time we were given a complimentary half-pint carton of milk is if a paying student was absent. My brother, Rodger, devised a way to make sure he received a carton of milk nearly every day. He approached our new principal, Sister Grace Henneberry, who replaced the wicked sister Mary Oona, and volunteered to deliver the trays of milk cartons to each classroom in his grade in exchange for one leftover carton of chocolate milk if no one claimed it. Sister Grace agreed. It left a lasting impression on the endearing nun. Many years later, at Rodger's wedding, the retired principal, who had become a friend of the family, arrived at the reception hall at the Mundelein Holiday Inn, walked up to the bridal table during dinner and firmly set a carton of chocolate milk in front of the groom.

By the time I reached the fourth grade I had outgrown my Disney lunch box and carried my lunch in a brown paper bag. My mother prepared all the daily school lunches in her cramped little kitchen after my father went to work and while my brother and I were delivering our morning newspapers. She had a system. She laid out all the bread on top of separate pieces of waxed paper wherever she could find a level surface. She went around the room, spread on the mustard, lunchmeat, maybe some Velveeta, and slapped a piece of bread on top, wrapped them in the waxed paper and stuffed them into the erected lunch bags along the edge of the Formica counter. If there were cookies or fruit from the previous Friday evening's grocery store run, she threw that in too. She wrote our names on each bag with a magic marker and we plucked the bags from the counter as we hurried out the door. On more than one occasion I eagerly unfolded the wax paper at my desk only to find two pieces of bread inside with nothing in between. I fumed at the thought that one of my siblings was enjoying a double helping of pimento loaf with cheese, while I was choking down a mustard sandwich on Wonder bread—with no milk to wash it down.

After lunch we went outside for thirty minutes—no matter what the weather. We had no playground equipment, or benches, or organized games. We simply stood around on the asphalt in the parking lot of the Church, or in the dusty baseball field across the street from the Convent. The girls played hop-scotch or jumped rope; the boys engaged in a rough house game of "keep away"—a cross between rugby and nothing else. Two teams tried to keep a tennis ball away from each other by running, passing, and catching the ball. Once the holder was tackled by the other team, he had to turn the ball over. There were no goals, no points, no scoring. I saw no point to it at all and rarely participated. I mostly wandered around the lot singing to myself.

Catholic grade school was, above all, regimented. Discipline was strictly enforced and I had my knuckles rapped with the edge of a ruler more times than I can count. Every priest, nun, and lay teacher had a reputation among the students. Some were nice and approachable, others you avoided at all costs. Sister Ann Dorothy, my fifth *and* seventh grade teacher, was kind and fair, although she wouldn't let me go out to the parking lot at recess with everyone else. When Sister Ann Dorothy discovered I possessed a modest amount of artistic talent, she insisted that I stay in the classroom after lunch and draw illustrations on the chalk board using special "artist's chalk" she purchased just for me. Each week I had to fill a twelve foot length of the chalkboard that ran along the side of the classroom, with colorful scenes from the Bible and I had to explain to the class my interpretations. When we returned to class the following Monday, the board had been washed clean and I had to start all over again. This continued for several weeks until the artist's chalk "mysteriously disappeared" and I was back on the playground practicing the latest Beatles songs that I learned from listening to my mother's radio while doing dishes the night before.

CHAPTER 31

༄

THE DAY SISTER SYLVESTER FELL TO EARTH

O N THE OPPOSITE END OF the spectrum from sister Ann Dorothy was Sister Sylvester, whom I had for seventh grade Algebra. She was big, really big! She had a crooked bill for a nose with a wart on the end of it, and jagged, yellow teeth. When she spoke, she expectorated and she sounded like the Wicked Witch of the West from "The Wizard of Oz." Mostly, she was just a mean and frustrated old woman. "I was terrified of Sister Sylvester because as she taught, she paced between the rows of desks and always managed to come up from behind me and whack me on the back of the head with her algebra book if I didn't know the correct answer to a math question," I told Sister Grace Henneberry years later. "I didn't get algebra, but I did get hit on the back of the head several times a week." Sister Grace smiled and softly touched my arm.

"Kevin," she replied, "we were *all* terrified of Sister Sylvester!"

"You're going to learn algebra, Mr. O'Donnell, if I have to beat it into you!" Sylvester insisted. No matter how many times she beat me, I still didn't get algebra. But I did get even and launched my diabolical plan to pay back Sister Sylvester for all the abuse I took.

The old nun addressed the class from the lectern at the front of the room with her hands grasping onto the front of the table where she placed her teaching manual, books, and notes. With her hands on top of the lectern and her foot braced upon the base, she gently rocked the heavy oak dais front to back as she taught. One day during recess, I loosened the wing nut that adjusted the pitch of the table top. When she returned for afternoon class, she put her considerable weight onto the lectern as usual. She and her books went sailing over the top of it, taking out the first four desks in the row. It looked like a train derailment. She broke her fall by plunging onto Karen Altergott's desk as the wooden structure toppled to the floor.

On another occasion, during lunchtime recess, I surreptitiously placed the contents of an entire box of thumb tacks on the seat of her chair behind her desk. All the pins were facing strategically upward. After lunch, she sat down at the desk to prepare her next lesson. I fully expected her to spring off the chair with 50 or so thumb tacks stuck into her backside—but she never flinched. I was awestruck. Just how many layers of clothing *do* these nuns wear? When she finally stood up and faced the chalkboard the round, shiny tack heads stood out like a star field against a black sky. She paced back and forth as she wrote on the chalkboard in perfect cursive handwriting. The class stifled their laughter and everyone looked around the room to see who could be responsible for such a prank. The tacks eventually lost their grip, and one-by-one dropped from her habit and bounced across the linoleum floor. We were all quite entertained. Sister Sylvester never realized they were even there—or at least she never let on.

When we reached the seventh grade, we had to change classrooms throughout the day for different subjects. This was done in silence and with discipline and precision. As one classroom lined up along the outer wall of the narrow corridor, the other class orderly vacated the room in single-file line and waited along the opposite wall. Sister Sylvester cut a swath between the two lines as she paced up and down the hallway, making sure everyone behaved.

On a fine spring day around Easter time we performed the switchyard maneuver in preparation for science class. Peggy DuPont brought a clutch of fertilized chicken eggs to school which we were going to incubate and watch hatch before we recessed for Easter week. I heard the familiar sound of swishing polyester and the rhythmic clicking of rosary beads tethered to Sister Sylvester's habit coming up from behind me. I made a spontaneous and irrevocable decision to exact my final revenge for all the thumps I took to the head compliments of the old woman. At the precise moment she passed, I boldly jumped out of line and waddled behind her in a mocking fashion. Screams of shock and delight arose in our wake as we proceeded down the hall.

In all the chaos and hysteria, no one saw the broken eggs on the floor that Peggy DuPont dropped on the way to class. Suddenly, Sister Sylvester became completely airborne when her feet were taken out from underneath her as she slipped on the gooey mess. The next few moments took on the super-slow-motion quality of a Brian DePalma film. I looked up just as the writhing mass in endless yards of black and white polyester executed a near-flawless double pike with a half-twist, descending toward me. We locked onto each other's terrified gaze as she turned her head in mid-fall. Emitting a silent scream, I raised my hands, extended my arms, and turned my head to the side in anticipation of what was sure to be a brutal impact. We crashed to the floor—and for a moment, I completely disappeared. All was quiet as I struggled to free myself from the tangled mass that enveloped me. I felt knotted-up and compressed, unable to gain my bearings, like I was tumbling through the surf of a tsunami. Limbs were flailing in every direction. Surely, I was going to Hell for touching and pushing on body parts that no human had ever come in contact with before. I cringed at the sensation of each squishy lump and wondered if I would ever again see the light of day and breathe uncontaminated air that didn't smell like a mixture of Ben Gay and Gorgonzola. At last my arms were free but I was pinned under the still tumbling servant of the Blessed Virgin Mary. I looked up from the floor and saw the zombie stare of Michael Lis, hovering over me. I grabbed his ankle in an attempt for rescue, but he twisted free. After what seemed like hours, I managed to stagger to my feet and Sister Sylvester bobbed upright. We were both completely covered in egg and dirt and humiliation. Her voice trembled as she pointed and squawked, "everyone to the parish hall, immediately—and Mr. O'Donnell I want you front and center!"

No one dared to whisper a word as we shuffled into the parish hall, a large, musty room lined with metal folding chairs in the basement of the old school building. After a few minutes Sister Sylvester entered, pacing in front of the entire seventh grade class. As she passed, she glared suspiciously at each and every student like a commandant at a POW camp. She was trembling and we all awaited the onslaught of her wrath. I tried to hide inconspicuously in the back row. She stopped and turned. She scanned the room. "Mr. O'Donnell?" she said, in controlled fury.

I raised my hand and slowly stood up. She nodded and emphatically pointed to the center seat directly in front of her. I tiptoed to the front. She grabbed Timothy Sullivan by the collar of his shirt, yanked him from his seat and tossed him aside. I quickly slipped in behind him and took his vacant chair. He scurried to the back of the room. I sat with my head to my chest and began silently reciting "Hail Marys." I sensed the vicious reprimand she was about to unleash. This could only mean one thing: expulsion. She was going to stand me in front of the entire seventh grade and strip the SMdP insignia right off of my chest, like they do to Johnny Yuma every week in the opening credits of the TV series.

I feared what my parents might do to me once they found out what a horrible thing I had done to a woman of the cloth who was so close to God—far closer than I was ever going to be! My mind began to race as I whispered "Hail Marys" faster and faster, as if their quantity was going to help me in my desperate hour of need. Then, the old woman began to speak in a slow and measured tone—.

"I have given my life to honor and serve our Lord," she said. "I have forsaken all my worldly possessions in sacrifice to God. He has called upon me to be a teacher of His children, children who don't know how to behave, children who would rather mock me and ridicule me than say a kind word to me or include me in their prayers. I did not ask to come here and teach you children. It was God's will and I have obeyed Him—which is more than I can say for any of you—you heartless, thankless, mannerless gits!" Her voice was quivering now and she stood directly in front of me. She was picking up momentum. I thought she was going to pop, or worse, *explode*! I quickly segued from "Hail Marys" straight into "Our Fathers" for a better shot at forgiveness, a quick absolution, and a painless death. And *if* I survived, she would surely have me excommunicated—banished from ever attending a Catholic school or church again! My mind began to race: my family would disown me; I would be shunned by the community. We would have to move *again*! I would force my family into yet another witness protection program in some suburb even more remote than Mundelein!

Her face was beet red, "All the inconsiderate, rude, and thoughtless behavior I can imagine doesn't even come close to what I witnessed here today!"

I could feel my heart pounding in my chest. A lump rose up in my throat and I began to tremble. I felt a whack from something far heavier than a math book coming—maybe a Bible—certainly that would be punishment worthy of my actions.

"Sister Sylvester has sacrificed everything for you! And what thanks do I get in return? I get made a laughing stock! Shameful! SHAMEFUL!" she shouted. "Not a one of you had the manners to help a poor, old, and pitiable servant of our Lord as she lay helpless on the floor. No one had the decency to even *try* to help her to her feet . . . "

She paused, " . . . except young Mr. O'Donnell here."

With those words she ripped me from my chair and spun me around to face my peers.

"And lead us not into temptation, but deliver us from evil—I'm sorry, Sister, I'm so sorry!" I pleaded as I covered my head.

"No need to be sorry, young man. You did the honorable thing. I could have been hurt had you not tried so chivalrously to save me from my fall."

Wait a minute? Did I hear her correctly? A loud and incredulous "huh?" rose up from the entire seventh grade class. I could scarcely believe it myself! I felt the warm glow of a bright shaft of light shine down upon me from the heavens as a choir of angels chanted in harmonic chorus. Alleluia, I have been saved! What a stroke of good fortune! My prayers *were* answered!

My classmates rolled their eyes and shook their heads in disbelief. I smiled back proudly and looked up at Sister Sylvester as I batted my eyelashes in cheesy humility. She returned a warm, yellow-toothed smile of gratitude.

She never again hit me with her math book. And she avoided calling on me in class—and even though I managed a passing grade, I still don't get Algebra.

Hallway of Santa Maria del Popolo School in 2008, virtually unchanged since the day Sister Sylvester fell to Earth directly in front of the drinking fountain forty years earlier.—*Photo by author.*

CHAPTER 32

༄

A NEW CAR

W E ANXIOUSLY WAITED IN THE parlor for my father and brother, John, to return from Sessler Ford in Libertyville with our new car. My sisters squealed as they noticed the gleaming 1965 Ford Country Sedan Station Wagon ease up the driveway for the first time. We all ran outside to greet, oohing and ahhing as we piled across the bench seats. Dad was very proud. It was the first new car he ever purchased. It was sleek and pure white with shiny chrome trim. It had a unique tailgate: one with a roll-down window and a door that pulled down *and* swung open.

A few days later, as it lingered pure white and sexy in our gravel driveway, I crawled in and sat behind the wheel, pretending, as many young boys do, that I was driving. I breathed in deep to take in the new car smell and admired its luxurious appointments: the blue vinyl bench seats and the wide assortment of instruments and switches that lay before me on the dashboard. It was busy and sophisticated like a Gemini Spacecraft. I pulled out a drawer and found an ashtray stuffed with several of my father's Raleigh Cigarette butts. There was a black knob next to it. I pushed in the knob. Nothing. A few seconds later, it popped back out. I pushed it in again and it popped back out again. I pulled on the knob and it came right out of its socket. I gasped. I thought I had broken it. It felt warm. I looked closer and saw that the underside was glowing orange. I wasn't sure if I should touch it but was curious to see how hot it actually was. I carefully held the black knob between my fingers and thumb and pressed the glowing orange coil directly

227

onto the vinyl seat between my legs. Immediately, a trail of smoke rose from the seat as it burned all the way through the vinyl to the foam cushion beneath. I yanked it out. I looked at the core of the knob again. It was no longer glowing. Still afraid to touch it, I pressed it to the vinyl seat a second time. When I removed it, there was a circular band branded into the vinyl. I continued my experiment across the length of the front seat another eight or ten times until the knob no longer left a mark. Wow, that's interesting, I thought. Then, reality set in. Oh no! What if my father notices? How could he not! I had left well-documented evidence of my experiment beginning on the edge of his seat, directly under the steering wheel and it continued in fading succession all the way across to the passenger's side. I replaced the glowing orange-knob-thingy into its socket, quickly looked around for any witnesses, slithered out of the car, and ran down the street. When my father discovered the vandalism, I thought he would go apoplectic with rage. I went with ignorance and stupidity as my only defense in overwhelmingly convincing fashion.

Most of our neighbors had asphalt or concrete driveways; ours was composed of dirt and crushed limestone gravel. It was always full of ruts and weeds that often grew up through the small stones. One year my father had a dump-truck full of gravel added to it. It sat like a gleaming white mountain in front of our listing garage. My brothers and I had to spread the gravel, rake it, and level it to a depth of two inches for the entire length of the driveway. We spent several days filling wheelbarrows full of the dense gravel and transporting it down the driveway only to spread it with a couple of broken-down bow rakes. My father supervised from behind the wheel of his station wagon—driving back and forth to compress the gravel and checking for low spots. He ordered us to add a few shovels full of gravel to where he pointed. It was backbreaking work and I detested it. A few days later, as I was walking by my father's car, I flipped open the door to the gas tank filler pipe, removed the cap and carefully funneled several handfuls of the white gravel into his gas tank. Consequently, every time my father made a turn in his new white chariot, you could hear the rushing sound of the gravel slide and skitter along the bottom of the tank, from one end to the other. I stared out the window and pretended that I couldn't hear the noise whenever he pointed it out to me. He was completely mystified by the sound and how the noise changed pitch depending on how much fuel was in the tank and by how quickly he turned—which I found to be both interesting and entertaining.

He never made the connection nor did he have a mechanic at Rouse's check it out. As long as the car ran, he didn't care to spend any more money than necessary on repairs. Amazingly, it didn't seem to have any adverse affect on the car at all.

CHAPTER 33

✧

ALTAR BOY

A TRIO OF PRIESTS RAN SANTA Maria del Popolo Church and school during the years I attended. Our "holy trinity" consisted of Father Murphy, Father Wilkins, and Monsignor Meaghan. They lived together in the Rectory next to the old school on the corner of Lake and Crystal Streets.

I liked Father Murphy the best. He was always friendly and his homilies were short. His Masses were under an hour. When I was in the 2nd grade and recovering from hernia surgery at Condell Hospital in Libertyville, Father Murphy came to visit me. He handed me a scapular of the Sacred Heart of Jesus and told me that if I wore it, Jesus would always protect me. I thought this was a pretty good idea and I asked him if I could have one for my parents and for each of my brothers and sisters. When I told him I needed seven, he laughed and set them on the nightstand. I wore that scapular for years and carried it in my wallet until recently, when it simply disintegrated. Father Murphy went on to become rector of Saint Mary of The Lake Seminary in 1973[76] and was promoted to Bishop of the Diocese of Great Falls-Billings, Montana, shortly thereafter. He became the Archbishop of Seattle, Washington, in 1991, and was much-loved by his flock for bringing peace to the Archdiocese after the tenure of his contentious predecessor.

Father Wilkins was a pleasant priest, but rather dull.

Then there was Monsignor Meaghan. I wasn't quite sure what a Monsignor did other than intimidate parents and frighten children. His status in the church hierarchy was a "tweener," somewhere between a Pastor and a Bishop, what I understood in my eleven-year-old brain to be analogous to a Webelos—higher than Cub Scout but not quite a Boy Scout. He must have been special; he was after all, a prelate conferred by Pope Pius VI himself.

Monsignor Meaghan had a long black Cadillac that he drove with all the subtlety of a Formula One racecar. He kept his gleaming Coup de Ville parked under a custom canvas canopy. It stood near the school's side entrance, where many of us congregated in the morning to line up for class when the bell rang. No one dared go near Monsignor's car. We all knew the *real* story why Brad Weidner and his family suddenly "had" to move to Minneapolis, Minnesota. The scuttlebutt circulating around the school was that Brad accidentally crashed his bicycle into Monsignor's black beauty and he and his family were excommunicated.

Every schoolchild was terrified of Monsignor. Even the adults of the parish feared him. He was a huge man, tall with a perpetual red nose, ornery scowl, and booming voice. He dressed in the old style—a button-down cassock that extended to his shoe tops and he wore a black biretta with a purple pom. He looked like a giant, upside-down exclamation point. He was very dramatic and his sermons were endless and rambling. He often chastised the congregation during Mass for not donating enough, not participating enough, or not singing loudly enough. If the singing wasn't to his satisfaction, he made us sing the hymn from the beginning.

"Again with the singing? Who does he think we are?" my father asked during Mass, "Lutherans?"

"Whisht!" scolded my mother in reply.

Meaghan definitely had issues and did his best to instill a heaping portion of Catholic guilt on all of us. Looking back on it now, I think alcohol might have played a key role in his bizarre behavior.

The only denizen of the school more terrifying than Monsignor Meaghan was the janitor, Mr. Baumgartner, a German immigrant who had no patience for children, or anyone else for that matter. My father said, "the old kraut is just a sore loser." I didn't know what that meant. The surly Mr. Baumgartner seemed to spend most of his time hiding out in the school's various dark, dank utility closets. When he emerged from his lair, he sure yelled a lot. He yelled about the mud or the slush left behind from the stampede of children entering the school. He yelled whenever a kid—unable to make it to the bathroom in time, vomited in the classroom. He yelled if kids ran through the halls. He was a very unhappy man but a very good yeller. He had a prosthetic left arm, at the end of which was not a hand, but a stainless steel mandible connected with cables. He manipulated it with great dexterity. Clasping a Folgers's coffee can filled with sawdust and clay, he yelled as he spread the dust down the aisle over some unfortunate student's regurgitated breakfast.

"What are you looking at!" he barked. I stared down at my desktop. I didn't dare look at him. He didn't like to be looked at and if he caught you staring at him, he held up his "claw" and *snapped* the steel jaws together—click, click, click! He was every bit as frightening as the infamous "one armed man" on the television show "The Fugitive," popular at the time.

Although I could usually avoid the creepy Mr. Baumgartner, there was no avoiding Monsignor Meaghan. He was in charge of, among other things, the school's altar boy program, which he ran like a prison warden. Becoming an altar boy was a badge of honor among Catholic schoolboys in my day. Like my brothers before me, I began to serve Mass when I was in the 6th grade. What motivated me to join the ranks had nothing at all to do with my Catholic duty as a "soldier of Christ." It was because we got to go on a field trip one day during the school year, and we got to go on regular visits to the seminary and swim in the indoor pool in the basement of the Gymnasium Building.

The one and only field trip I attended in my eight years of grade school began on a bitterly cold Friday morning in January, 1967, the week after the "big snow." As the rest of the students gathered in the parking lot and filed into class, Monsignor Meaghan herded all of the altar boys onto a school bus. I had never ridden on a bus before. We lived within a mile of school and didn't qualify for bus transportation like the kids who lived on the outskirts of town. We had to walk to and from school every day.

The rickety old humpbacked bus coughed out blue smoke from its chattering tailpipe as I eagerly awaited my turn to board. I looked up at the side of the bus and saw the name "Ritzenthaler" emblazoned in black letters. A jolt of fear ran through me. I had heard stories, none of them good, about the crazy old Ritzenthaler bus driver. I had seen him of course, coming and going into various taverns—always in a stupor, while I waited for my father outside one of his numerous haunts around town. I didn't question whether or not I should get on the bus. I was more terrified of the consequences of questioning Monsignor Meaghan's judgment than I was of a bus crash with (whom I wrongly assumed was) Mr. Ritzenthaler at the helm. All the other boys seemed oblivious to the risk. But how could they have known? They didn't wait in the car for their fathers outside the places I waited—and hadn't seen the things that I had. My classmates clambered onto the bus. They were boisterous and full of energy. I sat quietly. I had no idea where we were going, how long it would take, or what to expect. I said a silent prayer in the hopes that "Mr. Ritz" had not yet started drinking this early in the morning, and if he had, maybe, just maybe, he was half as scared of Monsignor Meaghan as I was, and he would sober up long enough to get us to where ever we were going and back, safely.

We gleefully tossed around in our seats as the chain-smoking driver navigated the drafty bus between the mountains of snow banks along Route 83 south of town, under the careful eye of the old priest. The windows soon frosted over from the lack of heat.

As the bus hobbled into a remote corner of a parking lot, I scraped the ice off the window. Through the streaky glass I made out a marquis: "Randhurst Theater." We were in Mount Prospect, fourteen miles from home. This was the site of what I had heard many of my classmates describe, in a never-ending stream of superlatives, as the eighth wonder of the modern world, Randhurst. It was the only enclosed shopping mall in the Midwest. I recalled when it opened in 1962. It made front page news. I remembered the pictures and reading about it in the Tribune on the parlor floor one morning while bundling up newspapers with my brother. Now I was actually at the historic site! It sprawled out in all directions beyond the theater—100 stores under one roof. Remarkable! I was wide-eyed and overwhelmed. How could my day get any better than this?

We walked single file into the empty movie theater and we were treated to the 1957 classic, "Old Yeller." The heat had been turned down in the building overnight and we watched the movie through our breath, wrapped in winter coats, scarves, hats, and mittens.

I wasn't familiar with the plot of "Old Yeller," but enjoyed how the main character, young Travis Coates, a year or two older than I was at that time, was left in charge of the family ranch with his mother and younger brother while his father went off on a cattle drive. When a yellow mongrel came for an uninvited stay with the family, Travis reluctantly adopted the dog. After a series of scrapes with raccoons, snakes, bears and all manner of animals, Travis grew to love and respect Old Yeller. I loved Old Yeller too, right up to the end. That is, until the boy killed the dog by shooting it in the head after it became infected with rabies from a wolf encounter. That's right. The God damn dog dies at the end of the movie. There's a real bright spot in any boy's day. Half of us were crying coming out of the theater and the tears froze to our cheeks as Monsignor Meaghan hurried us onto the bus for the long, depressing and quiet ride back to school.

Randhurst, "the eighth wonder of the modern world," is at present scheduled for demolition.

When altar boy orientation came around, I somehow missed the formal training. I learned "on the job," or as best I could remember from observing other boys I envied, those who got to serve in prime-time, 9:00 and 10:30 Mass on Sundays. We were grouped in pairs: first by grade, then by height. I was odd-man-out and paired with Ken Roden and Fred Rhode. We were the three smallest kids in the class. Without a fourth, we alternated assignments. Each acolyte was issued a black cassock and a plain white alb to wear over it. We were responsible for keeping them clean and in good repair; I had to iron my alb every day before Mass. Monsignor insisted we look our best: black trousers, dress shoes, hair combed.

Our responsibilities included lighting the candles, filling the incense urn, placing the cruets of water and wine on the side table, and having the correct Epistle and Gospel marked with the right colored ribbon in the Bibles—both on the altar and on the lectern. We also had to help the priest dress in his vestments and hang them up again after Mass. We had to know the difference between a surplice and a rochet, a stole and a chasuble. We memorized numerous cues, when to stand, when to kneel, and when to ring the Communion bells. We had to know all the routine prayers and hymns without looking in the Misselette.

My first few Masses were a complete disaster. But Father Murphy didn't care and he patiently pointed out what I needed to do to improve my game. But my inexperience and ineptitude must have been communicated to Monsignor Meaghan because I saw my name appear less and less frequently on the Sacristy roster as Ken and Freddy were often paired together.

We checked the schedule every Friday for our assignments for the upcoming week. The 8th graders were an elite group. They got all the high-profile jobs: weddings, which often came with tips; funerals, for which you got out of class; and the special ceremonial events like Midnight Mass, May Crowning, Stations of the Cross, and Confirmation. I was a long way from earning such a selective schedule. Then, during Lent, the inevitable happened. I panicked as I read the schedule—

O'Donnell, Kevin / Mon-Fri / 7:00 AM / Meaghan

What? Only losers served daily Mass during Lent—the worst of the worst! It was like being sent down to the minor leagues, Single A ball. But the real fear came in knowing that I had to serve with Monsignor Meaghan. I pleaded with my brother, Rodger, to give me a crash course in the nuances of daily Mass which was held in the little chapel, not the big church across the street. Over the course of the weekend we had rehearsed the entire Mass several times until I felt I was ready for my debut with the boss.

Monday came and I had to get up an hour earlier than usual to complete my paper route in time to make it to the chapel by 6:45 AM. I was late and Monsignor muttered under his breath as I nervously apologized. Ken Roden arrived before me and prepared the altar. As Mass began, I concentrated so hard on what Rodger told me that I missed several cues. Monsignor was clearly irritated. The defining moment came when I poured wine on his shoe tops during "the preparation of the gifts."

After Mass Monsignor Meaghan grumbled and groused and I trembled with fear and intimidation as I helped him out of his vestments. He brushed me aside spewing some derogatory insult that I did not understand. I broke down and cried. I explained through my tears how I missed the orientation class, how I studied the other boys, and how Rodger and I rehearsed the Mass over and over and over again, and the pressure I felt to be as good as the others. I felt like a complete failure because I did not meet his approval.

The lumbering priest breathed a deep sigh and sat down in front of me. He laid his massive hands on my shoulders to calm me. Then in a soft and sincere voice, he said, "look, being an altar boy is a lot like . . . playing baseball. You play baseball, don't you, son? Sure, you do. Who is your favorite player? Hmm?"

"Billy Williams, Monsignor," I said sheepishly.

"Billy Williams. Yes, he's a very good player. You don't think he was *always* that good do you? No. That's right. He got to where he is now by practicing . . . every day, batting, fielding, running. All those skills are important if you want to become a good ball player. It took Billy Williams many hours of practice to get that good. Do you think that if you practice at the skills of an altar boy you can become good, too?"

I nodded affirmatively, wiping my nose and blinking back tears.

"Sure," he said. "Of course you can. Now, run off to class and remember what Monsignor told you."

I felt invigorated from Monsignor's inspiring consult and a surge of motivation came over me. I was going to become the best altar boy Santa Maria ever had! Who knew this lumbering giant, whom we secretly referred to as "meanie Meaghan," had such a gentle and understanding side? My fellow classmates certainly would never believe it!

I took a Misselette from the pew on my way out of the chapel. I made sure I genuflected when I crossed the altar and blessed myself with the holy water from the font at the front of the chapel (just in case Monsignor was watching) before I raced down the empty hall to class. I studied the daily Mass in the Misselette that night and every night in my bedroom that week to familiarize myself with the subtlest intricacies of the altar boys' duties. Every morning I looked forward to 7:00 AM Mass and felt real and substantial improvement in my abilities with each passing day. I sensed Monsignor Meaghan felt it too. We were lockstep, as precisely choreographed as one of those dance numbers on the Lawrence Welk Show that my parents loved to watch.

By the end of the week I was beaming with confidence. I helped the old Irish priest replace his vestments into the wardrobe and confidently asked, "Well, Monsignor, I'm getting pretty good at this aren't I?"

He glared down at me and sardonically declared, "kid, you're never going to make it to the World Series."

I was crushed. What a horrible and mean thing to tell an eleven- year-old. I had tried so hard. It meant so much to me to gain his approval. None of that mattered to him.

For a brief time, a seminary student by the name of Thomas Job (pronounced *jôb*) helped with duties around the church and school, including the altar boy program. Every week during the winter months, Deacon Job selected a few altar boys and drove them on Thursdays to the seminary after school for a swim. I was thrilled when my turn came. My classmates and I were in awe of the seminary's big gymnasium; unlike the Publics, our school didn't have a gym. We raced each other across the wood floor, picked up some basketballs and immediately began shooting baskets. A few minutes later the deacon signaled us over and we followed him down a dark set of steps to the basement locker room. We modestly began changing into our swim trunks and the deacon exclaimed "swim suits are optional, boys!" We giggled. He loitered around until each of us changed and ran into the pool room. He followed us in. We all enjoyed being picked up by the burly deacon and thrown into the pool, and he wrestled with us under water. Afterwards, he hung around the locker room and snapped a wet towel at us as we changed back into our school uniforms before driving us all home.

Several weeks later Deacon Job stopped me in the hall after school and asked if I would be willing to help him do some yard work on Saturday at his parent's house in Elgin. How could I say no? When I came home, I asked my mother if I could go.

"You most certainly can," she said as she sat at the dining room table pasting pages of S&H Green Stamps into little booklets. "It's your duty to help a priest when he's in need of you help. Your brother, Rodger, can deliver your papers that afternoon," she said.

Deacon Job picked me up on Saturday at nine o'clock. It was a long drive to the city of Elgin and we turned down a maze of unfamiliar country roads through towns I'd never been to before: Lake Zurich, Barrington, Carpentersville, until we finally arrived at his parents home. I was surprised to see how elderly his parents were. His mother made us lunch while the Deacon and I began cleaning up the yard of debris that resulted from the previous winter's "big snow." I giggled whenever his mother called him "Tommy." We only worked for an hour or so when the Deacon declared it was time to leave. On our way home he told me of a family he knew near Barrington who had an indoor pool. He asked me if I would like to go swimming as a reward for my hard work.

"But I don't have any swimming trunks, Mr. Job," I said.

"That's okay, neither do I. Maybe they have some there we can borrow," he said.

I never did answer him. He pulled into a long driveway that led to a huge, sprawling house. It was the biggest and fanciest house I had ever seen. There were horses grazing in the front yard. He went to the door. I waited in the car. The woman who answered was surprised but happy to see him. They talked for a few minutes and she pointed toward what looked to be like another house on the property. It was the pool house. We drove up to it and Deacon Job invited me in. There was no one else inside. He chatted calmly, stripped down to his underwear and dived into the pool. He kept encouraging me to take my clothes off and jump in. I reluctantly did as I was told by the soon-to-be priest, but I was very uncomfortable and swam away from the Deacon whenever he approached me. After a few minutes I ran out of the pool. He followed me. As I quickly tried to dry off and change into my street clothes, I realized that I had to take off my wet underwear. I did so quickly. He sat beside me and pulled me onto his knee. I was a pre-pubescent eleven-year-old; he was a full grown man. He tried explaining that it was alright to be naked in front of him, "After all, Adam and Eve were naked in front of God in the Garden of Eden," he said reassuringly.

"Yes, but Adam and Eve were ashamed of their bodies in front of God once they had sinned and were driven out of the Garden of Eden," I snapped.

He stared at me. I sat with my head down and my hands over my crotch, embarrassed and terrified. He must have sensed my fear. He handed me a towel and told me to get dressed.

I was *so* ashamed. I never told my parents what happened and I never went swimming at the seminary with the altar boys after that. I avoided Deacon Job at all costs.

Then I did something that was unheard of in altar boydom—I quit.

Shortly thereafter, Deacon Job was no longer at our parish. He was suddenly, and without explanation, re-assigned to another church.

Santa Maria del Popolo Chapel, where I failed as an altar boy. The church seats about 150. This is where my children were baptized; my sister, Sheila, was married; and funeral Masses for my mother and my father, my sister, Maureen, and my brother, John, all took place.—*Photo by author.*

CHAPTER 34

∽

MY FATHER THE BARBER

M Y FATHER INVESTED IN A well-used, professional grade, Wahl electric hair clippers and fancied himself a decent barber. He was alone in that opinion. What he called a *good* haircut my brothers and I called tragic, and most others called comedy. His self-ascribed artistry more often resembled the work of Jackson Pollock, rather than that of Floyd the Barber. Whenever my brothers and I were due for a haircut, we remained on our best behavior. We did not want to contribute to my father's frequently foul moods at a time when he decided to release his frustration at the business end of his hair clippers.

When the weather was fair, he conducted the shearing ritual in the driveway beside the back porch. Otherwise, he set up shop anywhere in the house we could find room. Perched on top of an old metal stool that had a cracked maple seat, we had to position ourselves on the stool in just the right manner and sit perfectly still. Failure to do so resulted in a vise grip butt-pinch when the two pieces of the loose seat teetered together. This was likely to happen at the most critical juncture of the proceedings. Extremely painful, it caused us to flinch, which, in turn, made my father slip with the shears. The result: a conspicuous divot somewhere to the back of the head.

The sheers were housed in a weighty, stainless steel casing held together with multiple applications of electrical tape. My father kept it and the rusty accessories in an old shoebox on the top shelf of the hall closet. Many times my brothers and I pondered confiscating them or hiding them in the trash to be picked-up by Obenauf Disposal *"Purveyors of fine garbage"* on their regular Friday rounds. But we could never work up the courage for fear my father would find out and punish us with a patchwork haircut we called a "baldy-sour," and we would be mistaken for a chemo patient.

My brother, Rodger, holds the honors for the worst-ever haircut. My father hacked it so unfashionably short one evening that Rodger stubbornly wore a wool stocking cap the entire summer. He reasoned that he would rather suffer the relentless ridicule and teasing from the neighbor kids for wearing a winter hat in the summertime than remove it and reveal my father's handiwork.

I could always tell how artful my father would be with his shears by his attitude and his sobriety. Each episode was an experiment. He wrapped an old bed sheet around me and secured it snuggly around my neck with a diaper pin. Standing behind me, he adjusted the pitch and yaw my head with his fingertips placed on either side of my face. "There," he said, gently slapping my cheek. He plugged the sheers into a ratty, tangled extension cord that snaked through the house to one of the few outlets that wouldn't blow a fuse. He puffed on a Tareyton cigarette that dangled precariously from his lips. The smoke wafted up into his eyes from the growing grey ash as he applied the heel of his hand to the top of my head. He flipped the switch and I heard the menacing hum draw closer to my ears. Pressing the cold, vibrating steel to the nape of my neck, he dragged it upwards. The distinct aroma of 3-in-1 oil and burnt hair filled my nostrils as I watched what little personal identity I had fall in clumps around me and tumble in slow-motion down the sheet.

CHAPTER 35

ojo

THE DEVIL IN THE BOTTLE

F RIDAY. PAYDAY. MY FATHER AND I dropped off my mother
and sisters in front of the Piggly Wiggly grocery store. Afterward,
he and I drove a few blocks north on Seymour Street to the First National
Bank of Mundelein. My father cashed his check, paid the mortgage and
argued with the teller regarding the balance in his account. From there we
walked across the street. He put his arm around my shoulder as we crossed
Park Avenue. I recoiled with embarrassment and hoped that no one I
knew from school saw me. My father sighed. He handed me fifteen cents
to go into the Rexall Drug and buy a Green River. I sat at my usual place
at the counter on one of the green vinyl and chrome swivel stools—second
from the end. I sipped on the sweet, carbonated lime soda that Mr. Lyter,
the store owner, concocted, and let Karen Azzato flirt with me. I liked the
attention. Karen was a much older woman—a freshman in high school and
a friend and former grade school classmate of my brother, John. I slurped
my cocktail, loudly sucking the last few, syrupy drops through my straw,
hoping Karen noticed. I arose and said goodbye in as suave and urbane a
manner as I could formulate and sauntered out of the store. Certain that I
had left Karen breathless by my charm, I confidently walked down a few
storefronts. I passed Abernathy's Clothiers, Yopp's Meat Market, and the
True-Value Hardware Store, before I came to Lad and Helen's Tap next
door to the boarded up Central Hotel. I stood in the doorway, peered into
the dark, smoky bar, and waited for my father to notice me. The bar phone

rang. Before picking it up the bartender surveyed the patrons to get a count of head nods of those who said they were there, and those who said they weren't. It's the universal sign known to all bartenders everywhere. "Lad and Helen's," the bartender barked. "Who?" pointing to a patron in the middle of the bar. The man shook him off. "Nope. He ain't here. Nope. Haven't seen him. Sure, if I see him, I'll tell him." He hung up the phone. Conversations resumed. The barkeep tapped my father on his arm and motioned to the door. Dad turned and saw me, finished his last sip of his beer, picked his change up off the bar, and shooed me out of the doorway. I backed out on to the sidewalk. He checked his watch. I reluctantly held his hand as we crossed the busy street and hurried back to the car in the bank parking lot.

My mother gave my father a dirty look as we walked briskly into the Piggly Wiggly. We were late, as usual. She had been waiting in a corner of the store with a mound of groceries in a cart. They argued in Irish whispers (loud enough for unintended ears to hear), unaware that my sugar-charged sisters were shrieking as they chased each other around the cart and between my parents' legs. "Give me the Goddamn money," Mother insisted. But my father *never* let my mother have cash. We walked to the check-out line. My father flirted mildly with the girl at the register as he paid for the groceries. This infuriated my mother—all the excuse she needed to start drinking after she returned home, put away the groceries, and slid the cookie sheet of frozen fish sticks and tater tots into the oven.

Alcohol was central in my childhood experience. With few exceptions, the saddest, darkest, and most negative recollections of my boyhood were all complicated by, and attributed directly to, alcohol. Both my parents suffered from distinctly different forms of alcoholism, and both died as a result of their dependency. They each accused the other of being an alcoholic in many of the long, drawn-out drunken arguments they had, yet neither saw it in themselves, and if they did, they never admitted to it. On several occasions their arguing frightened my siblings and me to the point that we huddled together in one of the upstairs bedrooms until one of us ran across the street, usually in the middle of the night, and called in our neighbor, Rhoda Meyer, to come over in her nightgown and robe. She refereed the escalating proceedings before they came to blows.

My siblings and I learned to cope with our parents' dysfunction in several different ways in an effort to maintain some sort of normalcy within our home and sanity within ourselves. The effect their insidious and escalating disease had on each one of my brothers and sisters and me would prove to be diverse, permanent, and tragic.

My father was a maintenance drinker whose preference was for boilermakers. He drank nearly every day but rarely appeared visibly intoxicated. He seldom missed a day of work because of his habit and as far as I know, never drank before or during work. His drink day began right after work with a shot of Early Times Whiskey and an Old Style chaser, a seven ounce draught beer in a glass "shell." He generally stayed with beer after that. He always stopped off at a bar after work and most nights headed out again right after dinner, sometimes not coming home until long after we were in bed. At times my mother gave me the humiliating task of calling around to different taverns in an attempt to smoke out my father and tell him to come home. Sadly, I had most of the telephone numbers memorized and no matter where I called, the response was always the same: "Who? Nope. He ain't here. Nope. Haven't seen him. Sure, if I see him, I'll tell him."

Countless times I accompanied my father on his errands in the evening. They were nothing more than thinly disguised excuses to stop at the tavern. He said he had to go to the store, or out for cigarettes, or to the milk machine behind Stinson's Shell Station where the old North Shore Train Station stood on the corner of Prospect and Hawley Streets. (Milk machines were giant yellow refrigerated vending machines that dispensed gallon-sized waxed cartons of milk for fifty-five cents. After Rouse's dairy closed and we no longer had milk delivered, we made frequent use of the town's milk machines.) No matter when or where we ran errands, they always ended the same—with my father stopping for a shot-and-a-beer and conversation that sometimes lasted for hours. I usually waited in the car and listened to whatever songs I wanted to on the radio without the fear of criticism from my father. When he finally did return to the car, I quickly pushed the preset button back to the only radio station he listened to, WGN.

There wasn't a tavern owner in town that my father didn't know or who didn't know him. He was a dream customer, always welcome, always polite and cordial, if not friendly. He was never loud, obnoxious, or vulgar, and he didn't engage in impolite conversation. Above all, regardless of how tight the money was at home, he *always* paid for his drinks before he left the bar. Each of my father's favorite watering holes had for him a unique appeal and ambiance with regular customers with whom he visited depending on his mood. Some were "stag bars"—men only. Most were dives:

The Chug-A-Lug—at a half mile away was the closest tavern to our house—a flimsy old depression-era shack on Lake Street. Torn down (without much effort) in 2005;

Emil's Continental Tap—visited mostly on holidays or Saturday nights to pick up beef bomber sandwiches (they *still* have the best Italian Beef I've ever had);

The Lakewood Lounge—(later called The Barracuda Lounge, a "biker bar," and currently Jake Moran's) conveniently located directly across the street from the Chug-A-Lug;

The Happy Hollow—the old Hackett's Place Hotel on Diamond Lake Road, ancient and dungeonous with a small beach that we sometimes patronized. It overlooked the lake across from Bud's Fix-It Bike & Mower Shop;

Diamond Lake Bowling Alley—a seven lane hole-in-the-wall located at the end of Diamond Lake Plaza next to a coin Laundromat;

Ted's Tap—owned by the Ganicks, our neighbors up the street;

Lad and Helen's—a Friday night favovrite, located next to the boarded-up Central Hotel on Seymour Street. Currently Gregg's Olde Town Tap, owned and operated by Eddie Poleska's son;

The Dutch Mill (later called the *Irish Mill*)—on the outskirts of town on Route 83, the other side of West Shore Park. My father occasionally tended bar there to make ends meet when Goodyear went on strike;

Weich's Inn—in Ivanhoe, northwest of town. A sign reading "No Pizza" hung outside for more than 40 years. My father took my brothers and me there for a Friday Night Fish Fry if we had been on good behavior.

On his way home from work, my father often stopped at either:

McCormick's Restaurant—a past-its-prime steakhouse on Route 41 Frontage Road in Lake Bluff; or

Art's Old House—a roadhouse tavern and restaurant and site of a famous train robbery in the 1890's. Art's sat nearly on the edge of the tracks in Rondout, a crossroad of multiple rail lines east of Libertyville on Route 176 (the old Hiawatha Trail). Rondout claimed to be the busiest rail town in America with nearly 200 trains a day traversing through the one horse town during its heyday. Art's was the place where my father bought me my first legal beer in 1974, when I turned 19—then the legal drinking age in Illinois. My second legal beer was bought for me by one of Art's "regulars," former Chicago Cub's third baseman, Ron Santo, who had been recently traded to the Chicago White Sox, and lived nearby. He often held court at the corner of the bar. Art's Old House mysteriously burned down in the early 1990's.

There were other, less frequented joints my father was known to support: like *Little Nick's, Mike & Gwen's, Spina's* . . . you get the picture.

Whenever Brian Cissie Rodgers, my father's cousin and close friend, came to town, usually unannounced and unplanned, all bets were off. The two of them ran the gambit of my father's haunts in town only to return falling down drunk in the wee hours of the morning. This set my mother off and further validated her own drinking. My mother never liked Brian Rodgers—she claimed he was a bad influence.

Mother was a binge drinker. Her habit dated back to her teenage years in Bayonne, New Jersey. Incapable of drinking socially or in moderation, she was the reason my father moved his family to Illinois in 1956 in an attempt to assuage her habit and relieve his stress. There, she became an adroit closet drinker. She surreptitiously pocketed change from the grocery store money my father gave her and dimes and quarters from the laundromat fund, along with any "found money" from pants pockets. When she patiently saved enough money to buy a few bottles of beer, she walked uptown in the middle of a weekday when we were in school and my father was at work. She slipped into "the beer store" next to Diamond Lake Bowling Alley and bought a few quart bottles of the cheapest beer she could find, Meister Brau. Her compulsive drinking resulted in consuming as much alcohol as she could, as fast as she could. She hid opened bottles in the kitchen cupboards or in her dresser drawers and then passed out in bed, only to stagger to her feet minutes before my father came home. Her level of intoxication determined what, if anything, she fixed for dinner. Most evenings we had a bowl of boiled potatoes glazed over in salt, and "minced meat," a combination of ground beef, onion and peas—smothered in ketchup.

When we were very young and my mother was having particularly bad alcoholic episodes, my father, at wits' end and fearful for our safety and well-being, herded my brothers and sisters and me into the station wagon and drove us to the Benedictine Convent. He lined us up in one of the pews, gestured for us to kneel and fervently whispered, "Pray, children. Pray hard. Pray for your mother, that she will be better," as she lay at home in bed, unconscious from drink.

My father's desperate attempts to heal my mother through prayer came at all hours of the day and night. On more than one occasion he swooped us out of our beds and carried us to the car. In the dead of winter we walked quietly into the darkened chapel wearing little more than rag-tag pajamas and bulky rubber boots.

My parents sought counseling from the only person within the community thought to be qualified to address such a malady, Monsignor Meaghan, our drunkard Parish Priest. There were no such places as treatment centers or recovery programs, or cognitive therapy for drug dependency within the medical profession. That concept was not to be administered and accepted for another fifteen years. At the time, alcoholism was not considered a disease at all—but a social blight of the weak-willed, a family's embarrassment, a family's secret—and I wore it well. It carried with it such a terrible stigma that I admitted it to no one. During my formative years, it ranked right up there with gonorrhea, adultery, or incest in the realm of social acceptance.

If you were a hard case and had the right insurance and the right connections, you could be admitted to Elgin State Mental Health Facility for "treatment." Built in 1872 and originally called the Northern Illinois Hospital and Asylum for the Insane, the "hospital" underwent a name change in 1961 to enhance its image. You can put a pig in a prom dress, but it's still a pig. "Elgin" became a regional euphemism for the place where they keep those on the fringe of society locked up. It was full of schizophrenics, wards of the state, drug addicts, and the criminally insane.

In January, 1970, during my freshman year in high school, my mother entered Elgin on the advice of our family physician, Dr. Dolan, who didn't know what else to do with her. My father visited her on the weekends. She pleaded with him to let her come home. She was terrified of what she saw and heard within the confines of that dark, decrepit, Victorian estate. After three weeks, my father acquiesced. She remained sober for several weeks and I recall that it was the merriest time in my childhood. We finally had a normal family. But it was not long before my mother slipped into her old routines and habits, and the weight of the world fell back upon everyone's shoulders.

I loved my mother, truly, I did—but as a child and adolescent I was embarrassed by her drinking and the behavior it caused. Consequently, I rarely had friends over at the house.

I was more tolerant of my father's drinking because he was generally capable of executing his head-of-household responsibilities. When he drank to excess, however, it brought out the worst in him.

Early in the summer of 1970, I went to stay for a weekend with Uncle Brian Cissie Rodgers and his family in Lake Forest. The Rodgers' household was not much different than mine, except alcohol abuse always seemed more prevalent there.

My father came to pick me up on Sunday. He was sullen and quiet. He didn't speak a word all the way home. He dropped me off and barreled back down the driveway as soon as I got out of the car. My brother, Rodger, approached me before I entered the house.

"What's going on?" I asked.

Rodger told me the horrific details that unfolded while I was gone.

After Uncle Brian and I left the house on Friday night to return to Lake Forest, my father, fresh from carousing with Brian, got into an argument with my mother over her use of the telephone. She had also been drinking—at home, as she always had—while my father and Brian made their rounds around town. He accused her of having her friends and neighbors bring her booze while he was at work during the day. (My mother never got a driver's license and never drove a car, a blessing in hind-sight.) What ensued, Rodger described, was a drunken argument of epic proportions, that precipitated into violence. My father became enraged and ripped the phone off the kitchen wall taking the plaster along with it. Picking up the receiver he repeatedly hit my mother with it.

"The police came and took Dad away in handcuffs. He didn't come home until the next morning. I think they put him in jail," Rodger said.

"Is Mom okay?" I asked.

Rodger began crying. "She's in our bedroom," he said.

I quietly walked upstairs and into our bedroom. My mother was huddled in my bed with the window shades drawn, lights out, and the covers pulled up over her shoulders. I knelt beside her. She turned around and I could not believe what I saw. Her entire face looked like a rotting eggplant, grotesquely swollen—purple and green with bruises and abrasions. One eye was completely swollen shut. She pulled the covers down and I could see where the bruises extended all over her neck, shoulders, chest, and back. I screamed in shock and disbelief.

"Your father did this to me," she whispered as her entire body trembled.

I began crying uncontrollably—yelling and cursing my father. My mother had no reaction.

I did not speak to my father for a very long time; none of us did. Even though we never talked about it afterward, many things changed irrevocably in our house as a result of that night. Rodger became fiercely protective of our Mother. For the remainder of her life he treated her like a queen and lavished her with gifts, vacations, and items for the house—all the things my father never could or would indulge in. He also bought her beer whenever she requested it and was able on some level, to moderate her consumption.

My parent's relationship changed, too. They barely spoke to each other after that, and when they did, it was only to exchange necessary information. She made his breakfast, fixed his tea, and packed his lunchbox as she always had, but never addressed him or engaged him in any conversation. They never went anywhere together except for their children's graduations and weddings. But the most remarkable thing that resulted from that horrible night was that, until the day she died, my mother never, ever, slept in the same bed with my father again. For the next thirteen years, she spent every night alone on the couch in the parlor.

Both Mother and Father denied their disease their entire lives. Even when my mother became ill in the summer of 1983 she dismissed the doctor's diagnosis and insisted that he keep her true illness from us. We all witnessed her horrible death on October 16th of that year. She told us she had cancer. The cause of death listed on her death certificate read: "cirrhosis of the liver."

Four years later, on the evening of August 24th, 1987, my father stopped at the Chug-A-Lug for his usual shot-and-a-beer. His cronies told me he never sat down. He stared at the drink on the bar, and without taking a sip, picked up his change and walked out. He died peacefully in bed that evening. When we found him, the covers were tucked neatly around his waist, his Celtic cross at the end of its chain lay in the middle of his chest, and the radio on the dresser with the volume turned low was tuned to WGN.

CHAPTER 36

⟡

CHILD LABOR

I AM WHAT THE IRISH IN Chicago call a *narrowback*, a disparaging colloquialism used to describe the children of immigrant parents thought to be unfit for the hard physical labor typically performed by those in the country of their ancestral origin.

But between the ages of eight and eighteen I had no less than twenty-seven jobs. They started when I inherited my brother's paper route, but I did just about any chore to earn spending money. I don't know what I spent the money on as a kid, other than buying junk food. At one point I rode my bike up to Diamond Lake Super Market nearly every day, and for eleven cents, wolfed down a twin pack of Hostess Twinkies. I also bought most of my own clothes from Abernathy's and Grant's Department Store from the time I was twelve. We bought our school uniforms from Abernathy's. They also had a fine selection of Levi's for $6 a pair. I bought them skin tight and above my shoe tops as was the style in the late 60's. In 1968, my rural, mid-west version of haute couture consisted of tight Levi's and white socks from Abernathy's, Cordovan penny loafers from Fenwick's Footwear and a Madras shirt from Grant's.

My earliest childhood occupations ranged from shoveling snow off the neighbors' walks and driveways to mowing the lawns of the widow ladies in our neighborhood—Aunt Ida, Mrs. Dane, Mrs. Pfister, and Mrs. Kane in West Shore Park. Each paid about $1. I had to buy my own gas and oil and maintain the mower and I pulled it behind me on my bike as I made my way through the canopy of Dutch Elm trees that lined our neighborhood. I enjoyed going to Mrs. Kane's house to mow her lawn. She always invited me in for Kool-Aid and cookies and I sat at a metal TV tray she set up for me in her parlor. I stared at the huge oil painting that hung above her couch. The idyllic scene depicted a horse-drawn hay wagon along a dirt road. Children were playing around the wagon and riding on top of the stacked hay bales as the horses plodded up the winding road toward a large white farmhouse. I recognized that farmhouse. It stood in the middle of a trailer park on Route 83 west of Diamond Lake Road. It was the house Mrs. Kane lived in as a child. She pointed to a little girl in the painting running behind the wagon. "That's me," she said. "This was my family's farm. It was painted in the 1880's by a traveling artist."

I escaped into that painting and tried to visualize how innocent and carefree those days must have been. I was happy to be among those children.

When I wasn't mowing lawns or shoveling snow, I talked people into newspaper and magazine subscriptions to win trips to Wrigley Field or Riverview Amusement Park in Chicago. I opened lemonade stands, raked leaves, took care of people's pets when they went on vacation, and I cleaned out garages. I produced neighborhood plays and I auctioned off Ginger's puppies.

During my high school years, I sold some of the artwork in my portfolio, painted pictures of local businesses, and sold them to the stores' owners, including Rick's Country Corner Market in Diamond Lake and Rouse's Standard Oil Station. I babysat little kids. At fourteen, I caddied at Hillcrest Country Club in Long Grove, an all-Jewish private club, where the members' golf bags were as tall as I was and weighed about the same. It paid well (about $18) and I got to play golf for free on Mondays. I hitchhiked to the golf course because it was too far to walk, and at fourteen, I was too cool to be riding a bike. I pumped gas at Ed's Highland Gas in Diamond Lake along with my brother, Rodger. Gasoline at that time was twenty-seven cents a gallon for regular and twenty-nine cents a gallon for Ethyl (premium). Crazy old Mr. Kruckenberg, who lived in the farmhouse across the street from Ed's his entire life, came over to the station on weekend mornings, bought a quart of goat's milk and drank it right from the carton as he regaled my brother and me with stories of the Diamond Lake Church and School and the local railroads before 1900.

I cleaned out stables at Mrs. Horton's horse farm in Long Grove and tended to her gardens. During my sophomore year in high school I grilled hamburgers behind the counter at Burger King on the corner of Seymour and Hawley Streets in downtown Mundelein.

The summer between my final years at Carmel High School, I worked for Helke Landscaping in Lincolnshire, ten hours a day, six days a week, along with twenty-eight Mexicans who couldn't speak a word of English. My first day on the job, my *amigos* and I laid over 500 yards of sod and installed a drain tile around a private tennis court in Winnetka, covering the drain tile with countless wheelbarrows full of gravel. My second day on the job I couldn't get out of bed. My employer, Norm Helke, threatened to fire me over the phone. My father grabbed the phone and came to my defense. He explained to Helke that I was physically unable to get out of bed but that I would be at the pre-arranged pick-up point the following morning at 6:00 AM. Helke gave me a second chance, and I didn't miss another day of work all summer. Working as a landscaper was an extremely rewarding job on many levels. I learned to speak Spanish that summer out of necessity and consequently breezed through my second year Spanish class the following school year. I also developed a deep and abiding interest in horticulture. Occasionally, I drive past a spot in the town of Libertyville where I had planted several Colorado blue spruce back in the summer of 1972. It was the property of International Harvester back then. They made earth-moving equipment. The trees are *still* there, along an old fence line where the North Shore Interurban once rumbled past, between the Des Plaines River and a railroad siding, directly across from a car dealership. It's at this location, where Route 176 crosses the Des Plaines River, that Peter Shaddle portaged his canoe and walked west along the Hiawatha Trail until he found his paradise, one hundred and thirty-seven years earlier. The once stately trees that I had planted have become derelict over the years. But I dug a place for them and I rolled the bagged and burlapped saplings into each carefully prepared hole and I nurtured them through an entire summer. Seeing them now, nearly too weak to support themselves, gangly, crooked, and overgrown from years of neglect strikes me as sad.

During my senior year, I bagged groceries at Sunset Foods in Lake Forest with three of my high school friends: Dan Cantwell, John Schenning, and Jim Roy. We got into plenty of mischief there and were frequently reprimanded by the store manager because of our shenanigans. We were prone to smoke in the restroom, play soccer in the aisles, inhale the gas from cases of whipped cream canisters, use sides of beef in the butcher shop cooler as punching bags, and flirt with the cashiers. The four of us got into a fair amount of mischief outside of work as well. One of our favorite pastimes included driving to the "wrong side of the tracks" in the area's poorest town, North Chicago, illegally purchasing a bottle of liquor at a dive bar called The Cat and Fiddle, then ducking into the sleazy Admiral Theatre next door to watch 1940's and 1950's "stag" films, as we passed the bottle around. Afterward, we drove to Waukegan harbor and trespassed on the government pier, walking the length of the treacherous catwalk out to the lighthouse at the end of the breakwater. There we drank what booze we couldn't finish in the musty theater. We tossed the empty bottle into the harbor before we drove home. Those were reckless times.

I worked in the projection booth at the Elm Theater in Wauconda only because I had a crush on several of the owner's daughters. They were all named after queens: Victoria, Mary, Antoinette, and Elizabeth. The theater was owned by the Archdiocese of Chicago and they only ran G-rated movies, most of which no one wanted to see. It is where my parents took me to see my first movie, *The Song of Bernadette*, when I was five. The mostly empty theater was later torn down to build a new, modern Catholic church, Transfiguration.

In August of 1973, I sold children's shoes and boys' clothing at Marshall Field & Company at the newly opened Hawthorn Mall. Straight out of high school I worked in a factory owned by a beer-swilling friend of my father's. I inhaled ethylene chloride and methyl ethyl ketone vapors all day from the solvents they used and I learned how to operate a lathe. I injured my back lifting a large stainless steel roller intended for a printing press a few months into that job and ended up in the hospital for four days. I quit soon afterwards.

The following year, I spent a sweltering summer at the Goodyear Tire & Rubber Company Hose Plant in North Chicago where my father worked, and for the first and last time in my life became a member of a union. I rode to and from work with my father and listened intently to the news on WGN radio regarding the Watergate cover up and Nixon's ultimate resignation. I dreaded every hot, smelly day in that factory, working in 105-degree heat and braiding hydraulic hose. I made an astonishing $4.75 an hour, twice what my friends were making at their jobs. I worked in Department 721 and was responsible for the continuous operation of twelve braiding tables. As the hose uncoiled from a pan below, it was pulled up through the middle of the table where sixty-four spools of nylon-reinforced thread interwove at high speed, braiding the hose in Maypole fashion. There were no safety guards or emergency switches on the equipment. Getting a hand caught between the spools meant certain disaster. It was deafeningly loud and extremely dangerous work.

Working at Goodyear proved to be both a miserable and enlightening experience. It exposed me to a cross-section of society that I had not been exposed to before: poor, uneducated folks, many of whom were illiterate and who maintained strong segregation ties to their southern communities and ethnic origins. I wondered how my father could stand to go there everyday and how he managed to fit in and get along with such people. They were unlike anyone I knew growing up in my sheltered Catholic schools and all white town. I realize that he managed as he always had.

"You've got to go along to get along," he often said.

And he was a master at getting along. Since he was a boy he was always an outsider—an islander, a Mick, a foreigner—but he always persevered and always got ahead of others at his station by working hard and minding his own business. Those at the Goodyear plant were not his friends. They were coworkers and he treated them accordingly. He was cordial and polite, but he never befriended them. I saw that this had earned him a high degree of respect among all the races and nationalities within the factory.

I had neither the skill nor the patience of my father. I was an impetuous nineteen-year-old, killing time, waiting for the next best thing to come along. The highlight of my work day came at lunchtime when I sat with my father in the cafeteria. I learned my first day on the job that everyone sat in the same seat at the same table, every day. The white women sat among themselves at separate tables, as did most of the blacks and Hispanics. My father convinced the other men at his table to rearrange their seats so that I could sit across from him. We were both uncomfortable in front of each other whenever the conversation degenerated into profanity-laced sexually explicit banter, as it frequently did. Some of the men seemed genuinely amused by the fact that my father and I pretended not to hear them.

A wild-eyed dockworker with ratty blond hair and green teeth, whom everyone seemed to dislike, tried to goad me into such conversations on several occasions. I did my best to dismiss him. One day he leaned in toward me over his cafeteria tray and in an accent as thick as the Bluegrass from his native Kentucky hills, he shouted down the table at me, "Hey kid, kid, had ye ever et pussy before?" Conversations at the table stopped. All eyes were on me. "Well, kid," he laughed, "had ye? You know, ever et pussy?"

I looked up at my father looking at me wondering if I knew what that meant. I looked at him wondering if *he* knew what that meant. Everyone awaited my response.

My father's eyes telegraphed to me not to respond. But I had had enough of this ignorant man's taunts and could no longer tolerate the vulgarities directed at me. Against my father's advice, I decided to stand my ground.

"Just once," I said, "and your momma told me that I was much better at it than you."

I casually returned to eating my lunch. The others howled with laughter, slapped the table and congratulated me as they got up and filed back into the dusty plant. Old "green teeth" slithered out of the lunchroom and never bothered me again.

My father smirked. I shrugged. I waited for him to say something. He never did and we never again spoke of the incident.

♈

I was eventually fired from Goodyear—the only time in my life that I was fired from a job. I contend that it was because I was left handed. The braiding machines were designed for right-handed operation and maintenance. It was a constant and futile battle in frustration for me as I was unable to produce my daily quota. The conditions were so deplorable in that hose plant that I vowed never to work in a factory again, and I never have. I felt bad for my father. He worked there for twenty-five years. He used his influence to get me that job and I failed him. I know he was disappointed in me. I was obviously lost and aimlessly searching for some identity and purpose. Convinced that I was not cut out for manual labor, or manual laborers, I decided the surest way out of my miserable existence was to go back to school. I enrolled in the fall semester at Lake County College at the encouragement of my girlfriend, whose name, Diane Amann, my brother Rodger poignantly painted in cheap white paint across the back of the house a couple of months earlier.

CHAPTER 37

ⴄ

ROUSE'S SERVICE STATION

IN DECEMBER, 1974, SHORTLY AFTER I enrolled as a full-time student at Lake County College, I landed a job at Rouse's Service Station. I changed oil and fan belts, repaired flat tires and installed new ones. I replaced faulty thermostats and fuses, pumped gas, operated the car wash, and drove the tow truck to help stranded motorists. The hours were flexible and it's how I earned my way through school over the next three years. I was older than most of the pump monkeys that worked there by a few years, but considerably more mature and infinitely more dependable. J.R. Rouse soon promoted me to night manager. I enjoyed working with and talking to J.R.'s father, the Old Man, who, more than fifty years after his horse-drawn wagon accident on the grounds of the seminary, continued to work six days a week. He always kept an oil rag in the back pocket of his overalls and he never thought himself too high and mighty to work the pumps. He proudly raised the American flag at sunrise every day on the corner flagpole and insisted that whoever was working at sundown respectfully take down the flag, fold it, and leave it for him on a shelf. Despite his age and pronounced limp, he was often the first one out the door as soon as a car pulled onto the apron. "Ding-ding, ding-ding," the bell chimed each time a car rolled over the air hoses alerting us inside that a customer had pulled up to one of the eighteen gas pumps.

The Old Man came in around 4:30 every morning along with his wife, Libbie, a petite woman who never acknowledged anyone; she just quietly made her way upstairs to keep the books. She left after a few hours, taking the previous day's proceeds to the bank where my sister, Sheila, a bank teller at the time, often handled her deposits. Mrs. Rouse returned around lunchtime in her gleaming Oldsmobile to pick up the Old Man and drive him home. They lived in a meticulously kept brick house on Courtland Street, by Santa Maria, just west of Lincoln Street. J.R. and his brother, Mac, worked long hours at the station. Bruce, the most animated of the brothers, was a big man with a bombastic personality and several successful business interests of his own, including multiple service stations in Libertyville. I didn't see him very often except when I had to drive over to one of his stations to retrieve a needed auto part. Rouse's had a reputation for unparalleled service. Every car that pulled up to the pumps had its own pit crew, a minimum of three attendants: one to pump the gas, one to check the oil, and one to wash all the windows. The goal was to be at the vehicle within ten seconds after it pulled onto the apron. It was a very successful business model. Rouse's charged more than everybody else in town, but you got first-rate service. As a result, they were always busy.

On the day I started, I had to inform a woman, upon investigating the source of smoke billowing out from under her hood, that she had a dead cat smoldering on her manifold. I peeked around the opened hood and regretfully asked, "M'am, do you own a cat?"

"Aaaagh!" she shrieked, "Oh my God! Not my little Tinker Belle!"

She was in complete hysterics as she wedged herself out of her car. I stepped in front of her to spare her the hideous sight that lay under her hood.

"Tinker Belle! Tinker Belle!" she cried as she bulled her way past me.

She waddled around to the front of the car. Peering through her sausage-like fingers that she had stretched over her face, she saw the sizzling feline. She paused.

"That's not Tinker Belle," she said matter-of-factly, "that's the neighbor's cat."

She put her hands over her chest, looked to the sky and breathed a sigh of relief.

Surly Eddie Poleska casually walked over and peeled the carcass from the exhaust manifold, carried it around back and flung it into the dumpster.

"Thank God!" the woman laughed, patting my arm, "Oh! Thank God!"

She then squeezed back into her car and sped off.

A few weeks later, an Asian lady who drove a Buick Electra 225, poorly, swerved into the gas station with a big, old fashioned hay wagon turn. Protocol dictated that whoever was the first out the door had the responsibility of talking with the customer. The attendants nearly ran each other over as they darted the other way—into the car wash and mechanical bays, pretending they had something else to do as the Buick screeched to a halt at the pumps. I zipped up my jacket and walked briskly out to her car.

"Yes m'am," I said cheerfully.

I noticed no one else followed me out. She shouted her demands through the rolled up window. I raised my hand to my ear and shook my head as if I couldn't hear her. (I didn't respond to customers who acted out their requests in filling station charades. I figured that if I walked out to their car in the freezing cold to give them what they wanted, they could at least have the courtesy to roll down their window and tell me. I especially enjoyed playing stupid with those who repeated their animations two or three times until they gave up in frustration—not realizing how ridiculous they looked and how much satisfaction I gained from the experience.) Annoyed, the woman rolled down her window about an inch and put her mouth up to the open space.

In a heavily accented voice, she barked her demands. We went back and forth several times before I understood her. "Fill it up with Premium, check the oil, check the tires and . . . rotate the air in all my tires." Apparently, every time she filled her car up with gas, she insisted that the attendant let all the air out of her tires and replace it with "new" air. After my first encounter with the woman I, too, became a member of the ranks of those who scampered off to the back room and left the "checkie-tire lady," as she was known, to the revolving door of rookies.

The best part of the job at Rouse's was driving the tow truck. I liked helping people who were in desperate need of *my* assistance. Some were more desperate than others. I once got a call from the Mundelein Police Department to impound a vehicle from a residential property. When I arrived, the police were in an armed stand off with the owner. "Go ahead kid, just back 'er up there and get that car. We'll cover ya," the policeman told me.

"The hell, I will," I mumbled, got back in the tow truck, and returned to the station without it. There was no way I was going to put myself between the cops and some drunk with a gun.

One bitterly cold January night I got a call from a regular customer who was stranded about three miles north of town at the Doe's Motel. His battery was dead. I approached his Cadillac and saw a woman in his car I knew not to be his wife. She wore heavy make-up, a fur coat, and clothes like those I ogled in the Fredrick's of Hollywood catalog, revealingly askew and completely inappropriate for January. I pretended I didn't notice. The man acted nervous and impatient. After I jumped his battery and closed the hood of his car, he slipped me a $50 bill and said, "You never came out here and you never saw me. Got it?"

"I never left the station, sir," I said, tucking the bill into my coat pocket.

When I wasn't working at the station I hired out as a house painter and milked the better part of the summer of 1975 painting J.R. Rouse's home on the south end of town. J.R.'s son, Jimmy, and his first cousin, Billy Rouse, Bruce's youngest child, were all of ten or eleven years old. They were a couple of hellions, constantly around the house and yard, mostly unsupervised, and engaging in destructive mischief and name-calling. They taunted me as I painted. But they were only children and I did my best to ignore them.

J.R. used to reward his employees who showed ambition and exemplary service. In the summer of 1975 he motioned me aside and asked,

"What are you doing Saturday night?"

"No plans," I said, "why? You need me to work?"

"No. Listen, I'd like you to come with me and a couple of other guys. I want to treat you to dinner. A nice steak at Marino's in New Munster. It's over the border in Wisconsin. Ever been there?"

"No, heard of it though." I said.

"Prime rib big as your head—bigger than the plate they bring it to you on," he said laughing, "be here by 6:30."

The following Saturday J.R. drove us north on Route 45 in his red 1966 Cadillac Fleetwood. His brother, Bruce, was also in the front. I squeezed in back with two other guys. Once into Wisconsin, J.R. took a series of county roads until we finally pulled into an old Wisconsin farm town. The roadhouse restaurant was in the middle of "downtown," a half-a-block stretch of turn-of-the-century frame buildings. J. R. had accurately described the steaks and I left more on my plate than I ate. After dinner, J.R. and Bruce whispered something about entertainment. They both looked at me. We piled back into the Caddy. It wasn't long before I noticed we were not headed home. J.R. turned down one cornfield-flanked road after another, further and further out into the bucolic Wisconsin countryside. Soon there were no farms, no lights, and no cars. We came upon an isolated two-story farmhouse at the end of a long, dirt driveway. I had no idea where we were. I nervously walked up to the farmhouse with the others.

"Whatever you want boys, it's on me," J.R. said.

A woman greeted us at the back door. She acted as if she knew us. She led us down a stairway and through a series of doors that opened into a cellar. There were craps tables, a roulette wheel, slot machines, poker tables, and a small bar. J.R. and Bruce waited for my reaction. I tried to act cool. The others I was with seemed familiar with the place. There were a few other patrons—rough looking characters who glared at us when we entered. Several women approached us; one, who looked old enough to be my mother, put her arm around me and led me to the bar.

"What would you like to drink, honey?" she purred.

"A beer, ma'am," I replied. "Just a beer."

I clutched the glass bottle with both hands as I delicately deflected her strokes and caresses. I was completely grossed out. What did I get myself into? I could scarcely see my other dinner companions through the dimly lit room. Some were gambling, others were at tables in shadowy corners—all had women hanging on them.

J.R. must have sensed how uncomfortable I was. About twenty minutes into my nightmare, he and Bruce led a charge up the stairs.

"Let's go," he said.

I was the first one to the car. The others were chuckling as they came up behind me.

"You don't tell anyone about this place, got it?," J.R. insisted.

CHAPTER 38

༄

THE ROUSE MURDERS

HREE YEARS AFTER I LEFT Rouse's Service Station, the serenity and innocence of my village was lost forever. On the night of June 5, 1980, Bruce, the youngest son of Libbie and G. Hardin Rouse (the Old Man), was murdered along with his wife, Darlene, in the bedroom of their sprawling home a few miles away near Libertyville.

There was a severe thunderstorm on that spring night which provided two of the Rouse children, 15-year-old Billy and his 16-year-old sister, Robin, with an explanation of why they never heard any gunshots despite sleeping directly above their parents. "Amazing luck," said First Deputy Chief James Donaldson, who headed the investigation. Authorities doubted that the killer would have been able to time the shotgun blasts with the thunderclaps, and the children were immediately suspected. Investigators reasoned that if the children were not involved directly, then they at least knew something about it.

Robin was the one to discover the bodies at 8:30 the following morning when the manager of one of Bruce's gas stations called wondering where the workaholic owner was.[90]

"It was a hate killing," said Lake County Sheriff Tom S. Brown. "The way the bodies had been treated—brutally—it must have been a crime of hate."[91]

Police ruled out robbery as a motive, because Darlene was still wearing several expensive rings. Bruce's wallet containing $300 in cash was still on the dresser. Nothing else appeared to be missing. Nothing, authorities noted, except for several weapons from Bruce's collection of shotguns.

The night she died, Darlene went to dinner with friends then spent the evening with her bridge club. Bruce and his younger son, Billy, spent most of the evening installing a spray paint booth at one of his auto repair shops. They arrived home around 10:30 PM, a half-hour before Darlene came home. Bruce, who started his workday around 6:00 AM, went right to sleep; Billy said he dozed off in front of the television in the family room. He told police he awoke sometime during the night and went upstairs to bed.

Robin said she was already asleep by the time her parents came home, and the oldest son, Kurt, 20, was probably asleep in his apartment in the former servants' quarters adjacent to the house.

By outward appearances the Rouse family was a classic American success story. Bruce and Darlene were active in the community and were well known for their philanthropy. Beneath the surface, however, there was trouble in the family which came to light during the subsequent homicide investigation.

Like their father, each of the Rouse children was intense and driven. My few dealings with Kurt Rouse were not pleasant experiences. I found him to be a spoiled teenaged bully, overbearing and ill-tempered. I never met Robin, but Billy, I had observed, was an obnoxious brat.

"The whole family didn't get along together," an investigator told the press, "there was trouble among everyone."[92]

Having worked for the family for a few years, I was not surprised by this revelation, but I was surprised how well the family was able to keep it from the public eye.

Kurt was a state-ranked wrestler in high school and starting lineman on the Lake Forest Academy football team. Unfortunately, by 1980, it appeared that he had already peaked. He didn't have a steady job, and with no college ambitions, Kurt was resisting the pressure his parents put on him to join the military. When their relationship became strained, Kurt moved out of the family home on Milwaukee Avenue just north of Peterson Road and into the detached barn that had been remodeled into a living quarters for hired help.

Robin was the apple of her father's eye. She was a good student and was rarely, if ever, in trouble. Her relationship with her parents was solid, but she was not on good terms with Kurt, according to police.

While Kurt was unmotivated and ambivalent about his future, Billy, the baby of the family, was trouble. He had an undiagnosed learning disorder that kept him from reading at grade level and found it more fun to cause havoc than to apply himself to his studies, although he was a good athlete. Billy had been expelled from the local school district for vandalism and was attending a "correctional school" at the time his parents were slain. Billy had been a drinker for many years and had graduated to marijuana by the time he was a teen. His drug use, vandalism, and truancy became a major point of contention between him and his parents.[93]

Kurt was unaware of the killings until police woke him up at his apartment. He seemed confused and disoriented.

Billy, however, was helpful to investigators, something that immediately set off alarm bells.

"Intuitively, you pick up on a lot of things," said Kurt Proschwitz, an investigator, "from the onset there was suspicion."[94]

One of the first indicators that Billy knew more than he was saying was his concern that the funerals and other arrangements would keep him from participating in a soccer tournament that weekend. From the beginning, police suspected one or more of the children were involved; within hours of the slayings each of the children lawyered-up and refused to cooperate in the investigation. They were all summoned to appear before the coroner's inquest and the grand jury. Detectives thought that reviewing the grisly details might provide a break in the case and perhaps cause one or all of them to confess. But before both panels the children remained silent at the insistence of their counsel. It was their right under the U.S. Constitution and it could not be used as evidence or as an implication of guilt in court. But it drew additional suspicion from the police who considered that three children who refused to share what they know about their parents' murders likely had something to hide. The evidence in the investigation supported their suspicion:

- Two of the three children were allegedly asleep directly above the room where two people were gunned down with a shotgun, yet neither heard anything.
- None of the children would take a polygraph test or talk to investigative authorities under oath.
- Robin did tell a detective that one of her brothers committed the crime, but refused to speak further.
- The family's Labrador retriever never barked.

- There was a quarter-sized dollop of blood on the exterior of Bruce's car.
- There were bloodstains in the trunk of the car as if someone had put bloody clothes there.
- The windshield wipers on the car were in the on position although it did not rain until 3 AM—long after Bruce and Billy returned home.
- The doors to the home were locked from the inside and there was no sign of forced entry.
- The items "stolen" from the home—five shotguns and some jewelry—were all later recovered nearby, at the bottom of the Des Plaines River days after the murders.
- Neither the knife used to kill Bruce, nor the shotgun used to wound him and kill Darlene, was ever found.[95]

Police were never able to come up with any motive beyond the problems the children were having with their parents and within weeks, the investigation was at a standstill.

"I have no idea when we will have a suspect," Sheriff Brown said. "It will not be an immediate arrest."[96]

Police had narrowed down the suspects to three: Kurt, Robin, and Billy. But with no murder weapon and only circumstantial evidence, they could not positively link any of them to the murders. With the surviving Rouses united in their stonewalling of the probe, authorities could not even offer one of them immunity to discuss what he or she knew for fear one would claim complete responsibility.

"The problem is not so much that we have to find who did it, but we have to be able to show that no one else *could* have done it," Brown said six months after the killings. The investigation stalled with lack of further evidence and the unwillingness of the Rouse family to cooperate.

The Rouse children subsequently inherited much of their parents' $1 million estate and they each went their separate ways. The case file was soon collecting dust among the frustrated detectives in the squad room of the Lake County Sheriff's Office. Fifteen years elapsed before there was a break in the case and the crime was solved.

CHAPTER 39

‍⌃‍

CHICAGO, REVISITED

THE TRENDY DEPAUL AND LINCOLN Park neighborhoods that my father had become so accustomed to after the war were visited by him again during a period from 1978 to 1982 when he accompanied me to the bars in the city.

My long and bittersweet journey into music began in January, 1978, the snowiest month on record in Chicago's history.[97] Over three feet of snow blanketed the ground that season when I tried to navigate through the clogged and unfamiliar city streets in search of a little Irish Pub called Finn Mac Cool's one Wednesday night. The run-down tavern was on the northeast corner of Clark Street and Wellington, across the street from the old Ivanhoe Theater. Like my father's Aunt Scottie's Tap of the 1960's, Mac Cool's was long, dark, and narrow. It smelled of stale beer and misery. A small, unlit stage was adjacent to the front door. I introduced myself to the bartender-owner, Jim Guilfoyle, and asked if I could audition. He nodded and pointed in the direction of the stage. I quickly set-up my gear and strapped on my guitar. I perched on a bar stool with my back to the front window. I nervously sang a few songs to the disinterested Guilfoyle and a few silhouetted patrons hunched over the bar, nursing their beers. I sang my heart out. No one applauded. Guilfoyle sauntered over to the stage.

"Here's the deal kid. I *got* a guy, but he's out with a broken leg. You can play from nine until two. I'll give you forty-five bucks a night, cash under the bar and what ever tips you make, you keep, but you buy your own beer. You start tomorrow," he slurred.

I accepted his proposal. It wasn't much, but it was a start. Every weekend for a month, I drove fifty miles from home to the city and played what few Irish songs I knew, most of which my father had taught me as a child and I loosely transposed to guitar. I performed them to a revolving group of rag-tag patrons that ranged from hookers to construction workers, gay men to a street woman with a pack of feral dogs, who, one night, pulled out a knife on a man at the bar. It was a rough place—but I didn't know any better. I was an optimistic twenty-two-year-old bent on single-handedly revitalizing the waning Lincoln Park folk music scene, and it was my first experience playing bars in Chicago. Although I would come to play a number of taverns throughout the city over the next fifteen years, few proved to be as memorable and none were as rough or as dangerous as Mac Cool's.

My father often tagged along, "for safety," or so he said. I'm sure he was just grateful to get out of the house and make new acquaintances, drink on the cheap, and listen to his son perform the songs he had taught him.

Guilfoyle, a heavy equipment Teamster by day—bar owner by night—often invited my father and me into the basement after closing time, to participate in a drink of "the holy water." We descended down a steep, rickety staircase under a trap door behind the bar and entered a musty maze of cramped, dark aisles filled with moldy cases of empty beer bottles, broken bar stools, cob webs, and old advertising signs. The basement was a speakeasy back in the days of prohibition when Al Capone and rival gangster, "Bugs" Moran, wreaked havoc on the city. The infamous St. Valentine's Day Massacre occurred just a few blocks south of Mac Cool's, at 2122 Clark Street, forty-nine years earlier. Guilfoyle led us to an ice box built into the building's brick wall foundation. It had a thick oak door with a heavy-duty padlock. Guilfoyle fumbled with his keychain, unlocked the door, and entered the dark cooler. He emerged with a bottle of precious eighteen-year-old Jameson Irish whiskey and a shot glass. The three of us took turns toasting this-or-that, threw back the whiskey, and commented on how special it was. That is how I was introduced to fine Irish whiskey.

My tenure at Mac Cool's was brief, with a new and unpleasant adventure nearly every night. I learned quick and valuable lessons about playing club dates, dealing with those who frequented them, unscrupulous bar owners, and loose waitresses.

I had the distinct displeasure of observing the dynamics of the room from where I sat and every night I watched the unseemliness unfold. Guilfoyle, for example, suffered from a common malady of bar owners everywhere; he was his own best customer. His Polish waitress, Sophia, I observed, appeared also to be his mistress. They fought and made up several times during the night—every night. He became so angry with her one early morning after closing that he wrapped his arms around a freezer in the back of the room (which apparently belonged to her), picked it up by himself, and dumped it out into the snow-clogged alley.

At Mac Cool's, I watched drug buys under the tables and pick-ups in the parking lot. I successfully eluded sexual advances from both women *and* men and witnessed the occasional bar fight. I played there three nights a week, every Thursday, Friday, and Saturday—every other month for six months. I soon became dejected and was ready to move on. I told myself that I was going to give up pursuing music altogether if the gigs didn't get any better. Fortunately, most of them did. The accumulation of bad experiences for the remaining twenty-two years of my playing career did not come anywhere close to what I experienced in those first six months, with one exception—October 31st, 1984.

By the early 1980's I had achieved a good reputation and steady work on the Irish music scene in Chicago and teamed up with a South Side accordion player by the name of Jimmy Thornton. We billed ourselves as "Blackthorn." Jim had strong ties in the Irish community. His brothers were both city policemen and his father, a retired Chicago Police Captain. As a result, we reaped the benefits of a vast number of city events and political gigs.

Jim booked a Halloween job for us at a north side watering hole called the Dingle Bay Pub. It would be the first time (and the last time) we played there. The owner, Peter Hennighan, and his pleasant but clueless wife, Angie, were hosting a Halloween costume party and they asked if Jim and I would judge a "best costume contest" at midnight. The prize was $200. Whatever. I just wanted to play music. Most of the patrons participated in the loosely organized event, and the costumes were less than imaginative—except for one, "Staggers the Clown."

"Staggers," whose real name was Michael Kilcoyne, kept all the patrons entertained with his antics in between our sets, throwing back drinks, and never speaking a word. At the corner of the bar sat a scantily-clad woman who nursed several free drinks given to her by the over-attentive Peter

Hennighan. Jim and I observed their obvious and intimate connection. I had seen such behavior countless nights before, in classier places than the Dingle Bay Pub. No matter. It came with the territory and was none of my business.

Shortly before midnight, Hennighan pulled Jim and me aside.

"Listen," he said. "I want you to vote that woman at the bar there, the winner of the contest."

"The one dressed like a hooker? Are you serious?" I asked.

Jimmy Thornton, a hot-tempered and muscle-bound Kerryman, who bench-pressed four hundred pounds, didn't take any crap from anybody. He was a good partner to have in the rough-and-tumble Irish pubs of Chicago. His police connections came in handy on occasion, too.

"Forget it," Jim laughed. "This guy has kept all these customers in your joint all night long. He's been brilliant. Look at him—how he works the whole room. And you want us to throw the contest to your tart at the bar? Screw you!"

"Just do it!" the owner insisted as we hopped back on stage.

Midnight came and Jimmy and I included the audience in helping us make the decision as to who should be the winner of the contest and the $200 prize.

By process of elimination, Staggers won, hands down. The owner was furious. As Jimmy and I belted out tunes, Hennighan paced behind the bar breaking empty beer bottles against the floor. The object of his affection at the bar hastily slinked out the front door. Staggers collected his winnings from the enraged bar owner and declared, "drinks are on me!" Those were the first words he had uttered since he arrived hours earlier, and they came much to the delight of the raucous, late-night crowd.

A few weeks later, Jim and I saw Angie Hennighan at a North Side Irish wedding reception where we were booked to play for the evening.

"Do you remember the clown from Halloween night?" She asked in a serious tone.

"Sure." I said. "Staggers, Michael Kilcoyne. Wasn't he great? We had a nice chat with him after. He said he has a brother who is a professional clown with Ringling Brothers and Barnum & Bailey Circus. And since his brother was in town with the circus down at the Stadium, he borrowed one of his costumes, makeup and props and . . . "

"Yes. Well, someone shot him Halloween night . . . in the back . . . on the front steps of his apartment," she said. "He's going to be okay, thank

God. They robbed him of what was left of his two hundred dollars and they left him for dead."

I don't judge contests anymore.

I spent the next few years playing bars, restaurants and festivals throughout the city and suburbs—from Reilly's Daughters Pub at 111th and Pulaski on the far south side, to Grandpa's Place on the north side, across from the train station in Glenview. But it was in the Irish Eyes Pub at 2519 North Lincoln Avenue in the Lincoln Park neighborhood, where I honed my skills and learned how to work an audience. My father still insisted on traveling with me. Most nights I called him up to the stage to sing. He always sang the same song, *Today While the Blossoms Still Cling to the Vine*. Audiences loved to hear my father croon and he was *never* shy about hamming it up. Sometimes we stopped for breakfast at the Seminary Restaurant on the corner of Lincoln, Halsted, and Fullerton, to sober up on coffee before making the journey home. My father pointed out how the diner had changed very little from the time he used to frequent it in the 1940's.

From my boyhood days of Saturday night hooleys, I knew that performing was what I wanted to do more than anything else in the world. I hoped to make a career out of playing the Irish music I grew up on, but reality and responsibility dictated otherwise. Besides, "there is only one way to make a million dollars in Irish music," the late, great Tommy Makem once told me, "start with two million." Still, I tried for twenty-two years to become an overnight success. To Tommy's point, I played at wakes and weddings, and funerals, christenings, parties, and pubs. In 1986, I founded and fronted a band (named Arranmore by no strange coincidence). Over time, we worked our way into the concert and festival circuit. The former we referred to as the "blue-haired ball" because of the overwhelming attendance of elderly women. The latter we called the "manure tour" due to all the mid-west fairs we played. I enjoyed the few, limited moments I had in the sun—the most memorable of which were the concerts I worked with Tommy Makem.

By the early 90's, Arranmore was opening for Tommy at shows throughout the mid-west. We usually joined him on stage at the close of his set to perform a couple of songs together and to back him on his signature song, *Four Green Fields*, to close the show. I loved to watch him work a crowd. He was a theatrical, old-school performer, as engaging off-stage as he was on. Nothing pulls at my heartstrings quite like the emotional despair drawn from a good song sung well. Few have ever been able to do that as masterfully as Tommy Makem. "When the music is in your blood Kevin, it's hard to resist the roar of the greasepaint and the smell of the crowd," he said. Adding, "wait a minute now, I may have that backwards." Off-stage, Tommy was always a gentleman, thoughtful, polite, and beguiling; an aging hipster and intellectual gadfly who, if the mood hit him, blurted out poetry or burst into an obscure song in the middle of a conversation or in the middle of a restaurant. Tommy was well known and well loved and his music reflected that. Among his closest friends were Bob Dylan, they came up together in Greenwich Village in the 60's; Cindy Lauper, a Jersey girl who grew up, as I did, on Tommy's music; and Bono, who recognized the brilliance of *Four Green Fields* and said it was his favorite Irish song. You, too, were among his closest friends if he happened to be talking to you. He always gave everyone he met, fan and celebrity alike, his undivided attention and respect.

I worked with other notable performers along the way and I had some mild success as a songwriter. But none of it was enough to keep me in the game. As the years passed, success seemed more and more elusive and my musical satisfaction was replaced with a growing cynicism. Music was for me an addiction dating back to my childhood. I've been clean and sober now since 1999. Given the chance to do it over again, I wouldn't. I would instead choose to redirect that time and energy toward something more substantive and rewarding—like spending it with my children.

Relaxing backstage with Tommy Makem (right) before a St.
Patrick's Day concert in suburban Chicago, 1996.

CHAPTER 40

⚜

THE WAKE

B Y 6:00 PM THE ROOM at Kristan's Funeral Home is nearly full. A steady stream of family and friends file in to pay their last respects and are waiting patiently in the receiving line mentally organizing their condolences and words of comfort for my siblings and me. Most don't know what to say. It's awkward. They stutter, pause, or make random gestures. Whenever I see someone having difficulty with the moment, I verbally step in and tell them how grateful we all are that they took the time to pay their respects. They seem relieved.

Father Aguirre from Santa Maria stops by and directs those in attendance through a brief prayer service. Afterward, he leads me aside to go over some details for the funeral service.

"Now, Kevin, you know that Mass of the Resurrection will be in the small chapel tomorrow at 10:30," he said while searching his coat pockets. "Now let's see . . . afterwards, we'll make our way to Ascension Cemetery. We'll congregate at the chapel there—too messy to go graveside, I suppose, what with all the rain. There will be a brief internment rite, at the conclusion of which I will make an announcement, yes, an announcement that the family has asked *me* to invite everyone back to the parish hall for a small reception where the women of the bereavement committee will provide lunch, or words to that effect and . . . so on and so forth."

He continues to search his pockets.

"Whatever Father, that's fine. Can I help you find whatever it is you're looking for?"

"Ah!" he exclaims. "No, thank you. There it is." He pulls out a piece of crumpled paper and ballpoint pen from his inside pocket. He flips the paper over a few times.

I turn toward the priest, "Listen, Father, about the music tomorrow, it's very important . . . "

"Yes, yes, yes. Debbie Titus told me to tell you *personally* that she'll have a small choir in the balcony at the rear of the chapel."

The absent-minded priest adjusts his glasses and tries to scribble a check mark on the paper.

"Tsk. The paper, it's a little damp . . . the weather and all. Just want to make sure we have all the right songs. Let's see? You wanted 'Amazing Grace' for the entrance hymn is that right?"

I nod. He makes another check mark and continues,

"And 'St. Patrick's Breastplate' during the offertory" (another check mark). "Oh! And 'Morning Has Broken' during communion?"

"Absolutely," I reply. "Father, did you know that that is an old Irish song? My father learned it in Irish when he was a boy back in Ireland—the words are different and it wasn't considered a hymn . . . "

"Is that a fact?" he says politely while shaking his pen to get the ink to flow. He makes another check mark. "Now, what about this last one Kevin, the processional 'Today?' What's this 'today?'"

"Today While the Blossoms Still Cling to the Vine," I say.

He shakes his head in dissent.

"What's wrong with it?" I ask sharply.

"Well . . . it's not in the hymnal I'm afraid, and I don't think Debbie knows it. How about 'On Angel's Wings' instead? Do you know that one? That's always a *good* recessional hymn."

My voice begins to build. "I don't care if it's in the hymnal or not, and I don't want a good one. I want, *we* want, 'Today.'" I motion to everyone in the room. "I don't care about any angel's wings. I don't like angel's wings, Debbie knows the song, I know she knows the song because she and I have sung it together before." (A lie.)

My brother, John, steps in and grabs me by my shoulder. "Whoa, hang on there Hoss," he says. "What's goin' on?"

Everyone in the room is looking at us.

Father scratches a note on his paper. "Today," he says in agreement. "Just tying up a few details for tomorrow." He walks away to mingle with some parishioners in the back of the room.

John guides my outside onto the front portico. We each light up a cigarette. There are flashes of lightning in the sky toward the northwest, in the direction of Mechanics Grove School. I notice the lights are out throughout the neighborhood. "Goddamn rain," I murmur. "Is it ever going to stop?"

I see a young woman in a piper's uniform emerge from the dark parking lot. I arranged for a piper from the Midlothian Bagpipe Band to come and play a few airs. I introduce myself to her as she walks up the steps. I finish my cigarette. I flick the butt onto the driveway and escort the young woman inside. John follows. The crowd parts, allowing the young woman to make her way to the front. She pays her respects to the stranger in the coffin and steps to one side. She raises her pipes, primes the bag, and with a sharp strike from the heel of her right hand, tucks the bladder under her left arm. The sweet, mournful wail of highland pipes envelopes the room. She plays three tunes: *For Ireland I'll Not Tell Her Name*, *Hills of Urich*, and a Strathsbey called *The Shores of Loch Catrine*. As the music swirls around us, I walk over to the coffin. I reach into my suit-coat pocket and pull out a dram bottle of Jameson's Irish Whiskey. I hide it in the palm of my hand and lean over my father. In the centuries-old Galún Uí Dhomhnaill tradition, where Aodh Roe O'Donnell declared that his excess drink is to be shared among weary travelers passing that way, I gently slide the bottle inside the breast pocket of Dad's Donegal Tweed jacket.

"Now," I whisper, "you owe *me* one. And I fully intend to collect."

Then I pat him lightly on his shoulder and adjust his tie.

EPILOGUE

∽

"Cast a cold Eye on Life, on Death. Horsemen, pass by!"

—William Butler Yeats

My father and me at Yeats' grave Drumcliff, Sligo, Ireland, 1985.
—*Photo courtesy of Sheila Miller*

M UNDELEIN IS NO LONGER THE prosaic village of my youth where a mile in any direction from the center of town cornfields reached to the sky. It is indistinguishable from most other American towns, sprawling with housing developments, strip malls, and chain stores, cluttered highways, and a languishing town center. These are the economic realities of modern American life that some call progress.

They have planted houses in the fields and fens we called the cowpath. Hobo Jungle is now the 500 block of Cardinal Place, intersected by Pershing Avenue. And curiously, the house on Farina Court that occupies the very spot where the Lightning Tree once stood continues to be struck by thunderbolts, while the surrounding neighbors suffer no damage at all.

As I drive through the old neighborhood, I notice *one* remaining vestige of my childhood, the Pin Cherry tree in which my brothers, Billy Schafernak, and I made our tree fort. Like a former glamour queen, it stands tired but graceful, adorning the yard between houses that stand shoulder to shoulder in what once was our neighborhood frontier. On the opposite end of my childhood realm, Suicide Hill and the surrounding wetland have long since been filled in and renamed Lewendowski Park.

The sprawling Rouse's Service Station was sold and leveled after the Old Man passed away, replaced with a ubiquitous mini-mart filling station. In many respects, Rouse's represented the social as well as geographic center of the village, and it played an integral role throughout my young life. Nowhere was this more evident than on a quiet November evening in 1975. I was working the night shift. I casually strolled out to a red 1966 Ford Mustang as it pulled up to the pumps. I couldn't know then that that chance encounter would forever change my life. Her name was Jan Johnson. She was a Public. She lived in Fairhaven. I passed her house twice a day, every day, when I attended Carmel High School for Boys, but had never before seen her. We were the same age, grew up in the same small town, and knew many of the same people. We began dating almost immediately after we met. A few months later we were engaged. Eighteen months after our first encounter, we got married at the same Lutheran church where I attended kindergarten. Although we are no longer wed, I will always be grateful to her for the two extraordinary children we had together.

I still enjoy the peaceful pleasure of taking a leisurely drive around St. Mary's Lake through the cardinal's seminary. There are currently more

than 35,000 residents in the village of Mundelein. I am certain most are
unaware of what a magnificent treasure exists right in their own community,
or what serenity lies just off the highway behind the formidable iron gate
entrance along what once was the Hiawatha Trail. Proportionately few have
ever bothered to explore and appreciate this extraordinary property. The
distinctive neo-Classical edifices appear like Brigadoon out of the woods,
imposing the lines of a Latin Cross, laid out in perfect symmetry—with The
Immaculate Conception Chapel at its heart. The road that meanders around
the 100 acre lake remains essentially unchanged since it first opened in
1926. The edges of the lake are spanned in various sections by five elegant
arch bridges. Old-growth woods canopy the road in many places, providing
stunning views and glimpses of the campus at various points around the lake,
and a sense of what the countryside must have been like for centuries before
the Europeans came. I recently shared with my sister, Sheila, some winter
photographs I took of the seminary. She wrote back to me saying, "What
peaceful hours once enjoyed and how sweet the memories are still."

Each of my siblings continue the tradition our father started and escort
friends and visitors through the circuitous labyrinth of roadways and the
tree-lined lane around the crystal-clear lake. They share with them *their*
childhood memories and the seminary's secrets, beauty, and rich history.

I have developed a far different opinion of George Cardinal Mundelein
at the end of this book than I had at the beginning. I have a new-found
respect for his vision and for all that he accomplished in his lifetime, but
there is no mistaking his larger-than-life personality. Even in death, Cardinal
Mundelein's ego lives on. Leaving nothing to chance, he pre-planned his
own internment in the Sacristy behind the marble altar in the Immaculate
Conception Chapel on the grounds of his beloved seminary. However,
the burial crew had to make a last minute "adjustment" and chisel away
additional marble along the edges behind the altar during the funeral service
in order to accommodate his massive coffin.

Cardinal Mundelein's seminary serves not only as his final resting place
but, as one of his contemporaries pointed out, "a permanent memorial to
his patriotism and his faith."

As the Village of Mundelein approaches its centennial anniversary of
incorporation, they are about to reacquire a unique piece of its history: their
first fire truck, given to the town by its namesake. The 1925 Stoughton,
affectionately referred to as "Old #1, was recently discovered buried beneath

decades of dust and neglect and filled with hay seed and field mice in the barn of a collector. It changed hands many times over, traversing the United States from Maryland to southern Illinois after the village sold it in 1945. It was rescued only days before it met the scrap heap by retired Mundelein firefighter, Jim Carew, and has been hibernating for the past fourteen years in his Wisconsin barn less than twenty miles from its original home at the Mundelein Village Hall. Village officials have purchased the truck and have made arrangements with Carew to restore it to its original condition in time for the Mundelein Centennial Celebration in October, 2009.[98]

I am certain the benevolent cardinal would be deeply saddened to learn that his institution became the center of a scandal that rocked the Archdiocese of Chicago and served as a breeding ground and safe harbor for dozens of pedophile priests. Since 1950 more than sixty-five archdiocesan priests and deacons have been removed from public ministry on substantiated allegations of sexual misconduct with minors.

Thomas Job, the Deacon at Santa Maria del Popolo during my grade school years, was ordained a priest three years after my stint as an altar boy. His first assignment was at St. John Vianny in Northlake. From there, he was given additional assignments by the Archdiocese including St. Cletus in La Grange and at St. Joseph in Libertyville, where he became pastor. In October, 2005, the Archdiocese of Chicago announced that it had reached a settlement after admitting to substantiated allegations of sexual misconduct with minors involving twenty-four adult victims who accused fourteen priests of molesting them when they were children. One of those priests named was Thomas Job. The abuse was said to have occurred in the early 1970's. Yet the pedophile priest was allowed to continue his ministry with "unfettered access to scores of children" for nearly twenty years before he resigned, in 1992.[99]

Likewise, Father Jim Ray, our family friend, was removed from ministry while at Transfiguration Parish in Wauconda (site of the old Elm Theatre), on allegations of sexual misconduct involving a minor at his previous assignment at St. Peter Damian in Bartlett. I did not believe the scandalous reports that filled the newspapers or the belaboring television news accounts describing all that he had allegedly done. Then, he abruptly confessed to all of it. I felt betrayed. I was outraged. I began to search my memory and realized that there were numerous times throughout the years when he hugged me too close, or too long, or with too much affection, which I summarily dismissed. And while the allegations arose in 1991, the Archdiocese of Chicago states that Father Ray was "removed from public ministry in June 2002," citing "substantiated allegations of sexual misconduct with minors," as determined by the archdiocese's Professional Responsibility Review Board.[100] To date, the Archdiocese of Chicago has paid $65 million to settle approximately 250 similar claims over the past thirty years.[101]

The aftermath of the Rouse murders continued to decimate the founding family and sully the character of the town. Robin Rouse died in 1983, in a curious car accident in rural Racine County, Wisconsin. She was traveling at high speed when she clipped an oncoming car, lost control and struck a utility pole. Sheriff Tom Brown's successor, Robert "Mickey" Babcox said her death dealt her parents' murder investigation a serious blow. "I do feel that she was one of the closest ones and best to deal with," Babcox said. "She was there when it happened."

Billy Rouse continued to run afoul of the law. He had a series of drug- and alcohol-related legal scrapes over the next several years and was living for a time in a transient hotel in Key West, Florida. Neither Kurt nor Billy cooperated with authorities who periodically looked into the killings. After all, police surmised, there was nothing that could be done until one or the other confessed, implicating the other or their late sister. By 1984, no investigator was working on the case except to keep track of the brothers' whereabouts. That year Billy was arrested for attempted murder in a stabbing over a chess match. Convicted of misdemeanor battery, he received sixty days in jail. Eleven years later, Billy was arrested again as an accomplice in a pair of South Florida bank robberies. By 1995, he had squandered his inheritance and had been jailed at least four times on various drug-related charges. He had been married and divorced and was living in a run-down houseboat with several other itinerants.[102]

A Key West police lieutenant, who had been in contact with the Lake County, Illinois, cold case squad over the years, contacted Lake County authorities regarding Billy's bank robbery arrest. The cold case detectives rushed to interrogate Billy once more. This time he was willing to talk.

On October 12, 1995, Billy, in a 37-minute rambling and profanity-laced admission of guilt, confessed to killing his parents.

"I expected you guys a long time ago," Billy told Sgt. Fagan, one of the original investigators on the case. "I think I really might have done it." Billy agreed to take a lie-detector test. He discussed in detail his final argument with his mother over his drug use and became incensed when she told him he was heading to a military school. According to police testimony, after his parents went to bed, and while under the influence of hallucinogenic mushrooms and alcohol, Billy decided to kill them both. He considered using a steak knife, but decided instead on the shotgun.

"I decided I'm going to get rid of my mom. I said if I'm going to do it, I'm going to do it," he confessed. "I walked into the room, put the shotgun up to her head and the trigger went off." When his father awoke, he shot him, but not mortally. Billy stabbed his father to death stating that by doing so, "the shit I had to deal with then was gone."

In 1996, 32-year-old Billy Rouse was convicted of two counts of murder and sentenced to two consecutive forty-year terms in a Federal Penitentiary—the maximum penalty under the law at the time he committed the crimes.[103]

The "Rouse House" as it came to be known, continued its nefarious history after Bruce and Darlene's murders. It was sold several times, including to the Chicago mafia which operated it for a few years as a casino and brothel. During one two-week period in 1982, prosecutors said the operation raked in nearly $500,000 in a scheme that allegedly included Sheriff Tom Brown and others within the Lake County Sheriff's Department. It was also the site of a subsequent mob murder. Robert Plummer of unincorporated Libertyville was an independent bookmaker who refused to give a cut to the notorious Infelise crew of Chicago, who had been expanding their vice operations into Lake County. Plummer was bludgeoned to death at the top of the stairs.[104] Police found his body stuffed into the trunk of his Lincoln Continental in the parking lot of the Mundelein Holiday Inn eight days after his wife reported him missing. In January, 2002, the house locally referred to as "murder mansion," was destroyed in a mysterious fire that left nothing behind but a smoldering shell of ashes and bad memories. The structure was later torn down and today the property is vacant and overgrown with weeds.

As for Kurt Rouse, some say he's living quietly in northern California, others say he's in the construction business in Arizona. Regardless of where he is, he is the sole survivor of unspeakably sad and tragic family memories, those that he may not have had to recount if not for the bravery of a stranger who rescued him from a second story house fire behind his grandfather's service station on a winter's night in 1960.

When my father died, he left the 409 house to my brother, Rodger, who sold it a few years later to another immigrant family—this time from Mexico. I like to think that the new owner was fulfilling his childhood dream, providing a better life for his family than the one he knew in his home country. I think my father would have liked that too.

Death in my family struck mercilessly at regular four year intervals over a period of twelve years, beginning with my mother who died in 1983, followed by my father in 1987. My sister, Maureen, who never married, was a free-spirited and vibrant young woman obsessively fond of animals and environmental causes. She was well on her way to recovery from drug and alcohol addiction and making a new life for herself when she was diagnosed with ovarian cancer. She was convinced that she was being punished by God for all of her previous transgressions, including her teenage pregnancy in 1978. She gave her baby girl up to the sisters at St. Therese Hospital in Waukegan where Cardinal Mundelein's Catholic Charities placed the infant into a loving adoptive home. Maureen died of complications from cancer in 1991. My brother, John, or Jay, was never able to conquer his demons despite several attempts to defeat alcohol. He died behind the wheel of a parked car when he passed out with the engine running and his foot on the accelerator. The engine compartment overheated, caught fire, and engulfed my brother, too intoxicated to escape from the vehicle. His body was so badly burned that the only means by which the coroner's office could positively identify him, was by a thirty-eight-year- old x-ray still on file at Doctor Dulce's office in Waukegan, taken when we lived in Lake County Gardens and John suffered the compound fracture of his arm. I was told by Barbara Richardson, the Lake County Coroner at that time, that Jay's blood alcohol level when he died in 1995 was 0.56, seven times the legal limit.

My brother Rodger, upon witnessing the effects alcohol had on our parent's behavior, has never touched a drop of drink. Tisha battled alcoholism for several years but has been in successful recovery for more than two decades. Sheila has an occasional glass of beer, but never more than that. Daser lives estranged from the family and has battled the devil in the bottle her entire adult life.

It is indeed a wonder that *I* never fell victim to the sensuous allure of drugs and alcohol in the bars and clubs where I worked during my twenty-two year career in the music business. It was certainly there for the taking. But I always kept my guard up. Countless nights I witnessed from the stage the negative behavior it caused in a person. And I never wanted to be that person. I enjoy beer, especially European varieties, and fine wine as a complement to food. I seldom drink beyond that. Jameson's Irish Whiskey on the rocks in a Waterford tumbler is a rare treat for me. I drink it only on special occasions and the taste of it always brings me back to the cellar of Finn Mac Cool's on Clark Street, when Jim Guilfoyle and my father first introduced me to *na uisce beatha* (*na whishkee baha*, the water of life).

Even though I am what the islanders call a *"blow-in,"* Arranmore will always be a part of who I am. There is too much history and culture handed down to me for it not to be so. The island has experienced many changes from when I first arrived in 1979—most of which have been positive. Like the rest of Ireland, Arranmore has enjoyed a long stretch of prosperity, even though fishing has all but ceased and the young people continue to go off to *The Lagan* to look for work. The island population has diminished to about 500,—the lowest in more than three centuries—and unemployment is over fifty percent. Still, they persevere. The island now has a medical clinic and County Council housing for the elderly. Most homes have central heat and satellite TV. As of my most recent visit, a Secondary school has been built in Leabgarrow, the last of the roads have been paved with asphalt, and streetlights glow in the Atlantic mist among the hills and hamlets. But for all of its changes and modern conveniences, the independence of the island people and the character of the island itself remain intact. *This* is what beckons me to return time and again.

"You can't know where it 'tis yer goin', if ye don't know where it 'tis ye been," my father used to say. Not exactly John Steinbeck, but in his own humble, Irish way of looking at the world, he taught me that although heritage and circumstances can have a powerful influence on who we are, ultimately *we* are responsible for who we become. I wonder how different a person I might be without his influence, without my family heritage, without the music that runs through me, and without my small town, Catholic upbringing. Try as we may, we can neither change our past nor can we escape from it, and inevitably the most indelible part of who we are stems from the events that happened in years past—fadó.

The Pin Cherry tree that was on the edge of the cowpath where my brothers and I built our fort, is now surrounded by homes and incorporated into a garden landscape. February 2008.

All that remains of the Rouse Family estate. February, 2008
—*Photos by author.*

The central ceremonial pier, Saint Mary of the Lake Mundelein Seminary. April, 2008.

The longest of five bridges in St. Mary of the Lake Mundelein Seminary. This bridge, along with various other locations throughout the seminary were used in scenes from the 2009 horror movie "The Unborn."—*Photos by author.*

ACKNOWLEDGMENTS

ઌજ

T HIS PROJECT WOULD HAVE NEVER seen the light of day without the constant encouragement of my wife, Colleen. She made countless sacrifices over the past three years as she shared this experience with me. I could not and would not have completed this project without her inspiring support. She reviewed the manuscript more than anyone and listened intently to my storytelling. She deserved more attention than this project would allow and I am grateful for her understanding. Her advice, "just make sure the 94,497 words are not all about *you*," has helped to keep me honest.

My recounting of the history of Arranmore could not be told without the recognition of the late Barney Beag Gallagher, my father's former schoolmaster on the island and author of *Arranmore Links*; also, his son, Aiden, who updated and republished the book in 2004, and who graciously allowed me to reference extensive passages from it, particularly the events surrounding the Famine and the Arranmore Disaster. The writings of Breandan Mac Cnáimhsí, "*A picture of Arranmore Island during the Great Famine Period 1846-1848;* included in Barney's book, opened my eyes to the horrible time in the island's history and ignited the spark within. I am indebted to Lindel Buckle of New Zealand, whose help and excellent web site "Donegal Genealogy Resources" guided me to multiple documents including: *Life in Donegal during the 1830's, Extracts from the Ordnance Survey Memoirs of Donegal 1833-36, Parish of Templecarn, The 1837 Land Survey,* and the remarkable writings of Mrs. Asenath Nicholson, *The Annals of the Famine in Ireland in 1847, 1848 and 1849.* My thanks to the University Of Wisconsin Board Of Regents for their permission to copy Mrs. Nicholson's work. Genealogical records from Jim Sunkes and Jim Doran helped me bridge the gap of my 19ᵗʰ century family between Arranmore and Beaver Island, and I am grateful for their willingness to share.

My research in Ireland would not have been possible without the love and support of Brian and Rita Fisher who not only opened up their home to me in Dublin, but fed me as well, and helped to arrange interviews and travel itineraries and sourced historical information; my thanks for their hospitality and enthusiasm and for allowing me to stay and write in Castleknock for as long as I needed.

I hope the people of Arranmore, to whom I am most indebted and grateful, will look favorably upon the portrait I have painted of their island community. There's no other place on Earth I'd rather be. A special thanks to the following islanders for their help and guidance; Phil and Mary The Glen Boyle, Jerry Early, Peter Butty O'Donnell, Bridean O'Donnell, Bella Gallagher, Neilly Nancy Gallagher, Mary Gallagher, Robert Pfeifer, and Seamus Bonner.

I discovered that the gracious assistance provided by Dottie Watson, President of the Historical Society of the Fort Hill Country and Curator of the Fort Hill Heritage Museum in Mundelein, is the same Mrs. Watson of Hawthorne Hills whose morning paper I used to deliver on my paper route more than forty years earlier. Thank you, Dottie, for providing unfettered access to the museums resources and your personal documents.

My road to chronicling Mundelein's history began with Diana Dretske, collections coordinator at the Lake County Forest Preserves Discovery Museum Archives. She pointed me in the right direction. Thank you Ray Semple, Mundelein Village Trustee, for jarring my recollections of the Lightning Tree and the Mundelein Volunteer Fire Department. Stanley & Genevieve Rouse shared with me their memories of Mundelein, where they have lived for more than ninety years, and Brother Martin Schmitz, OFM CONV. of Marytown National Shrine of Saint Maxamilian Kolbe, unselfishly gave of his expertise. Research assistance and entertainment on these forays was provided by Kevin Crittenden. As I neared the finish line, I gained a second wind largely from the constant encouragement of family and friends: Sheila Miller, Trish and Mark Johnson, Amanda "Dolly" Johnson, Terence Healey, Steve and Gail Jones, and Patty Dwyer. I have benefited greatly from the patient and careful copyediting provided by my daughter, Haley O'Donnell, an excellent writer herself, and from the advice and fruitful suggestions of those who provided their comments and critiques to the excerpts I supplied including: Jim Roche, Kay Robb, Rich Ellinger, and Beth Nichols. Thank you *all* for keeping me on a righteous path.

A tip o' the hat to my author services representitive, Cleofe Miranda, and the team of design professionals at Xlibris for their patience in guiding me through the complex publication process. It has been a long, interesting, and satisfying journey.

Rory, this began at your request as your graduation gift from high school. I apologize that it has taken nearly three years to complete. You always seem to know how to bring out the best in people, including me. I want to be just like you when I grow up, and next time you suggest a gift, you might want to consider one with a return receipt.

Finally, thank you Bill Gates for Microsoft Word.

END NOTES

I list here only the books, articles, writings, interviews, and recordings that have been referenced in augmenting this memoir. This bibliography is by no means a complete record of all the works I have consulted. It indicates the primary source and is intended to serve as a convenience for those with an interest in further pursuit of the historical facts.

1   O'Donnell, Vincent. *O'Donnells of Tyrconnell, A Concise History of the O'Donnell Clan*. ed. 2000, p.48. Inver, Co. Donegal, Ireland: Dálach Publications, 2000.

2   O'Cléirigh, Lughaidh, *Beatha Ruaidh Uí Dhomhnaill*. 1616.

3   Internet Movie Data Base, *The Fighting Prince of Donegal*. Directed by Michael O'Herlihy. Walt Disney Studios. Distributed by Buena Vista. 01 October 1966. *http://us.imdb.com/title/tt0060408/*

4   O'Donnell, Vincent. *O'Donnells of Tyrconnell, A Concise History of the O'Donnell Clan*. ed. 2000, p. 62. Inver, Co. Donegal, Ireland: Dálach Publications, 2000.

5   Ibid., p.9.

6   *O'Donnell Coat of Arms and Family History*, http://www.araltas.com/features/odonnell/

7   O'Donnell, Vincent. *O'Donnells of Tyrconnell, A Concise History of the O'Donnell Clan*. p.42. Inver, Co. Donegal, Ireland: Dálach Publications, 2000.

8   Abbe, Donald R. "The History of Lynn County," *Panhandle-Plains Historical Review* 60. 1987.

9   Andrews, Hal. *X Marks The Spot—Chicago Gangland Wars in Pictures*. p. 27. Chicago: Maltese Publications, 1933. Public Domain, and *Bullets, Bombs and Blackmail*. Chicago Tribune, April 19, 1936.

10 Mc Manus, Seamus. *The Story of the Irish Race, A Popular History of Ireland*. ed. 1921. pp. 458-459. Grenwich, Connecticut: The Devin-Adair Company, 1979.

11 Forster, Nathan. *A Summary of the Foregoing Return of the General State of Arranmore, February 10th, 1823*. ms. 35,393. The Conyngham Estate Papers. Dublin, Ireland. Council of Trustees of the National Library of Ireland.

12 Ibid.

13 Ibid.

14 Gallagher, Barney. *Arranmore Links: The Families of Arranmore with Stories and Some History*. p. 142. ed. 1986. Barney and Aiden Gallagher, 2004.

15 Burke, Cormac, editor. *Gaeltacht and the Islands*. Take Off Magazine, 2008. p.41. Annagry, Letterkenny, Co. Donegal, Ireland. Foilseachán na Mara Theo.

16 Mac Cnáimhsí, Breandan. M.A. *A picture of Arranmore Island during the Great Famine Period 1846-1848*. Donegal Annual 1973, No.3, Vol. X and excerpted from Gallagher, Barney. *Arranmore Links: The Families of Arranmore with Stories and Some History*. pp. 112-122. 1986.

17 *Life in Donegal during the 1830's, Extracts from the Ordnance Survey Memoirs of Donegal 1833-36, Parish of Templecarn*. National Archives of Ireland.

18 Gallagher, Barney. *Arranmore Links: The Families of Arranmore with Stories and Some History*. p. 225. Barney and Aiden Gallagher, 2004.

19 *The Londonderry Journal*, April 29, 1846.

20 C.S.O., O.P., 1847, County Donegal.

21 Nicholson, Asenath, Mrs. *The Annals of the Famine in Ireland in 1847, 1848 and 1849*. University of Wisconsin Board of Regents. Public Domain.

22 Mac Cnáimhsí, Breandan. M.A. *A picture of Arranmore Island during the Great Famine Period 1846-1848*. Donegal Annual 1973, No.3, Vol. X and excerpted from Gallagher, Barney. *Arranmore Links: The Families of Arranmore with Stories and Some History*. pp. 112-122. 1986.

23 *Famine*. V. I.U.P.P. pp. 190-210. National Archives of Ireland.

24 Gallagher, Barney. *Arranmore Links: The Families of Arranmore with Stories and Some History*. p.122. ed. 1986. Barney and Aiden Gallagher, 2004.

25 Sharkey, Sally. *Arranmore Link: The Families of Arranmore with Stories and Some History*. p.122. B. Gallagher. 1986.

26 Gallagher, Barney. *Arranmore Links: The Families of Arranmore with Stories and Some History*. p.121. ed. 1986. Barney and Aiden Gallagher, 2004.

27 Nicholson, Asenath, Mrs. *The Annals of the Famine in Ireland in 1847, 1848 and 1849*. University of Wisconsin Board of Regents. Public Domain.

28 Gallagher, Barney. *Arranmore Links: The Families of Arranmore with Stories and Some History*. p.124. ed. 1986. Barney and Aiden Gallagher, 2004.

29 Nicholson, Asenath, Mrs. *The Annals of the Famine in Ireland in 1847, 1848 and 1849*. University of Wisconsin Board of Regents. Public Domain.

[30]   Ibid.

[31]   Gallagher, Barney. *Arranmore Links: The Families of Arranmore with Stories and Some History.* p.125. ed. 1986. Barney and Aiden Gallagher, 2004.

[32]   Nicholson, Asenath, Mrs. *The Annals of the Famine in Ireland in 1847, 1848 and 1849.* University of Wisconsin Board of Regents. Public Domain.

[33]   Ibid.

[34]   Ibid.

[35]   O'Donnell, Vincent. *O'Donnells of Tyrconnell, A Concise History of the O'Donnell Clan.* ed. 2000, p.92. Inver, Co. Donegal, Ireland: Dálach Publications, 2000.

[36]   Bonner, Seamus. *Arranmore Timeline.* 1999. http://www.arainnmhor.com/culture/localhistory/

[37]   O'Hara, Charlie. *Home on the Island,* DVD, Chapter 2. Directed by Tom Burke and Shane Brennan. Ireland. Moondance Productions. 2006.

[38]   Gallagher, Barney. *Arranmore Links: The Families of Arranmore with Stories and Some History.* p.126. ed. 1986. Barney and Aiden Gallagher, 2004.

[39]   Holland, Denis. *The Landlord in Donegal,* p.92. Belfast. 1858.

[40]   *A Poor-Law officials report on Glenties Workhouse.* Famine II, pp. 53 and 357. National Archives of Ireland.

[41]   Mac Cnáimhsí, Breandan. M.A. *A picture of Arranmore Island during the Great Famine Period 1846-1848.* Donegal Annual 1973, No.3, Vol. X and excerpted from Gallagher, Barney. *Arranmore Links: The Families of Arranmore with Stories and Some History.* pp. 112-122. 1986.

[42]   Doran, James. *Genealogy Report: Descendants of Daniel (or Hugh) Boyle.* Doran Family History and Genealogy, December, 2007. http://familytreemaker.genealogy.com/users/d/o/r/James-Doran/

[43]   Cole, Robert. *Home on the Island,* DVD, Chapter 3. Directed by Tom Burke and Shane Brennan. Ireland. Moondance Productions. 2006.

[44]   Doran, James. *Genealogy Report: Descendants of Daniel (or Hugh) Boyle.* Doran Family History and Genealogy, December, 2007. http://familytreemaker.genealogy.com/users/d/o/r/James-Doran/

[45]   McLaughlin, John Gerard. *Images of America, Irish Chicago.* p.vii. Chicago. Arcadia Publishing, 2003.

[46]   Kasting, Colleen, et al., *Memories of Mundelein: 75th Anniversary 1909-1984.* Diamond Jubilee. p.7.

[47]   Illinois Department of Natural Resources, Chain O'Lakes State Park.

[48]   Watson, Dottie. President of the Historical Society of the Fort Hill Country and Curator, Fort Hill Heritage Museum. Interview with author, February, 2008.

[49]   Kasting, Colleen, et al., *Memories of Mundelein: 75ᵗʰ Anniversary 1909-1984.*
       Diamond Jubilee. p.8.

[50]   Ibid., p.10.

[51]   Watson, Dottie. President of the Historical Society of the Fort Hill Country and
       Curator, Fort Hill Heritage Museum. Interview with author, February, 2008.

[52]   *Diamond Lake Church History.* P.3.

[53]   Cole, Robert. *Home on the Island,* DVD, Chapter 3. Directed by Tom Burke
       and Shane Brennan. Ireland. Moondance Productions. 2006.

[54]   Hipke, Deana C. The Great Peshtigo Fire of 1871. *http://www.peshtigofire.
       info/*

[55]   Marx, Christy. *The Great Chicago Fire—Great Fires throughout History.* Rosen
       Publishing Group.

[56]   1901 Irish National Archives Census.

[57]   Rodgers, Grace Rialta. Age, 93. Interview with author June 25ᵗʰ, 1985,
       Chicago

[58]. Kasting, Colleen, et al., *Memories of Mundelein: 75ᵗʰ Anniversary 1909-1984.*
       Diamond Jubilee. p.8-12.

[59]   Buckley, Lindel. Donegal Genealogy Resources, Events Affecting
       Arranmore Islanders.*http://freepages.genealogy.rootsweb.ancestry.com/~donegal/
       Eastlanddisaster1915.htm* and www.findagrave.com/cgi-bin/fg.cgi?page=gr&G
       SIn=Boyle&GScnty=705&GRid=16320694

[60]   George, Francis Cardinal. *The Cardinal I Never Knew: George Mundelein.* The
       Catholic New World, March 5, 2000. Chicago.

[61]   Walsh, James Joseph. *Our American Cardinals: Life Stories of Seven American
       Cardinals.* 1969

[62]   Lynch, Patricia. An *Architectural and Historical Tour of St. Mary of the Lake
       Seminary.* pp. 10-130. University of St. Mary of the Lake Mundelein Seminary
       Office of Institutional Advancement. 2003.

[63]   Kantowicz, Edward, R., *Cardinal Mundelein and Twentieth-Century Catholicism.*
       Journal of American History. Vol. 68. June 1981. p 51-68

[64]   Walsh, James Joseph. *Our American Cardinals: Life Stories of Seven American
       Cardinals.* 1969

[65]   *University of Saint Mary of the Lake Celebrating 75 Years,* University of St. Mary
       of the Lake Mundelein Seminary, 1996.

[66]   Rouse, Stanley and Genevieve. Interview with author, 19 April, 2008.

[67]   Lynch, Patricia. An *Architectural and Historical Tour of St. Mary of the Lake
       Seminary.* pp. 10-130. University of St. Mary of the Lake Mundelein Seminary
       Office of Institutional Advancement. 2003.

68 Ibid.
69 Ibid.
70 Ibid.
71 Ibid.
72 Ibid.
73 McLaughlin, John Gerard. *Images of America, Irish Chicago.* p. 48. Chicago. Arcadia Publishing, 2003.
74 *University of Saint Mary of the Lake Celebrating 75 Years,* University of St. Mary of the Lake Mundelein Seminary, 1996.
75 O'Donnell-Bennett, James. *Mighty Army of Peace Prays at Mundelein,* Chicago Tribune, 24 June 1926.
76 Rouse, Stanley and Genevieve. Interview with author, 19 April, 2008.
77 Mundelein, George Cardinal. Ad hominum delivered at Archbishop Quigley Preparatory Seminary, Chicago, May 18, 1937.
78 Kane, Francis, Most Rev., *The Lion and The Cardinal,* 20 March 2006, The Parish History of St. Joseph's Church, Wilmette.
79 Healey, Terrence. Interview with author, 05 December, 2008.
80 Rouse, Stanley and Genevieve. Interview with author, 19 April, 2008.
81 Watson, Dottie. *What's In a Name?* Historical Society of the Fort Hill Country Newsletter, 2007.
82 Emmet, Thomas, A., *Ireland Under English Rule.* Vol. 1., p. 101. Putnam, New York & London. 1903.
83 Cavanaugh, James, F. *Irish slaves in the Caribbean.* Clann Chaomhánach. Clann newsletter (ISSN 1393-1733).
84 Kasting, Colleen, et al., *Memories of Mundelein: 75th Anniversary 1909-1984.* Diamond Jubilee. p.17.
85 Pine Meadow Golf Course History. http://www.pinemeadowgc.com/welcome.htm
86 Lynch, Patricia. An *Architectural and Historical Tour of St. Mary of the Lake Seminary.* pp. 10-130. University of St. Mary of the Lake Mundelein Seminary Office of Institutional Advancement. 2003.
87 *Marytown History,* National Shrine of Saint Maximilian Kolbe. Libertyville, Illinois.
88 Ibid.
89 Historical Timeline of the University of Saint Mary of the Lake, http://archives.archchicago.org/photo.htm
90 Gribbon, M., *A Family Affair.* The Malefactor's Register, October 20, 2006.
91 Ibid.

[92]   Ibid.

[93]   Ibid.

[94]   Ibid.

[95]   Ibid.

[96]   Ibid

[97]   *Graphical Climatology of Chicago Temperatures, Precipitation and Snowfall (1871-Present)*. National Weather Service Archives on Climate. NOAA. http://www.nws.noaa.gov/.

[98]   Lissau, Russell. *Truck That Was Almost History Now Apart of It*. Daily Herald, October 5, 2008

[99]   Brachear, Manya, A. *24 Victims of Priests Settle—5 alleged abusers identified for 1st time*. Chicago Tribune, October 28, 2005., BishopAccountability.org http://www.bishop-accountability.org/news/2005_10_28_Brachear_24Victims.html

[100] Falsani, Cathleen. *Cardinal: I Should've Done More*. Chicago Sun-Times, March 21, 2006 http://www.suntimes.com/output/news/cst-nws-arch21.html

[101] http://www.washingtonpost.com/wpdyn/content/article/2008/08/12/AR2008081203091.html

[102] Gribbon, M., *A Family Affair*: The Malefactor's Register, October 20, 2006.

[103] Ibid.

[104] Mors, Terry, M., PhD., *The Rouse House Revisited: Unraveling the Enigma of Murder, Police Corruption, and Organized Crime*, American Mafia, July 2002. Cleveland, Ohio. PLR International.

My father, John Mary Hughie O'Donnell. Irish Fest, Navy Pier,
Chicago. August, 1985.—*Photo by author.*

Printed in the United States
154047LV00004B/1/P